CHRISTOPHANY

FAITH MEETS FAITH

An Orbis Series in Interreligious Dialogue
Paul F. Knitter & William R. Burrows, General Editors
Editorial Advisors
John Berthrong
Diana Eck
Karl-Josef Kuschel
Lamin Sanneh
George E. Tinker
Felix Wilfred

In the contemporary world, the many religions and spiritualities stand in need of greater communication and cooperation. More than ever before, they must speak to, learn from, and work with each other in order to maintain their vital identities and to contribute to fashioning a better world.

The FAITH MEETS FAITH Series seeks to promote interreligious dialogue by providing an open forum for exchange among followers of different religious paths. While the Series wants to encourage creative and bold responses to questions arising from contemporary appreciations of religious plurality, it also recognizes the multiplicity of basic perspectives concerning the methods and content of interreligious dialogue.

Although rooted in a Christian theological perspective, the Series does not limit itself to endorsing any single school of thought or approach. By making available to both the scholarly community and the general public works that represent a variety of religious and methodological viewpoints, FAITH MEETS FAITH seeks to foster an encounter among followers of the religions of the world on matters of common concern.

FAITH MEETS FAITH SERIES

CHRISTOPHANY

The Fullness of Man

Raimon Panikkar

Translated by
Alfred DiLascia

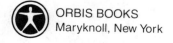

ORBIS BOOKS
Maryknoll, New York

Founded in 1970, Orbis Books endeavors to publish works that enlighten the mind, nourish the spirit, and challenge the conscience. The publishing arm of the Maryknoll Fathers and Brothers, Orbis seeks to explore the global dimensions of the Christian faith and mission, to invite dialogue with diverse cultures and religious traditions, and to serve the cause of reconciliation and peace. The books published reflect the opinions of their authors and are not meant to represent the official position of the Maryknoll Society. To obtain more information about Maryknoll and Orbis Books, please visit our website at *www.maryknoll.org*.

Library of Congress Cataloging in Publication Data

Panikkar, Raimundo, 1918-
  [Pienezza dell'uomo. English]
  Christophany : the fullness of man / Raimon Panikkar ; translated by Alfred DiLascia.
    p. cm. — (Faith meets faith)
  Includes bibliographical references and index.
  ISBN 1-57075-564-7 (pbk.)
  1. Jesus Christ—Person and offices. I. Title. II. Series.
BT203.P36 2004
232—dc22

                                                          2004014381

ἐν τῷ φωτὶ περιπατῶμεν
(1 John 1:7)

Ad lucem hoc in saeculo
peregrinantibus
qui sperant se ambulatores esse in luce

A quanti sono *peregrinanti*
per il campo (*per agros*)
della temporalità
nella speranza di
peregrinare nella luce

Portrait by Juliet van Otteren © 2001.

Raimon Panikkar
Tavertet, Catalunya

Contents

Foreword by Francis d'Sa, S.J.
Fullness of "Man" or Fullness of "the Human"?   xi

Preface   xix

Part 1
INTRODUCTION
The Christophanic Experience

1. A Challenge to Christology   3
    The Point of Departure   3
    The Situation of the World   5
    The Limits of Christology   6

2. The Task of Christophany   9
    Christology and Christophany   9
    The Literary Genre   13
    The Divine Manifestation   15

3. The Christophanic Experience   18
    The Cosmovision   18
    The World of Interiority   20
    Mystical Language   25

Part 2
THE MYSTICISM OF JESUS THE CHRIST
The Experience of Jesus

1. The Approach   39
    The Problem   40
    The Starting Point   46
    Three Anthropologies   54
    Existential Inquiry   74

2. The Expressions   89
    Abba, Patēr   90
    The Father and I Are One   106
    It Is Good That I Leave   120

3. The Mystical Experience of Jesus Christ   135
Eva Me Suttaṃ   135
"*Itipaśyāmi*"   137
"*Sat-puruṣa*"   138

Part 3
CHRISTOPHANY
The Christic Experience

Nine *Sūtra*   143

1. Christ Is the Christian Symbol for the Whole
   of Reality   144
2. The Christian Recognizes Christ *In* and *Through* Jesus   149
3. The Identity of Christ Is Not the Same as His Identification 153
4. Christians Do Not Have a Monopoly on the Knowledge
   of Christ   156
5. Christophany Transcends Tribal and Historical
   Christology   161
6. The Protological, Historical, and Eschatological Christ
   Is a Unique and Selfsame Reality, Distended in Time,
   Extended in Space, and Intentional in Us   165
7. The Incarnation as Historical Event Is Also Inculturation 170
8. The Church Is Considered a Site of the Incarnation   176
9. Christophany Is the Symbol of the *Mysterium Coniunctionis*
   of Divine, Human, and Cosmic Reality   180

Epilogue   185

A Final Word   190

Glossary   191

Bibliography   197

Index   207

Foreword

Fullness of "Man" or
Fullness of "the Human"?

FRANCIS D'SA, S.J.

Readers who are not familiar with Raimon Panikkar's writings are surprised at or irritated by his insistence on speaking of "Man" and not of "human beings." At a symposium organized on Panikkar by the United Nations Educational, Scientific and Cultural Organization, even one of his former students asked whether there is a way of avoiding the "non-inclusive" expression "Man." This betrays a serious misunderstanding of Panikkar's world. This book should clear away all such misapprehensions. For Panikkar Man is always more than Man. In this illuminating book he answers not only the question Who is Man? but also Who am I?

To say that *Christophany: The Fullness of Man* is a seminal book is to stress the obvious, since almost every book of Panikkar's has been a seminal book. Few of his readers will dispute this. Yet this particular book clearly stands out like the Everest in the Himalayan ranges of his publications. Not only because its approach to interreligious understanding does justice to the issues of such a difficult enterprise. Not only because it is christology at the crossroads—it persuasively makes the point that traditional christology is only a halfway house. Not only because it treats of the Trinity in an altogether new perspective—monotheism has no place for the incarnation, it says; it is only in a trinitarian "cosmovision" that the incarnation makes sense. No, the book is outstanding because phenomenological inquiry, philosophical reflection, and theological insight work in *advaitic* harmony to respond to the needs of our times in a unique manner. It takes the challenges of our technocratic age seriously.

Panikkar has never been satisfied with cosmetic changes. His writings have been consistently prophetic. The diagnosis they offer begins at the root of the problem. Panikkar's preoccupation is never at the level of symptoms. That perhaps is one of the reasons why some complain that it is not easy to understand him. They would like to read him as one reads any other author. But Panikkar's books, in spite of all their apparent similarities, are like the rungs of a ladder; the higher rungs presuppose the lower.

In his groundbreaking but much misunderstood *Unknown Christ of Hinduism* (London: Darton Longman & Todd, 1964) Panikkar broached the topic of the Trinity in the final pages. The few comments on Iśvara— "who points towards what we would like to call the Mystery of Christ, as being unique in his existence and essence and as such equal to God"—constitute a sort of overture of the Trinitarian Symphony that reaches its culmination in *Christophany: The Fullness of Man*. His *Trinity and the Religious Experience of Man* (1973)—the earlier version was called *Trinity and World Religions*—left no doubt about his wholehearted preoccupation with the Trinity.[1] The concentration there was on the Christian Trinity but with reflections connecting with the core of the Hindu and the Buddhist revelations. Those illuminating remarks opened the door for the first time to an interreligious understanding of the Christ and the Trinity.[2] The thematic insights of that booklet are now developed in an organic manner in *Christophany: The Fullness of Man*.

Before that, an unexpected but most welcome unfolding in Panikkar's approach to the Trinity took place through the publication of his "Colligite Fragmenta: For an Integration of Reality."[3] There he presented a "secularized" version, as it were, of the Trinity in his cosmotheandric (or theanthropocosmic) intuition. Its concern is not the "Christian" experience of the Trinity but the human invariants, namely, the cosmic, the human, and the divine dimensions that constitute reality. The cosmic is about the objectifiable dimension of reality; the human stresses the objectifying dimension; and the divine is the depth dimension that endows the objectifiable and the objectifying dimensions with a certain endlessness, a kind of infinity. Because of the depth dimension, neither the cosmic nor the human dimension has a limit. This cosmotheandric[4] cosmovision is trinitarian; each of the three dimensions is unique and irreducible but at the same time interindependent! "Everything that exists, any real being, presents this triune constitution expressed in three dimensions. . . . The cosmotheandric intuition is not a tripartite division among beings, but an insight into the threefold core of all that is insofar as it is."[5] Panikkar saw this as the emerging religious consciousness. He epitomized this radical revision of the

---

[1] I suspect, however, that Panikkar's "trinitarian preoccupation" was already operative long ago in his Spanish books *El concepto de naturaleza* (1951) and *Ontonomía de la ciencia: Sobre el sentido de la ciencia y sus relaciones con la filosofia* (1963)—books to which I have no access.

[2] In *Trinity and the Religious Experience of Man,* Panikkar also brought out briefly the trinitarian dynamic at work in the different types of spirituality of the Hindu traditions. The few pages dealing with this theme leave no doubt about the relevance of the Trinity to spirituality. Readers familiar with those reflections will at once see how much fruit they have borne in *Christophany: The Fullness of Man*.

[3] In *From Alienation to At-one-ness,* ed. F. A. Eigo and S. E. Fittipaldi (Villanova, Pa.: Villanova University Press, 1977), 19-91.

[4] That is to say, *cosmo-the-andric*, where world = *cosmos*, God = *theos*, Man = *anēr*.

[5] Panikkar, "Colligite Fragmenta," 74.

way we look at God, Man, and World in a revolutionary formulation: "God, Man and World are three artificially substantivized forms of the three primordial adjectives which describe Reality."[6]

One of Panikkar's many seminal contributions lies in his approach to myth. Myth for Panikkar is that *through* which you experience and understand and not that which you experience and understand. It is the universe of meaning in which one finds oneself; it is the horizon of one's being and understanding. Myth is not objectifiable, just as the horizon is not objectifiable, but it reveals its characteristics, its presuppositions, and its prejudices *in the way* we understand, decide, and act. But myth as the background can neither be experienced nor influenced directly. It is only seers (like Panikkar) who can draw our attention to the myth that is operative in a particular culture through its "myths." Panikkar, a mutational man according to Ewert H. Cousins, is symbolic of the emerging myth of our times. In almost all his writings the trinitarian myth (which makes possible the cosmotheandric experience) is discernible.[7]

Panikkar's cosmotheandric intuition, however fascinating it may be, is not the end of the road. The meditation continues and comes to fruition in *Christophany: The Fullness of Man*, which is about the christophanic experience (Part One), Jesus's experience (Part Two), and the christic experience (Part Three).

If christo*logy* focuses on the doctrines that are developed on the basis of the words that speak of the experience of Jesus, christo*phany* is the opening of the third eye, which brings one in touch with the experience that the christological doctrines refer to. Christophany does not separate philosophy from theology. That is why it does not reject christology but goes beyond it in much the same way that it does not neglect or ignore reason or the critical function when it employs the language of symbol and metaphor.

Panikkar illustrates the mystical language of the christophanic experience with the help of a poem of St. Teresa of Avila. The message she hears is dual: "seek for yourself *in me*; seek for me, in *yourself!*" Panikkar is keen on showing that mystical language of this kind is neither simply human nor purely divine but theandric, and neither monistic nor dualistic but *advaitic*—both important considerations for the chapters that follow. St. Teresa's poem is the springboard for presenting his christophanic approach.

Central to this book is the chapter on the experience of Jesus; it illustrates the *path* (but not the method) that christophany takes. It is not the *logos* that dominates here; what is required is an openness to the *phania*.

---

[6] Panikkar, "Philosophy as Life-Style," in *Philosophers on Their Own Work*, vol. 4 (Bern: Peter Lang, 1978), 206.

[7] Ewert H. Cousins, "Raimundo Panikkar and the Christian Systematic Theology of the Future," *Cross Currents* 29 (Summer 1979):143. For Cousins a "mutational man [is], one in whom the global mutation has already occurred and in whom the new forms of consciousness have been concretised."

For christology, unlike christophany, ignores the mysticism of Jesus Christ. Christian traditions have to a great extent neglected the mystical dimension of Jesus Christ. Focusing on his message, they have devoted their energies to safeguarding orthodoxy. Doctrines have taken center stage; and mysticism has taken a back seat. However, though texts are not the focus of christophany, it is through the texts that we approach the self-understanding of Jesus Christ in order to participate in his experience hinted at in texts like "Abba, Father!" and "I and the Father are one!"

Because christophany aims at experience, Panikkar asks: "Is Christian faith founded on an historical book or a personal experience?"(p. 51 below). For Panikkar, Jesus came to give life, not to hand down doctrines. It is this life that has to be lived and realized. Its lifeblood is the experience of the Ultimate (which for Panikkar is in fact mystical experience). The core of *Christophany: The Fullness of Man* deals with the mystical experience of Jesus. Not so much fidelity to words as to the eternal life that these words embody—that is christophany's concern. One can concentrate on the *individual* (historical) Jesus and come to the conclusion that "*he* is the Way," or on the *person* of Jesus and exclaim, "*You* are the Truth," or go still deeper into the *ādhyātmic* level and discover the Christ and realize that "*You* are the Life." The third is the mystical experience that we have to appropriate if we wish to experience what Jesus experienced, namely, the reality of the Christ.

Panikkar does a kind of phenomenology where the difference between *having* and *being* becomes clear. "Yes, I do have a 'me' but I am not identical with that me. 'My' 'I' seems to be found beyond that 'me'." Our "I" (Panikkar calls it "the small I") is neither relevant nor ultimate. The real I of our lives, or the I of my "me" is not my I. Rather God is the I and I am his you. I and you are neither separate nor one; they stand in an *advaitic* relationship. This is the core of the phenomenological reflection that acts as a preparation for what follows.

In his conscious pilgrimage to the center of his being, Panikkar realizes that he cannot identify himself either with his body or his mind or with what he is today, or yesterday, or will be tomorrow. Here he encounters a profound truth: the experience of contingency wherein we can "discover the tangential touch between immanence and transcendence" and realize that we participate in and are an integral part of the very flux that we call reality. "I am the point of the tangent in which those two poles [World and God] meet: I stand in between."

The point is subtle and therefore worth laboring, for "what I *am* is certainly not identical with what I *have*. The *me* I have, and with it I have everything else. The *I* I do not have, I am (it). What I am is neither creature nor creator. I do not know what I am. I know that, although limited, I have already in some way transcended the limits: consciousness that I am finite shows me the infinite. I am neither finite because I know I am such, nor infinite because I am conscious that I am finite." Furthermore: "But about

this 'I' which in a certain sense is inseparable from my 'me', I can say nothing—except, perhaps, that though it does 'remain' me, it is not *me*. . . ."

When in this context Panikkar asserts, "The I is prior and higher than
knowing who or what I am. In brief, I have succeeded in experiencing the
'me' as the *you* of the I," he is in fact drawing our attention to the different dimensions of Man, dimensions that tend to be overlooked, though
they are constitutive. The "me" of our daily lives is really a "you," which
is like a field of the I that cannot be objectified. God cannot be a you.
Rather "God is the I and 'I' the you," says Panikkar. "Yet, in moments of
difficulty, suffering, and testing in my life, I was led spontaneously to
invoke You, Father, Divinity—and even more frequently, Christ, my *iṣṭadevatā*."[8]

This Christ is the mediator between the infinite and me; it is the Christ
who dwells in the deepest center of our being. It is the same Christ that
Paul refers to when he confesses, "It is no longer I who live now, but Christ
who lives in me!" (Gal 2:20). The you that I am (and not the me) is Christ's
dwelling in the deepest center of my being.

After this preliminary but nonetheless essential reflection, Panikkar
proceeds to examine with deep insight three important utterances of Jesus
Christ. He undertakes to do what no christology has ever dared to do,
namely, to interpret them in a manner that could eventually bring one in
touch with the mystical experience of Jesus.

The key expressions here are cosmotheandric *perichōrēsis*, *koinōnia*,
filiation (a human constant), *creatio continua*, insightfully interpreted by
Panikkar as *incarnatio continua*, and *kenōsis*. *Christology* is *about* the
Christ ("He is the Son of God") and what he said and taught. Panikkar's
christophany is a way to *re-live* the mystical experience of Jesus Christ; it
is to "participate in the same spiritual experience, the same profound intuition that Jesus Christ had." "You are *my* Father insofar as you generate
me: you are nothing other than being Father" who "engages in no other
activity than this: generating." Here Panikkar aptly refers to St. Thomas
Aquinas: "By the same act through which God generates the Son he creates
the world."

This fathering, so to say, is the "I" of everything. This "I" (seen inter-
culturally also as Brahman of the Upanishads or the emptiness of Buddhism) brings forth a "You," the Son, the Christ, in whom and through
whom we [can] discover our filiation. Panikkar's brilliant interpretations of
crucial texts (like "Abba, Father!" and "The Father and I are one") argue
persuasively that, like Jesus, we too *are really* children of this Abba, not
just adopted children. Christophany in an ongoing invitation to realize that
we are immersed in and belong to the eternal process of the "I" "thou-ing"
the Son, a process in which the Spirit urges me/us to respond with "Abba,

---

[8] "An *iṣṭadevatā* is the most human way of carrying us close to this experience. We need
to find the divine icon with which we can communicate."

Mother!"[9] The process of generating is an eternal "thou-ing." Like Jesus, I too am the "you" of the Father. Here at the *ādhyātmic* level the I and the you "constitute the two poles of the same reality," where a nondualistic relation obtains. Unlike christology, then, christophany draws attention to the constant summons of the Spirit to realize with that "I and the Father are one"[10] but, as Panikkar qualifies, "to the extent that my I disappears, and my I disappears to the extent it allows itself to be shared by whoever comes to me, 'feeds' on me."

Panikkar's third text "It is good that I leave" brings out the truth of the Spirit. Our meditation is within the context of our trinitarian "nature." As in Indian raga, we return again and again to the same theme in new and refreshing ways, the theme here being: "This is precisely what the experience of the Trinity is: we know that we are inserted within a cosmotheandric *perichōrēsis.*"

When Jesus leaves, the Spirit arrives, the Spirit who will guide us to the whole truth. His going away means his presence in a new way. Every being is a christophany, a manifestation of that presence. But presence does not mean merely historical and temporal presence. The incarnation as the trinitarian vision of creation liberates us from such shackles. Just as *creatio* is a *creatio continua,* so too the *incarnatio* has to be understood an *incarnatio continua.* Our worth lies in the fact that we are unique participants in the *creatio continua* or, as Panikkar puts it, the *incarnatio continua.* And "if I do not desire anything for my I, I am everything and have everything. I am one with the source insofar as I too act as a source by making everything which I have received flow again—just like Jesus." Panikkar points to the eucharist, which is a work of the Spirit, and speaks of the resurrection as "the real presence of the absence." "The *I* will die and thus make room for the Spirit: this is Life and Resurrection." *Kenōsis* is the precondition of the resurrection.

Finally the chapters on the christic experience articulate what follows from the christophany. The Christ of the christophany is, for example, the Christ that was, is, and will be at work in the whole of creation, that is, in every single being and not only in Jesus. "Jesus is Christ but Christ cannot be identified completely with Jesus." Hence other traditions "have no need to call him by the Greek name." Similarly christophany opens our eyes to ecosophy, "listening to the wisdom of the earth," to not absolutizing history (and consequently realizing that the "Incarnation as historical event

---

[9] Panikkar offers here—as usual in passing—a profound insight. He says, "'Father' does not stand only for source, power, and person. It also signifies protection, especially love—and therefore Mother." Later on he comments: "As we have already said, the symbol father also stands for mother, for the woman who gives life, existence, nourishment and love, and signifies sacrifice, sharing, participation in the same adventure, and therefore equality." To this I would add only that going through such an experience one would today probably exclaim "Abba, Mother." Such a Father-Mother function is more Mother than Father!

[10] Panikkar adds: "We are *brahman* but do not know it."

cannot be considered a universal human fact" and that "Christianity too is a cultural construct"). Above all, "Christophany is the symbol of the *mysterium conjunctionis* of divine, human and cosmic reality."

To return to the title of this foreword. Panikkar states

> When I refuse to be called 'a human being', or when I criticize evolutionistic thought, when I claim to be unique and, to that extent, unclassifiable, I am reacting against the invasion of the scientific mentality which tends to obscure one of the most central of all human experiences: *being a unique divine icon of reality, constitutively united with the Source of everything, a microcosm that mirrors the entire macrocosm.* In a word, I am one with the Father, infinite, beyond all comparison and never interchangeable. The I is not me. I am not the product of evolution, a speck of dust, or even mind in the midst of an immense universe. Man, the integrally concrete, real man, is not an item in a classification scheme: it is he who does the classifying. (My italics)

Our age has problems with all three centers of reality: God, World, and Man. Science ignores God; Man does not care for the world; and now the world is fighting back. And our solutions are at best piecemeal and at worst cosmetic. It is on this background that *Christophany: The Fullness of Man* as a christophany undertakes a full-scale revision of our understanding of these three centers; this fullness is to be experienced, if at all, at the *ādhyātmic* level. It is a mission statement for the new millennium—a statement that can be understood only when read with the third eye!

Preface

ἰδοὺ ὁ ἄνθρωπος
Ecce homo
(John 19:5)

पुरुष एवेदं सर्वं
puruṣa evedam sarvaṃ
Man is certainly all this.
(Ṛg-veda, X, 90, 2)

This study constitutes an attempt to concentrate the *pathos* of an entire life into a few pages; I have been meditating and writing on this topic for more than fifty years. The first part of the work constitutes a reflection on the central figure of Christian consciousness and proposes a deepening of classical christology. This "new" discipline, named christophany, intends to offer to the contemporary world, characterized above all by a widespread scientific mentality and collapse of the religious and cultural frontiers of mankind, a response to the yearning for the fullness of life that burns in every heart.

The second part consists in an attempt, bold perhaps, to decipher the mystical experience of Jesus of Nazareth, since it is difficult to understand a message without knowing, to a certain extent, the messenger's heart.

The third part is limited to describing, in nine *sūtras*, the christic epiphany in the light of an experience that has passed through the scrutiny of the methodology mentioned in part one. Some readers might ask why citations are given in Greek, Latin, and Sanskrit—sometimes untranslated. The bolder the undertaking to set out on new paths, the greater the need to be rooted in one's own tradition and open to others, which makes us conscious that we are not alone and allows us to reach a wider vision of reality. Even the notes are intended to be an invitation not to forget the wisdom of our ancestors.[1] I do not intend to be "original," rather (perhaps) *originario*, in the sense of seeking communion with the origin from which we obtain our inspiration, not in order to repeat lessons more or less known but in order to participate creatively in the very Life of reality.

---

[1] With regard to classical texts, the ancient custom has been followed of citing the first division (book, part, chapter) with Roman numerals. In the case of biblical texts, citations follow contemporary style.

I have been asked why I have written this book with such commitment. Above all, I must say, in order to deepen the faith which has been given me by submitting my intuitions to the critical examination of the intellect and the wisdom of tradition, not for my own interest but in order to flow into that vital current that flows in the deep arteries of the mystical body of reality. The first task of every creature is to complete, to perfect, his icon of reality.

Second, this book interrogates the twenty centuries of christological tradition and allows itself to be interrogated by that imposing doctrinal corpus which needs both *aggiornamento* ("updating") and reform (*ecclesia semper est reformanda*, "The church must always be reformed").

It is *cum magno timore et tremula intentione* ("with fear and quaking intention")—to cite Hildegarde von Bingen's prologue to *Scivias*—that I bring my contribution to the rich two-thousand-year-old theological tradition concerning trinitarian and christological mysteries, since all dogmas are intrinsically related. A profound humility should accompany such a great ambition.

I am convinced both by the signs of the time and by the work of contemporary scholars that the world finds itself before a dilemma of planetary proportions: either there will be a radical change of "civilization," of the meaning of the *humanum*, or a catastrophe of cosmic proportions will occur. This leads me to see a genuine meeting of cultures as a first step toward a metanoia pregnant with hope.[2]

Third, but no less important, this study addresses itself to those for whom the name of Christ bears no particular meaning, either because they belong to other cultures or because, for various reasons, they have canceled him from their interest.

These pages constitute a reflection on the human condition in its deepest dimension, least conditioned by historical vicissitudes. There exists in each of us a desire for fullness and life, for happiness and the infinite, for truth and beauty that goes beyond religious and cultural contingencies. To avoid abstract or generic generalizations I have followed the thread of a two-thousand-year tradition whose symbol is the Greek translation of a Hebrew name. Note that I am not saying that Christ is the fullness of life but that this fullness, effective since the beginning, is one that the Christian tradition calls Jesus the Christ.

The theological translation summarized in these pages highlights a conviction I have been expounding for many decades; it is the task of the third Christian millennium to transcend abrahamic monotheism without damaging the legitimacy and validity of monotheistic religions. This task, initi-

---

[2] This is the impression the author derives from reading the rich and profound works of such admirable writers as Von Balthasar, Barth, Bonhoeffer, Brunner, Bultmann, Congar, de Lubac, Feuerbach, Garrigou-Lagrange, Jaspers, Lévinas, Lonergan, Mancini, Rahner, Scheeben, Schmaus, Tillich—to cite only a few of recent and contemporary authors.

ated at the Council of Jerusalem (Acts 15:1-33), entails not a denial of the divine but an opening to the great intuition of the Trinity—the meeting point of human traditions.

A sociopolitical translation would constitute an acknowledgment that the last half millennium of human history is so characterized by European domination that one may now talk of the europeanization of the world. In this way the westernization of life has been spread over the whole planet. But these Western values are inseparably bound to Christianity, which finds itself today ever more detached from any ecclesiastical organization, understood as a more or less open sociological body. What remains is Christ: *real* symbol of divinization—that is, of the *Fullness of Man*. (Some would prefer that I say "symbol of human Fullness," but this would not be correct; the fullness of Man is more than a human fullness. The complete Man is Man divinized; that unique being, athirst for the infinite, is not himself until he reaches his destiny.) Man is more than his "human" nature.

I would remind the third group of readers of the only scriptural phrase in which the word "divinity" appears: "For in him the whole fullness of divinity dwells bodily" (σωματικῶς) (Colossians 2:9).[3] This is the human vocation!

I wish to acknowledge all the friends who have read parts of the text in a first draft and have stimulated me to clarify certain points. In particular, I thank Milena Carrara Pavan, who has been by my side, with patience and dedication, throughout the long vicissitudes of the original writing of this text, which otherwise would never have seen the light. A special thanks to my friend Alfred DiLascia, the English translator, and Joseph Cunneen, without whose encouragement this book would not have come to this publication.

---

[3] It is sadly significant that the phrase "the body of Christ" (Col 2:17) has disappeared in numerous translations.

Part 1

Introduction
The Christophanic Experience

ῥαββί . . .
ποῦ μένεις
ἔρχεσθε καὶ ὄψεσθε

. . .

μείνατε ἐν ἐμοὶ
κἀγὼ ἐν ὑμῖν

. . .

Rabbi, . . .
ubi manes?
Venite et videbitis

. . .

Manete in me
et ego in vobis

Teacher, where do you live?
come and you will see.

. . .

You remain in me,
and I in you.
(John 1:38-39; 15:4)

1

A Challenge to Christology

The Point of Departure

Christ's knowledge (*gnōsis christou*, Philippians 3:8), that knowledge pregnant with eternal life (John 17:3), cannot be fragmentary. No partial knowledge can take us to salvation, to realization. Every knowledge is fragmented, not only when its object has become detached from the rest of reality but also when the knowing subject has shattered its knowing by reducing it to either sensible perception or rational intelligibility. It thereby forgets the knowledge of the third eye, on which more than one tradition, including the Christian (the eye of the flesh, the eye of the mind, the eye of faith) insists. Salvific knowledge. Christian *gnōsis* and vedantic *jñāna* constitute that holistic vision which assimilates the known to the knower, which scholastics call *visio beatifica* (the "beatific vision") when it has reached its fullness.

From an intercultural and interreligious perspective, the key question of the entire Christian tradition centers on the figure of Christ. The other religions ask Christianity, "Who is Christ? A supreme *pantokratōr*? A Western divine prophet? A universal savior? A Man like others?"

"Christology" is the word, over fifteen centuries old, with which theological reflection refers to the mystery of Christ. Since the first generation of Christians, christology has been the interpretation Christian hearts and minds have given of the impact the figure of Christ has produced on them.

We know that every interpretation depends on the context and the cultural approach of the person who elaborates it. We know, moreover, that Christians believe that their understanding of Christ is modeled on the faith that illuminates the Christian intellect so that it may grasp, as far as possible, the reality of Christ. But we also know that in every "revelation" it is up to us, limited historical beings, to understand the language of the "revealed words." The divine revelation is received by our limited human minds: *quidquid recipitur ad modum recipientis recipitur* ("Whatever is received is received in conformity with the modality of the receiver"). The "divine revelation" thus becomes also human revelation.

The christology of the first centuries was forged by the Christian faith against the background of Hebrew religion and Greek culture. Paul's

3

genius is the fruit of the creative intersection—not exempt from tensions—of his Hebraic heart, Greek mind, and Roman life. There is no need to elaborate further the obvious fact that the christology that has reached us today is the result of "Christian" faith in dialogue with Judaism and the Greco-Roman world, later with the mentality of the new European peoples, and finally with Islamic culture. The contribution of the Americas has been reduced, in terms of doctrine, to some modern adaptations, and that of Asia, Africa, and Oceania has been practically nil—with the exception of Latin North Africa, or the Syriac Asia Minor of the early centuries.[1] In addition, we should not forget the impact of popular religiosity on the Christian understanding of Christ, a fact that has rarely been taken into account by academic christology. Very often the Christ of ordinary Christians is not the Christ of the theologians.

We are far from the times when the Christian people at Ephesus, not content with the compromise formula that defined Mary as "mother of Christ" (rather than "mother of Jesus"), became enthusiastic over the formula that resonated in their "pagan" hearts—"mother of God" (*dei genitrix*, θεοτόκος). Modern popular understanding sees Christ with greater sympathy as "son of Man," probably without being too conscious of the trinitarian depth of this intuition: God has a human mother, and Man a divine son.

As they first encounter traditional christological images, it is understandable that the other peoples of the world have seen Christ as an exotic figure, more or less attractive, or as a suspicious construction associated with foreign conquerors and invaders, responsible for military operations that range from the Crusades to the *reconquista*, from colonialism to the Vietnam War. Christology is not a purely chemical property of the mind but possesses a *Sitz im Leben* that shapes the interpretation of what christology seeks to explain. In short, christology is a Western product bound to the history of a culture. This is a statement of fact, not a value judgment.

Undoubtedly contemporary christology has transcended the somewhat static character and no longer approaches the divine mystery with a treatise *De Deo uno* ("On the One God") independently of Christ and the Trinity. But the relationship between the *De Deo trino* ("On the Triune God") and the *De Deo Inarnato* ("On God Incarnate") is still weak.

The long discussions in the history of Christian spirituality that make a distinction between *la mystique du Christ et la mystique de Dieu*[2] still contribute to a mentality that, in order to save a rigid monotheism, tears Christ in two. New winds are blowing, however. Vatican Council II not only binds Christ to God, as Protestant theology emphasizes, but to Man as well: ". . . the mystery of man is seen in its own proper light in the mys-

---

[1] Among others, see a brief summary in Evers (1993).
[2] See Monchanin (1985) 157: "La mystique de Dieu est nécessairement au terme de la mystique du Christ."

tery of the Word incarnate. . . . This is true not only for Christians but also for all men of good will . . ." (*Gaudium et spes*, n.22). The most salient aspects of the council's "christological revolution" are four: the importance given to *kenōsis* (Philippians 2:5-11), "recapitulation" (Ephesians 1:10ff.), the historicity of Jesus Christ (Hebrews 5:8-9), and soteriological affirmations.[3]

My point of departure lies in traditional christology, one that began much earlier than a few centuries ago—perhaps one should say much earlier than a few millennia ago—as the ancients believed and as we read in St. Augustine (*Retractiones* I, 12). Justin, commenting on John 1:9, does not hesitate to write that all those who "have lived according to the Word are Christians" (*Apologia* I, 46), thereby demonstrating a *forma mentis* that sees the concrete as the manifestation of the universal. Hinduism, Buddhism, Islam, etc., offer us many other examples of the same "way of thinking."

The Situation of the World

Praxis is the matrix of history, even though, at the same time, it is *theōria* that informs the praxis. The existential situation of the world at the outset of the twenty-first century is so serious that we must not allow ourselves to be absorbed by internal political polemics or problems of a minor order (priesthood for women, protestant sacraments, ecumenism, sexual morality, modern rites, and so on). The world is undergoing a human and ecological crisis of planetary proportions. Seventy-five percent of its population lives in subhuman conditions; thousands of children die every day because of injustices Man has perpetrated. Since 1945 wars kill more than twelve hundred persons a day; religious intolerance is still all too alive throughout the planet, and the conflict among religions is still intensely inflamed.

What does contemporary christology have to say about all of this? What bearing does the Christian response have on the burning problems of our day, and how is all of this related to Christ? Must we reduce Christ's message to the promise of a private salvation for the individual soul? Must the Christianity that claims to be historical renounce history? A christology deaf to the cries of men and especially women today would be incapable of uttering any "word of God" whatsoever. The Son of Man was concerned with people. What is his manifestation, his epiphany today?

The situation of the world does not involve justice and goodness alone, but truth and beauty as well; as Marsilio Ficino (1433-1499) says, beauty is situated between goodness and justice *(De amore* II, 1). The often violent passion for justice and the rather mild approach to the search for truth and beauty is perhaps to be ascribed to the fact that, in the light of the modern

---

[3] González-Faus (1966) 107-11.

fragmentation of knowledge, we have forgotten the classical doctrine of the transcendentals (being-as-such is one, beautiful, true, and good). The degradation of beauty to a mere estheticism may be the sign of a similar forgetting. Here the intercultural contribution is important.

Human consciousness today cannot ignore the contemporary condition of intercultural reality—that is, the twofold fact that we are conscious of many cultures and of their peculiar osmosis with the technical and scientific character of the dominant culture that originated in Europe. The various cultures and religions may still proclaim their distinctive criteria of truth and beauty, but they cannot remain enclosed within themselves. The meeting of cultures is inevitable. Even the fact that there are Christians on all five continents is experienced as a dilemma by those very Christians, who are culturally marginalized by their historical-cultural roots. Either Christ may be extrapolated from the culture and history with which he has been identified until now, or these Christians must abandon their respective cultures if they wish to remain Christian. This is the challenge: either Christianity limits itself to being monocultural (while including a wide range of subcultures) or it renounces that right to universal citizenship which even a colonial period had acknowledged—although in a wrong way. Sensitive to the problems of the modern world and conscious of the responsibility of religions, I have been hoping for many years for a Second Council of Jerusalem (whatever the site might be) that would bring together not only Christians but exponents of the world's other human traditions.

Here are some of the topics to be confronted:

- the problems internal to every culture (historical concreteness)
- collective dialogue on the diverse worldviews underlying the different religions (human coexistence)
- the harmony with nature that must be restored by something other than simple ecological cosmetics. *Ecosophy* is a contemporary imperative of human consciousness (cosmic brotherhood)
- human responsibility in the face of a mysterious reality seen as either immanent or transcendent and which many traditions call divine (transcendence of human life)

Whatever be the case, we must begin with a few concrete, even though modest, steps, one of which is expressed by the word "christophany."

The Limits of Christology

Traditionally we spoke of Christ's function in the universal economy of salvation. Generally speaking, this was a question of a purely logical deduction from "Christian premises" without any critical reflection on those very premises, a deduction that entailed the absolutization of a certain logic that one believed could be extended to the whole of humanity. The contemporary intercultural challenge, however, has shown itself more profound than previously imagined. There is no doubt that classical christology does not have at its disposal categories adequate to confront these problems. Today's christology is neither catholic—that is, universal—nor is it necessary that it be so. Its content cannot be separated from the parameters of intelligibility that belong to a powerful yet single current of human culture.

We must be conscious of theological discussions of the past and the present regarding Christianity's role among the religions of the world and of Christ's function in the economy of salvation. Although this work does not ignore such discussions, it does not intend to be either polemical or critical of other positions; it simply presents a point of view. I am delighted to learn from others and always ready to learn better, in amplitude, extension, height, and depth, the love of Christ that transcends every knowledge because it belongs to God's *plērōma* (Ephesians 3:18-19).

The fact is that christology has been developed only within the framework of the Western world. Despite its trinitarian soul, christology has not really freed itself from the monotheism it inherited from the abrahamic tradition.

Let it be clear, however, that it is not a question of either supplanting traditional christology or of forgetting the tradition from which Christianity was born. What we need to do is to revisit the experience of the mystery of Christ in the light of our times—to recognize the *kairos* of the present, even though our need does not spring from an anxiety to be up-to-date. We have heard talk about a cultural sophism, as if philosophy should be merely an applied sociology.[4] We should remember St. Thomas's demanding phrase: *Studium philosophiae not est ad hoc ut sciatur quid homines senserint, sed qualiter se habeat veritas rerum* ("The study of philosophy does not aim at knowing the opinions of Men but rather the truth of things"; *De caelo* II, 3). After all, there is a middle path between a relativistic and an objectivistic conception of truth: relativity is not relativism.

The indispensable presuppositions to make the Christian message intelligible and acceptable were called *preambulae fidei*.[5] The first of these requirements, preambles to the faith, were said to be "a minimal degree of culture"—of a culture convinced of possessing universal value. In fact, however, that degree was the product of a very particular form of thought and vision of reality.

An example will spare us from dwelling on this point. The great sage Eihei Dōgen, the man who introduced zen into Japan, wrote a short treatise in 1233, the *Ghenjokan* (later inserted in his *magnum opus,*

---

[4] Borne (1987) 398.
[5] Cf. a criticism in Panikkar (1983) 321-34.

Shoboghenzo). In the first paragraph we read: "Inasmuch as all things are at one and the same time authentic, illusion and awakening exist, the activity of life exists, being born exists, dying exists."[6]

These words suffice for us to presume that neither Aristotelian logic nor linear time nor inert matter nor individuality enters into the conception of reality on which this text rests, not to mention so many other Buddhist beliefs: Man is one of the six manifestations of living and conscious beings; while things are nonsubstantial, a creator God does not exist. We are not interested in discussing whether these ideas are more or less true within a worldview that bestows plausibility on them. We simply ask ourselves what kind of meaning traditional Christianity might have in such a vision of the world. In order to bear witness to Christ, are Christians justified in undertaking the so-called *évangélisation de base*? Is it necessary to destroy all the other symbolic universes in order to initiate those presuppositions *(preambula fidei)* on which the Christian *kērygma* rests? There is the problem.

---

[6] Dōgen (1997) 13.

2

The Task of Christophany

Christology and Christophany

Although the word is Greek, I take the word "Christophany" to signify a Christian reflection that is to be elaborated in the third millennium. In this respect let us note that three phenomena characterize the contemporary religious scene: (1) the decline of the traditional religions along with the proliferation of new forms of religiosity, (2) the internal crisis of Christian identity, and (3) the external situation of a world in which cultures and religions meet on a planetary scale.

This meeting, however, almost always takes place within the matrix of the Western technoscientific world, which, at least in part, bears Christian origins. The christophany that I propose may be characterized in the following fashion. First and above all, christophany does not pretend to offer a universal paradigm, nor does it even say that historical Christianity should adopt this model. It leaves open the question whether Christianity should be a *pusillus grex* ("a small flock"), a "remnant of Israel" (Jeremiah 31:7), or a leaven that helps the whole dough to ferment (Matthew 13:33; Luke 13:20-21).[1] Christophany simply intends to offer an image of Christ that all people are capable of believing in, especially those contemporaries who, while wishing to remain open and tolerant, think they have no need of either diluting their "Christianity" or of damaging their fidelity to Christ. And christophany offers the same experience to all those who nourish an interest in that Man who lived some twenty centuries ago but still seems, to many people, to live.

Second, Christophany, which is obviously a Christian word, although open to universal problems in a concrete and therefore limited way, seeks to present this epiphany of the human condition both in the light of our contemporary situation and of what seems to originate out of something beyond Man—that is, the light that has accompanied *Homo sapiens* since his very first appearance on earth. This christophany, however, should be very cautious so as not to repeat the old error in which religions have constantly been engaged—cultural and nationalistic manipulation of the divine as in the phrase *Gott mit uns* ("God is with us")!

---

[1] See Panikkar (1992).

Third, the word christophany—in itself ambiguous—could be interpreted to mean a more or less docetic vision of Jesus, but this is not the meaning that we attribute to it in these pages. Instead, we employ the word in a sense that is in greater harmony with the *phaneros* ("manifestation") of the Christian scriptures—that is, a visible, clear, public manifestation of a truth.[2] Christophany stands for a manifestation of Christ to human consciousness and includes both an experience of Christ and a critical reflection on that experience.

Fourth, christophany cannot—better, must not—ignore or pretend to abolish the christological tradition of the preceding two millennia. Every growth requires both continuity and change, in the sense of the adage that the wise steward *nova et vetera profert* (Matthew 13:52). And this implies that a Christian who is both rooted in tradition and open to the new should recognize that we are talking about Christ. I insist on this fact of continuity. Despite the novelty of the name, christophany traces itself to those profound intuitions of traditional christology which it does not replace but, on the contrary, prolongs and deepens in fields hitherto unexplored and proposes new perspectives.

Fifth, unlike christology, the word "christophany" bears another value inasmuch as it suggests that the meeting with Christ is irreducible to a simple doctrinal or intellectual (*not* only rational) approach that is proper to christology. Yes, the *logos* is also God's *Logos*, but it is not the whole Trinity. In addition, although the Spirit is inseparable from the living Christ, it is not subordinated to Logos Christ. The word "christophany" appeals to the Spirit too. It is this that constitutes the capital difference between christology and christophany.

Christophany takes nothing away from christology but is open to the reality of the Spirit, which, without separating *logos* from *pneuma*, does not subordinate the latter to the former. Neither is it a "pneuma-logy," but it receives the Spirit's presence and action in a different form—the form of the third eye. We have already asserted that without a mystical vision, christophany does not acquire its full meaning.

The substitution of the word "christology" with "christophany" does not mean that we are forgetting the *logos*; on the contrary, we are suggesting the transcending of a purely rational approach and a thematic opening to the Spirit's action when we study the figure of Christ. "The Son of Man" is neither comprehensible nor real without the Spirit that gives him life.

The Spirit is irreducible to either a rational intelligibility or a feeling (or

---

[2] From the time of Aristotle (*Metaphysics* XII, 4) "to appear" has been construed to mean the revelation of being. See Heidegger (1966) 77: "Sein west als Erscheinen" (Being manifests its essence in what appears); the whole chapter "Sein und Schein" (75-88); also "das *legein des logos* als *apophainesthai*. zum-sich-zeigen-bringen" (130) (the saying of *logos* as manifestation). We record this text to underscore the profound cultural unity of the West—from Parmenides on.

other "sentiment") subordinate to reason.[3] Real human life is guided neither by the stoic *secundum rationem* alone nor by the biological *sequere
naturam* but also by the *secundum te* of liturgical prayer. Two words helps
us to communicate what we wish to say. The first is *phania*—that is, the
manifestation or direct appearance (without intermediaries) to human consciousness, which becomes conscious of something even though it cannot
understand it by reason alone, and even though reason does play an unsubstitutable role (not every manifestation is believable).[4] The second word is
"experience," understood as the consciousness of an immediate presence
and thus as the irreducible instance of any human activity whatsoever—
although even here we require verification from all other human faculties.

Sixth, in addition, christophany accentuates a disposition of spirit that
is more passive or feminine in receiving Christ's impact on the human consciousness in contrast to a more aggressive inquiry on the part of reason
which aims at intelligibility in and through rational evidence—as it were
fides "petens" intellectum ("the faith that 'prays' for understanding").
When we say "passive," we are thinking of the contemplative attitude of
the *pati divina* ("impact of the divine factor") and therefore of the mystical dimension.

Seventh, this notion of Christ must include both the figure of the historical past and the reality of the present. Christophany is not mere exegesis of "inspired" texts nor Christian archaeology, and not even an
exclusively analytic and deductive reflection of that historical reality which
Christians call Christ. Christ does not belong to the past alone. Christophany practices theology of the highest order and does not therefore accept
the dichotomy between theology and philosophy that has been practiced in
recent centuries.[5] In traditional language it is both *fides quaerens intellectum* ("faith seeking understanding") and *intellectus fidei* ("a [critical]
knowledge of faith"]. A philosophy without theology is irrelevant, and a
theology without philosophy is a more or less superstitious credulity.

Christology has been, in general, a reflection pursued by Christians
who, except in its first period of formation, have virtually ignored the
world's other traditions. Christophany, on the other hand, is open to both
a dialogue with other religions and an interpretation of that same tradition
on the basis of a scenario that embraces the past (including the pre-Christian) as well as the present (even what is called the non-Christian, including the secular). It is for these reasons that the new name is justified, for

---

[3] See Matthew 4:1 and Mark 1:12, which speak of Jesus as "guided by the Spirit."

[4] Φανερός (*phaneros*), as is the case with the word φανός (*phanos*) has as its first meaning "shining," derived from φαίνω ("to bring to light"). Φῶς (*phōs*) is light, primarily in the
sense of light from the sun, and comes from the root *bha*, whence we derive "evident," "manifest," "visible," "open"). In a different context I would have entitled the book *Christāloka*,
to indicate the splendor or light of Christ. Christophany would like to be the splendor of the
Mystery (which Christians call "christic") visible to all—although, to be sure, in different
forms.

[5] See Panikkar (1997) 25-37.

christophany is not only a christology modernized or adapted to our times. Christophany penetrates into every manifestation of the human spirit. In our time, for example, modern science, paradigm of the human spirit, has developed independently of both God—*etsi Deus non daretur* ("as if God did not exist") and the reality of Christ.

Perhaps today's shepherds still experience the announcement of the incarnation, although the magi of the present see and follow stars very different from the star seen in the east. Christophany is constitutively open to a dialogue with the contemporary scientific mind. It is not a discipline enclosed within either temples or academies; its epiphany, on the contrary, is "like a flash of lightning that comes from the east and manifests itself (φαίνεται, *phainetai*) all the way to the west" (Matthew 24:27).

Eighth, inasmuch as it is open to dialogue and seeks to integrate the figure of Christ within a wider cosmovision, christophany is not a discipline centered exclusively on a past event but one that tends to be a vision concerning "the way, the truth, and the life" (John 14:6; 1:14; 1 John 5:6), an *intellectus saeculi* ("understanding of the world").

What we have just said implies a thematic integration of the homeomorphic equivalents of that mystery which Christians call Christ. Christophany does not, in principle, exclude a priori any epiphany of the sacred and the divine without, however, neglecting the task of critical discernment. Not every one of the sacred's epiphanies is a christophany, although the latter does seek to distinguish grades and levels within every hierophany as it proceeds to study the ways different traditions have interpreted the Christian understanding of Christ and the respective interpretations of his homeomorphic equivalents. By the latter we understand symbols and concepts that in other systems of belief or thought exhibit an analogy of the third degree that makes them homeomorphic. What this means is that the homeomorphic equivalents discharge, in their respective systems, a function that is equivalent (not the same) to that which other notions (or symbols) discharge in their own system. The word of God, "God-talk," is not bound in chains: *Verbum Dei* (ὁ λόγος τοῦ θεοῦ, *ho logos tou theou*) *non est alligatum* ("The word of God is not fettered"; 2 Timothy 2:9).

Christophany should not be an exercise in Christian solipsism, a suggestion that pertains not only to individuals but also to the Christian church in its entirety, as well as to the historical intertwining of humanity, especially in our own day. Christ's manifestation also generates a cosmic repercussion. Christophany interrogates other cultures too, as they in turn interrogate it. The other religions are no longer treated as adversaries or "pagan" but are acknowledged in terms of their own self-understanding. This allows us not only to understand the other traditions better but likewise to penetrate more deeply into the very mystery of Christ, a mystery that is like a lamp shining from one end of the sky to the other (Luke 17:24). The dialogue leads to a deeper understanding of ourselves and to an integration of the interpretations of the others.

Ninth, the christophany that we propose considers the other religions of the world not as Christians have often interpreted them but as they understand themselves—as, to use scholastic language, *loci theologici*, proper and legitimate places for theological activity. How to understand another religion adequately is a problem in itself which at this time we can do no more than simply mention. In this sense, christophany dares to widen the concept of theology as "God-talk," *logos tou theou*, in the sense of the subjective genitive—that is, "the word *of* God," which we ourselves can discover in every authentic expression.

In the attempt to explain Christ to Buddhists and Hindus, not with the usual words *ad usum nostrorum* ("solely for our own use"), as if they were for Christians' private use, but by means of parameters that make sense for the partner in the dialogue, we find ourselves faced with the great difficulty of presenting the figure of Christ in a language in which the Christian does not feel betrayed. The contexts and the languages are different.

The Literary Genre

Readers accustomed to the analytic classifications proper to scientific thought will ask themselves to what kind of literary genre this writing belongs: exegetical work, theological study, edification, mystical effusion, poetry, intercultural philosophy, psychology, or autobiography. The truth is that I am trying to transcend the dilemma that underlies such a question. Modern culture seems to have virtually forgotten that simple intuition of things which is neither complex nor synthetic, since it is not a question of summing up particular kinds of knowledge. The whole is not just the sum of its parts, and we must be careful not to say "equal to the sum" because we would thereby fall into algebraic or merely calculative thought. For example, $3 = 1 + 1 + 1$, but this equation cannot be applied to the Trinity. Jesus speaks to us of the simple eye. Simplicity (Matthew 6:22; Luke 11:34) was one of the ideals of the first monks and has been regarded since antiquity as a sign of wisdom. If it were necessary to put a label on this study, it could perhaps be classified as intercultural philosophy, understanding the word "philosophy" also in an intercultural sense and not only as an *opus rationis*.[6]

This work intends to be a *studium*, in accordance with the Ciceronian definition (*De Inventione* I, 25). In the upanishadic tradition, it belongs to the order of the *nididhyāsana*, contemplation that entails the vital assimilation of what the elders have heard and personal elaboration with one's

---

[6] See the illuminating writings of Xavier Tilliette on the reflections of modern philosophers concerning the figure of Christ. See a summary in Tilliette (1990a) 424-30, and more specifically Tilliette (1990b and 1993); see also the brilliant pages of Milano (1987).

own mind.[7] If I were gifted, I might have summarized my ideas in a poem, but the reader would consider it to be more or less a metaphor or an individual testimony—nothing more. I have therefore felt obliged to place myself in both ancient and contemporary traditions by making forays into almost all the genres mentioned above in the light of my conviction that philosophy cannot be broken into separate specialized compartments without wounding its very heart. Theology (philosophy) must not be considered either a deductive or purely conceptual science. Rather, in accordance with the oldest tradition, it should be viewed as an activity of the contemplative intellect whereby "contemplation" does not mean *theoria* alone but also active participation in the *templum,* with all the lights and powers with which we are endowed. Philosophy or theology is thus a spiritual activity inseparable from the search for "holiness," a word that must be understood in the light of the very philosophy it professes.

What appears here is clearly a latent philosophical idea and a holistic vision of reality, and we do not avoid critical allusions to certain presuppositions and a personal interpretation of tradition. The thoughts of different traditions are not developed in greater detail so as not to lose the guiding thread of these pages, whose intent is to lead to a personal experience of that mystery which can guide one's entire life.

There are three reasons for maintaining a respectful distance from the complex, classical, and more or less orthodox classical christologies. The first is the impossibility of gaining an exhaustive knowledge of the profound reflections on the tension between the human and the divine in the figure of Christ. Moreover, the enormous number of interpretations bear testimony to a culture's vitality.

The second is my suspicion that we have arrived at a conceptual saturation that has covered virtually the entire spectrum of possibilities within a cultural tradition, however ample and profound it might be. Fortunately, the situation permits a certain synthetic vision for discovering, for example, that the myths of Western culture have exhibited a certain uniformity for at least twenty-five centuries and that the Christian imprint has been decisive. In this context Karl Jaspers was able to write, "We westerners are all Christians."[8]

The third reason, implicit perhaps in the preceding two, is the conviction that humanity is facing a crisis that involves at least the last six or eight millennia of human experience. This situation highlights interculturality, not in order to defend some impossible multiculturalism but to encourage a reciprocal fecundation of cultures. This christophany touches only implicitly on the important questions feminist theology raises. The new feminist vision

---

[7] The three classical moments of distinctly human activity, according to the *Upaniṣads,* are *śravaṇa,* the hearing of the word (of the Vedas or of the wise man), *manana,* the effort to understand (an operation proper to the mind—*manas*), and *nididyhāsana,* that contemplative assimilation by which one becomes what one knows, and hence entails praxis.

[8] Jaspers (1963) 52.

that is being developed not only offers us a hermenutical key for interpreting the politics of domination that males practice more or less unconsciously but also helps us see the profound meaning of a christology of liberation.[9] Although we cannot ignore the challenges that these problems raise, the perspective that we have adopted attempts to integrate feminist intuitions within a framework that embraces the masculine/feminine dualism.

The Divine Manifestation

For almost half a century I have maintained the proposition that every being is a christophany. It is a question not of converting the whole world to Christianity but of recognizing that the very nature of reality shows the nondualist polarity between the transcendent and the immanent in its every manifestation. Political life cannot be reduced to a selection of *means* (for what end?), nor religious life to the achievement of an atemporal *end* torn from the actual world.

Although it is a concrete form of expressing the universal, christophany liberates—perhaps one should say redeems—the figure of Christ from a particularistic culture. It also liberates from religious, political, and philosophical monotheism, as well as anarchical polytheism, both of which are at the origin of so many civil wars throughout the "created world."[10]

Neither is the Trinity a monotheism (it would then be a docetism) nor God a substance (it would then be a tritheism) or a simple universal concept (it would then be an atheism). Christ opens us to the trinitarian mystery. The divinization of man has constituted a human theme since at least the beginning of historical consciousness. The hellenic memory of this was still alive among the first Christians, and its echo is still evident when Pico della Mirandola writes that man was created after creation was completed. For this reason we do not possess a nature as all other beings do but remain free to construct our nature and thus to become the image and likeness of Him who *in se ipso verae rerum substantiae perfectionem totam unit et colligit* ("unites and gathers in himself the entire perfection of the true substance of things").[11]

A similar vision would liberate us today from an ideology widely diffused in the modern scientific community: evolutionistic anthropology. Even if our body were descended from less developed animals and our

---

[9] The work of Elisabeth Schüssler Fiorenza (1994) is only one example that might be chosen from an abundant bibliography.

[10] The contemporary mind is understanding more and more clearly the problem of the monotheistic incongruity within monotheism. In addition to Erik Peterson's *Der Monotheismus als politiches Problem* (1983, 1935), the bibliography is immense. See Congar (1981), Breton (1981), besides other works on the Trinity. The profound work of Corbin (1981) stands by itself. For a brilliant synthesis of the problems entailed by the passage from montheism to the Trinity, see Milano (1987).

[11] Pico della Mirandola, *Exposition*, v. 6 (*Opera omnia* [Basle, 1572], 300ff.; de Lubac presents other texts with a magisterial commentary (1974) 83.

souls were the product of a bioneurological evolution, real and concrete Man in any case is not a species of a genus "animal." The consciousness of our possible divinization—or, one might say, our aspiration for the infinite—makes us essentially different. As I shall point out later, a spirit exists in us that makes us enter into communion—into *koinōnia*, scripture would say (2 Peter 1:4)—with divine nature.

At the same time, this divinization of Man does not consist in an alienation so as to become a transcendent God—which we are not—but to become in fullness what we potentially are—*capax dei,* as the scholastics said, even though they were too subtle about the *potentia oboedientalis.* True divinization is full humanization. What else did the church fathers mean? They intended not to make Christ a second God but to discover what he reveals to us: that we too can become God. Christ "divinizes man" (θεοποιῶν ἄνθρωπον; *theopoiōn anthrōpon*).[12] This divinization makes sense only within the sphere of the incarnation and the Trinity; in strict monotheism it becomes impossible and blasphemous.[13]

Let us recall a few widely-known assertions:

- "God's Word became Man so that you might learn how to become God."[14]
- "The Word of God became Man and the son of God the son of Man, so that Man, united to the Word of God and receiving sonship, might become son of God."[15]
- "We were not made Gods at the beginning but Men, and at the end Gods."[16]
- "He (Christ) became Man in order to divinize us."[17]
- He became Man so that "I too might be made God."[18]
- "The incarnation makes God a Man through the divinization of Man, and Man a God through the humanization (ἀνθρωποποίησις; *anthrōpopoiēsis*) of God."[19]
- "That I may become God to the extent that he became Man."[20]
- "In each one of us the son of God becomes Man and the son of Man becomes the son of God."[21]

---

[12] Clement of Alexandria, *Protrepticus* xi.

[13] See the various articles in the *Dictionnaire de Spiritualité ascétique et mystique, doctrine et histoire* (Paris: Beauchesne, 1935-95): s.v. "Divinisation" (1957), vol. 3, cols. 1370-1459. There is also a brief article on "Union à Dieu" (vol. 16, cols. 40-61), and other articles on mysticism and grace. For a synthetic study of Meister Eckhart's fidelity to the patristic tradition, unlike St. Thomas's, see Woods (1992).

[14] Clement of Alexandria, *Protrepticus* I, 9, in Bouyer (1960) 334.

[15] Irenaeus of Lyons, *Adversus haereses* III, 19 (PG 7:939).

[16] Ibid., V (PG 7:1120).

[17] Athanasius, *De incarnatione verbi* LIV (PG 25:192). See Bouyer's commentary (1960) 496-501.

[18] Gregory Nazianzen, in Sherrard (1992) 26.

[19] Maximus the Confessor, *Ambigua* (PG 3:100a).

[20] St. Gregory the Theologian, *Oratio theologica* III, 19 (PG 3:100a).

[21] Eckhart, *In Johannem* (LW, iii, 118).

With a leap of almost twenty centuries, we may quote perhaps the last great scholastic philosopher, one who underscored the experiential dimension of Christianity:

> Man is a formal projection of divine reality itself, in a finite way of being God . . . God is transcendent in the human person insofar as the person is God in a deiform way. It is precisely as Christianity is a religion of deiformity that its *experiential* character constitutes its supreme *theological* experience.[22]

Christophany, however, does not focus on the divinization of man. The intuition is found, after all, in a great many religions. The texts that I have cited speak of the *admirabile commercium* between humanity and divinity. In the ancient formula *Accepta tibi sit . . . festivitatis oblatio: ut . . . per haec sacrosancta commercia, in illius inveniamur forma, in quo tecum est nostra substantia* ("May the offering of this festivity be acceptable to you so that through these sacred exchanges we may reach the form of him in whom our substance consists"), the Christmas liturgy prays. Christophany bears a double meaning: the humanization of God corresponds to the divinization of Man. Christ is the revelation of God (in Man) as much as the revelation of Man (in God). The abyss between the divine and the human is reduced to zero in Christ; and it is converted in us in the hope of reaching the other shore. In the Offertory of the Mass the union of water and wine symbolizes the participation of our humanity in the divinity of Christ.[23]

Christophany refers directly to this humanization of God. It speaks of the making of the new creature in Christ (2 Corinthians 5:17), of the new Man (Ephesians 4:24; Colossians 3:10), of the renewal of everything (Revelation 21:5). It would be important to add the vision of Ignatius of Antioch of Christ as "new Man," (καινὸς ἄνθρωπος; *kainos anthrōpos*) in *Ad Ephesians* 20:1, or as "Man made perfect" (τοῦ τελείου ἀνθρώπου γενομένου; *tou teleiou anthrōpou genomenou*) in *Ad Smyrnaeos* 4:2, which reflects the tradition of the ἄνθρωπος Χριστός; *anthrōpos Christos* of the Gospels,[24] as well as the vedic tradition of the "primordial Man" (*puruṣa*) in whom all reality is recapitulated.[25]

In a word, christophany projects us into the taboric light that allows us to discover our infinite dimension and presents the divine in the same light that allows us to discover God in his human dimension.

---

[22] Zubiri (1975) 62.

[23] *Da nobis . . . eius divinitas esse consortes qui humanitatis nostrae fieri dignatus est participes* ("Grant that we may partake of the divinity of the one who became a partaker in our humanity").

[24] For Jesus as Man, see Matthew 11:19; 26:72-74; Luke 23:4-14; and nineteen times in John.

[25] See *Ṛg-veda* X, 90 and other texts in Panikkar (1977) 72ff.

3

The Christophanic Experience

The Cosmovision

Christophany, as I have said, is not a simple extension of christology that attempts to explain—and even understand—the "fact" of Christ. Since it is more experiential, christophany concentrates its attention on the light in which Christ manifests himself to us. In this way we discover that not only do many of Jesus's statements create scandal by shaking our habits, but they seem to originate in a different vision of the world.

One striking example of this is Jesus's eucharistic speech (John 6:22-67). Scientific cosmology does not help here. If we restrict ourselves to such a scheme, the speech makes no sense; it could be accepted only as metaphor, and even "with a grain of salt." The same could be said of the cosmology of Jewish contemporaries of Jesus. They were "right" to be scandalized. We are dealing here with a dilemma of which we are not always conscious.

In order to accept in a human way—freely and consciously—any fact or event, we must seek to understand it intellectually. The famous problematic of Tertullian, *credo quia absurdum* ("I believe because it is absurd") is generally misunderstood; its *quia* ("because") does belong, after all, to the order of reason.[1] It gives us a reason to believe. The dilemma consists in this: because of the intellectual process of acceptance, we must either integrate such a fact into our vision of the world or modify that vision. To take one significant example, most medieval scholastics who believed in the saying *philosophia ancilla theologiae* ("philosophy as the handmaid of theology") did not take into account the fact that the theology of the time was no more than an essentially Aristotelian-Platonic philosophy that served to undergird and constituted the basis of Christian dogma. In adhering to the hellenic cosmology it converted theology into the *ancilla philosophiae* ("the servant of philosophy"). Even those who defend a *theologia crucis* ("theology of the cross") and are ready to insult reason, end up building another castle based on another philosophy, as happened with the earliest protestant theology.

---

[1] See Schestow (1994) 309-24, for an impassioned and intelligent defense of this attitude, about which more will be said below.

18

The christophany that I wish to introduce resolves the dilemma by accepting the second part—that is, by modifying its vision of the world. This is possible only if the faith that has allowed the reality of Christ to be revealed to us is strong enough to overturn the habitual parameters of our understanding: again we encounter the *antistrophe* that we have noted before, an *antistrophe* that is more profound than Nietzsche's *Umwertung* ("transvaluation [of values]").

The problem is central. The manifestation of Christ, the epiphany that stands at the basis of christophany, is so powerful that, inasmuch as it does not reenter the categories of the rational mind, it unsettles a merely rational cosmovision. Luther, among many others, had seen and suffered this dilemma, which in fact caused his antipathy to scholasticism inasmuch as he believed that its "theology" was only Greek wisdom, "foolishness before God" (1 Corinthians 3:19). In brief, christophany requires, in addition to the two eyes we use to deal with everyday experience, a third eye, which faith alone can open. The faith that moves mountains (Matthew 17:20) and dominates the plants and the elements (Matthew 20:21; Luke 17:6; Mark 11:22) may well modify our cosmovision.

What then is the change that is necessary to bring to "our" cosmovision?

The question makes no sense because worldviews are not changed at will: they constitute the omnicomprehensive myth that produces meaning and makes things and events coherent with its distinctive vision of the world. To allow this new vision to spring forth constitutes the great challenge of our times.

A cosmovision does not constitute the concept of the world we construct (cosmology) as much as the vision we have of reality as it presents itself to us, as we see it in a vital relationship that constantly moves between objectivity and subjectivity. The cosmovision changes as our eyes are gradually opened to new aspects of reality, aspects that in turn modify our categories of understanding.

With regard to the cosmovision inherent in christophany, we may begin with Jesus's nocturnal dialogue with Nicodemus. How is it possible to "remain"? How is it possible to be "immanent" in another? (John 3:9). What does this invitation to remain "in him" mean? To remember it is not enough. Neither those who say "Lord, Lord" (Matthew 7:21) nor those who pray with the mind and not the heart will enter the kingdom (Matthew 15:8); it is not the rituals that count but "the Spirit and truth" (John 4:24). What vision of reality do these words presuppose?

Jesus's answer to "the teacher of Israel" (John 3:10) is as unsettling as the archangel Gabriel's answer to Mary (Luke 1:37). It does not include any discussion of ideas nor offer any technical answer to the question of how; instead, it insists on the value of immediate and direct experience ("We testify to what we have seen," John 3:11). Christophany is the fruit of such "seeing," which then seeks to express itself in comprehensible language and draws insight from tradition itself, the fruit of a perception of the *phania* of Christ.

The problem is of capital importance. I have already referred to the atheistic hypothesis of the superfluous God: after all, the universe functions, regardless of whether or not God exists. This transcendent, absent God is completely useless. The same may be said of Christ. If "the mystery of Christ" leaves our cosmovision unchanged, it remains simply a private affair of "the faithful," with no real bearing on the world. Christophany's challenge and task are to present a vision of the universe in which the mystery of Christ finds its place. Otherwise, everything is reduced to pious and meaningless phrases.

The challenge is real. In what do we place our trust? In the words, for example, that tell us that Christ has risen, or in scientific categories that present the resurrection as a collective hallucination? If our "faith" is only belief in the words of others, it obviously cannot be accepted by the human intellect. If there has been a personal experience, however, it will try to find a suitable language that will be understandable only within a determinate cosmovision.[2] The challenge is no light matter.

The World of Interiority

The epigraph cited on page 1 may summarize all that I am about to say. Whoever in the past twenty centuries has heard about that young rabbi, either from John the Baptist, the latest popular preacher, from books or one's own mother, even from the stones themselves; whoever has heard the *kerygma*—to express the idea in a more academic form—has not allowed herself to be discouraged by the unworthiness of intermediaries but, moved by grace or simple curiosity, has sought him out by asking him personally, ποῦ μένεις—*ubi manes*—"Where do you live?" And she has heard the answer in her own heart: "Come and you will see for yourself."

> Come—that is, follow me, observe what, in the depths of your heart, you know you must do and be; take a first step, begin with action rather than in the head; do not begin from what others tell you but come and then you will see.

What counts is the vision, the direct experience, as the Samaritans told the woman at the well (John 4:42). This is often understood as an elitist theology that contradicts many other invitations of the teacher, such as, "Come to me" (Matthew 11:28); "let the children come to me" (Matthew 19:14; Mark 10:14, etc.). This leads many to believe that the experience of Christ—and therefore, his grace—was reserved for the few

---

[2] See Guardini (1953) for a passionate and intelligent defense of this position.

who reach the heights of contemplation and that ordinary people ("the little ones") can neither go nor see anything.

But what is involved here? Above all it is a question of "seeing," a personal experience, not a question of formulating a doctrine or even asserting that Jesus was a great prophet or the Messiah whom the people awaited. It is not a question of elaborating a theology of Christianity—that is, the "reception," the impact Jesus made, as it was elaborated by the rich and multiform Mediterranean culture. If "Jesus Christ is the same yesterday, today, and always" (Hebrews 13:8), then while respecting the authority of the *seniores* of every age, even we contemporaries, including those who belong to other cultures, have the possibility—and perhaps the right—to receive directly the impact of one who rejected neither the Samaritan woman nor the Syrophoenician nor the woman taken in adultery.

It has always been said that faith is a gift, but we should keep in mind that those who receive it must also be conscious of its reception. Such a consciousness is neither a doctrinal evidence nor a rational conviction; it is an experience of truth (1 John 1:1-3), not simply trust in somebody else's experience—no matter how important and undeniable that experience is. In a word, faith reveals to us that the name Christ is not only the name of a historical personage but a reality in our own life (Philippians 2:7-11). This is an experience that may be expressed in many and varied forms. Scripture itself confirms this when it asserts, "Nobody can say 'Jesus is the Lord' if not in the Holy Spirit" (1 Corinthians 12:3; cf. also 1 John 5:1). The one who makes this assertion makes it because she has "seen" something—she has had an experience—not because she has learned something in a classroom lesson.

At the basis of faith, therefore, is an experience of union. I do not wish to be misunderstood. The word "experience" is ambiguous and polysemic. In this instance it is not a question of a mere psychological experience, but of an ontological "touch," so to speak. It is an experience that transforms our entire being; we have a feeling that we have been taken over by a stronger reality that penetrates and transforms us. It is not yet the time to discuss what might be the criteria for establishing the authenticity of such a touch or the diverse forms this experience of human fullness might present.

But let us return to the question: What is seen? The evangelist who reports the question, "Where do you live?" and gives us an answer, as he plays on the same verb nine times in seven verses (John 15:4-10): *Manete in me*; μείνατε ἐν ἐμοί; "Remain in me." You no longer live *with* me as the first time, but *in* me, as intimately as I exist in the Source of reality and life."[3] Jesus's entire eucharistic speech (John 6:22-70) is centered on the

---

[3] It is worth noting the near-embarrassment of much modern exegesis in the face of the meaning of this verb, so crucial in the Johannine writings, which contain 66 of its 112 appearances in the whole New Testament. In fact, how is it possible for one to "remain" in another

same verb: "He who eats my flesh and drinks my blood remains in me and I in him" (John 6:57).

This is the mystery of Christ: the interpenetration, the *perichōrēsis* (*circumincessio* in Latin), as the church fathers would say, between the divine and the human, without forgetting that within the human there also exists the cosmic, as Jesus's entire speech here attests. *Manete in eo* ("Remain in him"), John reasserts as the last counsel to his "children" (1 John 2:28). What is the meaning of this term, which Paul will later interpret as a "living in Christ" (Philippians 1:21) and as "our life" (Colossians 3:4)?

The baptismal water poured on the head of many Christians has not reached the heart. A two-pronged road is thus opened that everyone must travel in accordance with the talents each has received: intellectual inquiry and inner journey. In other words, we must inquire of tradition who this Christ might be and at the same time ask our own hearts what he might signify. Unless the first road is linked with the second we shall not arrive at an authentic Christian life—and shall remain at most catechumens. Two variant interpretations can lead us to the heart of what *manere* ("to remain" one in the other) could mean. We might call one anthropological, the other philosophical.

The first is the universal phenomenon of falling in love. The vision of the person loved is transformed, though others don't see what the person in love sees. In addition—I am speaking of a genuine falling in love and not of a more or less superficial infatuation—those who love each other in a certain sense live one in the other. The sufferings and joys of the one affect the other. There is an interpenetration that is *sui generis*; it is not simply a matter of "one single flesh" as Paul would say, but above all of one single spirit.

The second, which is also a universal phenomenon, can be expressed by saying that everyone is open to transcendence. Each of us has a certain consciousness that in fact there is something else, something greater than what we can grasp by sight. In the history of ideas, this opening to the transcendent is defined, generally speaking, as religious faith; the most common name used to express the term of this human experience is called the divine—and very often God. It has frequently been noticed, however, that something of this transcendence descends into the inner depths of man and we speak of the immanence of the divine. God, the sacred, the numinous, or whatever we wish to call it, remains then in us—it is *immanent*. There is a *manere* of God in each of us. This creates a certain reciprocity: God is in us and we are in God. Paul, echoing Greek wisdom, preached to the Athenians that in God "we live and move and have our being" (Acts 17:28).

---

person in an individualistic and rational cosmovision? We should also call attention to a wholly different current of thought in Berdyaev (1933) 97: "At a greater depth it has been revealed to us that man does not save himself through Christ but in Christ."

In effect, experience of the divine immensity is such that nothing can be admitted outside of it. Our *manere*, our "ex-istence" is therefore in God. The relation between God and man, therefore, instead of being one of pure transcendence (which does not admit any relation) is one of immanence. God is the transcendent mystery immanent in us. Hence there is a conviction common to different religions that someone who claims to have seen the transcendent God is not telling the truth. In the *Sermo* (117, c. 3, 5 [PL 38:663]), St Augustine says, *Si comprehendis, non est Deus* ("If you understand, it is not God"), summing up the whole patristic teaching on the [un]knowability of God. It is in immanence that transcendence is discovered. We realize that we "remain" in something that, being within us, is greater than we are, transcends us. Mysticism speaks of this constantly. One need only cite the first (untranslatable) phrase of the *Īśa-upaniṣad*: "Everything that moves in this changing world is entwined by God."[4]

But this is not yet the christophanic experience, which is neither merely "human" like the first nor exclusively "divine" like the second. On the contrary, the christophanic experience reveals to us that, when they are authentic, the first is not merely human nor the second solely divine. In the christophanic experience it is neither God who remains in us nor we in him; it is rather a theandric or eucharistic presence that penetrates us and remains in us, and we in it. On one hand, it is similar to the anthropological experience of falling in love, but with a difference: the christophanic experience is not a mere human presence. It is the human and the divine in a union that is unique. On the other hand, it is a mutual *manere*, which assumes the nature of the two experiences just described. Here, in experiential form, is what various doctrines later elaborate. The encounter with Christ partakes of the encounter with both the person lived and the divine. Without the falling in love, without the silence of the *Abgrund* ("abyss"), there is no christophany—no christic manifestation. Christian mysticism presents this polarity, which is not free of tensions. Those who are inclined to knowledge, to *jñāna*, will see the divine aspect; those more sensitive to love, to *bhakti*, will see Christ's humanity as central.

In this sense christophany presents its own peculiarity. It is neither a mere theophany nor even the loving discovery of being loved. More than a synthesis which makes us think of a Hegelian *Aufhebung* of the two experiences, it is a nondualistic union, which in a certain sense constitutes their basis; the two experiences go together in life as well. Do not those in love tend to divinize the beloved? And is it not also true that even the most intellectual mystics tend to anthropomorphize the divine? The christophanic experience does not split Christ's immanence into one part human, one part divine: it is an *advaita* experience.

Perhaps the scriptural model of this christophanic experience is the meeting at Damascus (Acts 9:1ff.). Paul never saw Jesus with the first eye

---

[4] See Panikkar (1975a) 102-18 for commentary.

of the senses. His vision of the second eye (the mind) is that of a Jesus who betrayed the Law and thus deserved death. At Damascus the third eye (of the spirit) is suddenly opened, and he sees Jesus. It is therefore natural that, dazzled, he remains blind in the first eye until light slowly enters also into the second, and that later he will see with the third. After this transformation, which Jesus has come to effect, he will then be able to say that he has met the Christ in Jesus, and to speak with the authority of one who has seen.

Two examples from other religions are also worth reporting, although they also contain some differences. The Kṛṣṇa-bhakti offers something similar, though not the same. Kṛṣṇa is a human figure; interiorized and alive in our heart, he is immanent in us. But Kṛṣṇa is also an avatar, a divine descent, not an incarnation in the Christian sense. Kṛṣṇa is God in human form, not a Man-God, though in practice the differences tend to vanish. In Christian terminology this would be called docetism—which from a Hindu perspective makes no sense, since Vishnu is everything. The Kṛṣṇa of the heart, the living Kṛṣṇa is God who has taken human form, although this form is illusory.

In certain types of neo-Hindu spirituality the figure of the guru could be related to the christophanic experience, but here too the morphological differences are notable. Phenomenologically speaking, there may be many gurus, just as there are many avatars, whereas the notion of many Christs is contradictory, just as the idea of many Gods in a monotheistic sense is contradictory. There would be one sole God—though under different aspects. It is impossible to distinguish two supreme and infinite beings, for then they would not be two. Even though at times he is called *sat-guru* and *jagat-guru*, the *guru* in general does not pretend to be either unique or universal. The relation is very personal. The *guru* is what he is for the *śiṣya*, the disciple; his role does not pretend to serve a cosmic function—although recently, perhaps due to Christian influence, this tendency has made some headway. Insofar as every experience is personal, it lies beyond all comparison. When we express ourselves in a language that aims at being intelligible, however, we must draw on ideas derived from tradition.

The eucharistic life constitutes the concretization of this experience. It is not without reason that an important patristic tradition, which persisted in the medieval period and even up to the modern age, saw in the eucharist (certainly not in communion, as some pretended) the drug for immortality and the condition for resurrection (John 6:54ff.).[5] In the eucharist, Christ is encountered in the same way in which one enters into contact with a person—physically. The eucharist is material, yet at the same time is not any piece of bread or glass of wine, nor even an anthropophagy. It is an encounter that is also spiritual. Nor is it accidental that the primordial religions know similar rites of physical contact with the divinity, even though

---

[5] See Panikkar (1963), "La eucaristia y la resurrection de la carne," 335-52.

under different aspects than the eucharist. However this may be, in eucharistic spirituality, unlike the attachment to communion, we find the theandric form of the *manere*, one in the other, as the texts explicitly warrant (John 6:33-58).

But there is something else in the christophanic experience, and here I have to correct a certain piety, eucharistic as well as christic. Stated in concise form, Jesus is not God but God's son and, as son, "equal" to the Father because the Father retains nothing for himself. In our context, the *manere* of which we speak is a dynamic "remaining" that is also in a certain sense transient because, as ancient texts assert, Christ takes us to the Father and does not remain enclosed in us. We must remain in him as he remains in the Father, and go toward Him. As almost all liturgical prayers conclude, *per Christum Dominum nostrum*, "through Christ, by means of Christ." Not even a profound human love closes itself up in the beloved but transcends without leaving her or him. It is not an enclosed love, an *amor curvus*, as the Middle Ages would say, but a trinitarian love. Certainly, when the falling in love is real, it possesses the power to make us love others as well. The discovery of Christ's immanence does not stop at our ego but catapults us toward the Father and from him to the whole universe. As I hope to explain later, the christophanic experience opens us up to a cosmotheandric experience.

To sum up, christophany is neither the manifestation of God nor a meeting with the human beloved. It is a unique *phania*, whence the visceral reaction against every comparison by those who have experienced Jesus Christ. Nevertheless, critical thought is legitimate. The best description of Christian self-consciousness is found perhaps in Paul's final doxology in Romans 16:25-26: Jesus Christ, who "according to the revelation, kept silent for eternal centuries (κατὰ ἀποκάλυψιν μυστηρίου χρόνοις αἰωνίοις σεσιγημένου)," and in Colossians 1:26, Paul says, "has manifested himself now (νῦν δὲ ἐφανερώθη)." This "now" is what we have at heart, and the following pages constitute an attempt to immerse ourselves in this light.

Mystical Language

Much has been written about mystical language.[6] It is right to recall the condemnation of Meister Eckhart and others for using phrases *ut sonant* ("*as* they sound") without considering the context *ubi sonant* ("*where* they sound")—forgetting, moreover, that words *resonate* (in our hearts) only where they "resound." This distinction implies that there is no objective language, sometimes defined as "literal," in the interpretation of texts, whether sacred or not. Howsoever this may be, our linguistic observation goes beyond these polemics and would like to introduce an inter-

---

[6] See the virtually exhaustive volumes of Haas (1979 and 1996) on the *status questionis*.

cultural perspective, which is generally forgotten by the dominant modern culture. With the exception of poets, who are granted the right to speak metaphorically, such a culture utilizes language as a system of conceptual signs. It has been said of St. Thomas in late scholasticism, *formalissime semper loquitur divus Thomas* ("The divine Thomas always speaks in a rigorously accurate way"). In that age theology and even faith were discussed as if they were algebra. It is no surprise to find mystical language described—and by a sympathizer, not an adversary—as *obscurus, involutus, elevatus, sublimis, abstractus et quadam tenus inflatus.*[7]

A brief look at another culture will be enough for us to realize that language is not a conceptual algebra that indicates the *res significata* in a more or less universal sense but rather a system of *symbols* that evokes in the listener a synchronization and a special participation—and a double effort by the reader who neither sees nor hears nor knows the person who writes.

"Is not the failure in clarity (*Unklarheit*) of the language of (German) speculative mysticism above all a failure in clarity *in us*?" asks a scholar who has an excellent knowledge of the mystical tradition.[8] This does not mean that no criticism is possible or that a certain psychological empathy is not needed in order to understand the language of the other. It does mean, however, that every complete language is an objective-subjective, cultural and temporal system—above all, a system of levels of consciousness and knowledge. When traditional theology demanded faith in order to cultivate that science, it did not intend to exclude anybody out of elitist prejudice, but rather to remind us that, to use modern language, we must be on the same wavelength. Every expression that does not limit itself to repeating already established concepts and amusing itself with them but wishes to give visual shape to a profound experience must in a certain way create its own language, even if it be by means of words that have already been consecrated.

In the following pages I have tried to be as simple and clear as possible and have therefore avoided poetry and metaphor. Nevertheless, words are symbols, not concepts. A christophany that takes into account the other religious traditions of mankind cannot accept the conceptual algebra of the West as a neutral and universal paradigm. After Parmenides we seem to have forgotten that concepts are only surrogates of the thing—of reality. Ideas of Platonic origin are accepted even though, when emptied of their ontological consistency (perhaps through their Augustinian translation into divine ideas) they become simple algebraic signs.[9]

---

[7] The words are those of the Jesuit Maximilian Dandaneus published in 1646; see Haas (1979) 79.

[8] Kurt Ruh, in Haas (1979) 80.

[9] The displacement in the world of concepts (*der Verschiebung ins Begriffliche*) undermines the consistency (*die Substanz*) of the experience and transforms it into a mere name that then becomes a substitute for reality. See Jung (1963) 150.

The meaning of language has been said to reside in its use—but on whose part? Naturally, on the part of the one who knows how to impose himself, that is, on the part of power. The language of the strong has become a weapon. A Christian discourse should be conscious of this use (abuse) by those who hold power. "We shall be asked to give an account of every word that is unfounded—and thus vain, without force" ῥῆμα ἀργόν (Matthew 12:36).

Mysticism possesses a more direct and immediate language. Let me conclude this introduction with a comment on a phrase of St. Teresa of Avila that gave rise to a debate between her brother Don Lorenzo de Cepeda, John of the Cross, and other individuals and nuns in the absence of Teresa. The saint heard Christ speak the following words: *Teresa, búscate en mí, búscame en ti*[10] ("Seek for yourself in me, seek for me in yourself"). These words inspired a poem that seems to me one of the most beautiful expressions of christophanic experience. I quote two stanzas:

> Alma, buscarte has en Mí,
> Y a Mí buscarme has en ti.
>
> . . . .
>
> *Fuiste por amor criada*
> *Hermosa, bella, y ansí*
> *En mis entrañas pintada,*
> *Si te perdieres, mi amada.*
> Alma, buscarte has en Mí.
>
> . . . .
>
> *Y si acaso no supieres*
> *Donde me hallarás a Mí,*
> *No andes de aquí para allí,*
> *Sino, si hallarme quisieres*
> A Mí buscarme has en ti.[11]

We seek below to translate these stanzas and to comment briefly upon them:

> Soul, you must seek yourself in Me
> And Me you must seek in yourself.
>
> . . . .
>
> You were created for love
> Beautiful, gracious, and thus

---

[10] See Martin-Velasco (1995) 119-48, for a very valid modern commentary.
[11] From Santa Teresa de Jesús, *Obras Completas* (1967) 500-501.

In my heart painted,
Should you lose yourself, O my beloved,
Soul, you must seek yourself in Me.

. . . .

But if perhaps you should not know
Where you may find Me
Do not go hither and thither,
But, if you should wish to find me,
Me you must seek in yourself.

In commenting on the poem allow me to retain the form of the first person addressing another. Each of us is a pilgrim still on the way, a seeker, a "being" who is not yet, who is becoming.

Soul, seek, do not stop, do not deceive yourself: your being has not been achieved, is not perfect, is still unfinished.

This seeking constitutes the very dynamism of Life. It reminds us of the revealing phrase of Psalm 62:11 (Psalm 61 in older Catholic Bibles), the Latin translation of which has been widely commented upon in Christian mysticism. The famous words are *semel locutus est Deus, duo haec audivi.* Teresa was given only one word (*locutio*): "seek." But Teresa heard two invitations: "seek yourself, seek me."

Seek Yourself

All the wisdom of the world repeats: "know yourself," "ask who you are," "enter into your inmost self," "discover your heart." This is the invitation to the *autophanic experience,* to know the manifestation of the reality that we are and of which we must become progressively more conscious in order to become masters of our life: free. Free in order to reach our freedom—liberation, *sōtēria, mokṣa.*

Seek Me

Most human traditions invite us to open ourselves to transcendence. This human search does not end in ourselves. Instead, "seek God"; "begin your journey toward the infinite"; "open yourself up to *nirvāṇa,*" "leave yourself," "wake up," "move always ahead."

This is the invitation to the *theophanic experience,* to know the light that does not come from us, that illuminates and transforms us—so that we may fully become what we are called to be. None of this is new, but Teresa heard more—she heard two other messages: seek for yourself, *in me*; seek for me, *in yourself.*

This is the *christophanic experience* on which I would like to comment. It is not a mere search for oneself in one's self, a more or less egocentric introspection. Still less is it a simple search for the Other in a transcendence, a more or less total going out of ourselves. It is a search for ourselves in an icon which, because it dwells in our deepest self, does not alienate us: Christ is man like us, while he is at the same time infinitely superior to us. Christ is son of God, irradiation, splendor, ἀπαύγασμα, *apaugasma*, of his glory (Hebrews 1:3), and therefore does not allow us to enclose ourselves within ourselves. We seek ourselves in seeking Christ; we seek Christ in seeking ourselves.

The *búscate en mí* includes three moments:

1. "Seek for yourself in me—emptying yourself of yourself."

Otherwise you would not even be able to begin to seek: you would seek only yourself, with the danger of flowing into solipsistic self-divinization, egocentrism, and narcissism. You cannot seek for me if you are full of yourself—you most empty yourself. All traditions posit this as a primary condition: *Wu-wei, śūnyatā, asat,* μὴ ὄν, ὑπὲρ ὄν, πένθος, *nihil, Gelassenheit, desasimiento, noche oscura, abandano, indiferencia*—whatever interpretation is given to the origin of the élan—grace, karma, effort, destiny, profound nature.

This is the beginning of a properly human life, of Life. Without this initiation we remain just a species of the genus animal; we have not yet been born into our true nature. Virtually all human cultures know rites of initiation into life, but baptism makes no sense for an animal.

To search for "him" we must form an emptiness in ourselves. This act of self-emptying is equivalent to a death. Without this complete death to ourselves we cannot be resuscitated and we remain moribund throughout our temporal existence. It would be pathological to remain fixed in a negative, necrophilic, and perhaps even suicidal asceticism, yet without this first step, the monastic *compunctio cordis*, the Gospel's metanoia, or meditation on emptiness, there is no fully human life. In Christian terms, the removal of "original sin" constitutes the beginning of true Life.

2. "Seek yourself in me by going out of yourself."

Otherwise you will not find yourself. Your identity, what you seek, does not reside in yourself [as an individual]; you must go out toward the Other. You cannot seek me unless you abandon all that you possess—you must go out of yourself. But inasmuch as the other is Other, there is no road, there are no ways that have already been traveled and marked out. The great unknown cannot be sought as a known: *y por aquí no hay camino* ("going this way there is no passage"), *avijñātaṃ, vijñātām,* ἀγνωσία, *rayo de tiniebla, cloud of unknowing,* the *tao* named is not the *tao.*

We cannot attain transcendence, but neither can we remain enclosed within immanence; we must open ourselves to transcendence—open ourselves only because we cannot cross the abyss without destroying it. Once again despair opens us to hope.

> "How can this be done? I do not know man." I know neither the way nor the goal. Seek yourself in Me; I am this other; discover the unique Other who, not being strictly speaking other, allows yourself to be yourself—breaks your isolation while respecting the uniqueness of your being. And if you allow love to penetrate into you, you will discover that the Other is not another but Me—who is I.
>
> You will discover in Me a microcosm—not a small world but the world in small, miniaturized. Then you will begin to discover the whole world in Me, and this discovery will make you at one with the universe and reveal to you, in Me, all the levels of reality. You can no longer think of yourself as alone. You are a microcosm.

Thus, despite the negative meaning that the expression has acquired over time, *nihil mundani a me alienum puto* ("nothing in the world alien to me"), it will become connatural to us, and the inner will not be an enemy to the outer, as is said in the *Gospel of Thomas*.

Man is a pilgrim, but the *peregrinare* is not the same as traveling toward a known goal, much less a touristic excursion in search of exotic sensations. Human life is the undertaking of a journey toward the risky adventure of being or non-being, as an *upaniṣad* says (*astiti nāstiti* (*Kaṭha-upaniṣad* I, 1, 20). Abraham left Ur without knowing where he was going (Genesis 12:1; Hebrews 11:8). "Go and leave everything you have" (Matthew 19:21). All the literatures of the world speak of the same kind of adventure. It is necessary to go forth in search of the Grail, the princess, the treasure, heaven, the unknown, happiness—God.

3. "Seek yourself in me—discovering Me."

> Otherwise you will discover only a non-you. By discovering Me you will discover in Me a *mikrotheos*; not a small God but God in a human measure, an incarnate God. The journey toward Me never ends.

The ultimate reality escapes us, yet we slowly glimpse the reason: this reality is in us also; we also are ourselves and cannot alienate ourselves—that is, escape from ourselves. We then discover that this Me is not extraneous to us, that we ourselves are involved.

At this level objective knowledge is no longer possible: knowledge involves the subject as well. It is the mystical intuition, the vision of the third eye, the consciousness of the "realization" that never ends—in fact, is infinite.

God (the infinite, the reality, the absolute, or even nirvāṇa) is not an object of either thought or prayer. The third eye does not compete with the intellectual eye; it belongs to a different order. Not only do we discover the world of reality within us, but we also become conscious that we ourselves constitute reality. To consider ourselves "part" of this reality is a gross and overly spatial metaphor. We are, rather, images, icons, of the whole of reality. We lift the *velamen essendi* (Meister Eckhart's "veil of being") in order to catch a glimpse of the microtheos that we are. We find a very beautiful image in Clement of Alexandria: "Everything that appears veiled contains greater truth . . . as the forms . . . become more attractive when they allows us to glimpse this gracefulness under light tunics" (*Stromata* V, 9).

Here again we find a virtually universal theme. "The pearl is not far away, *Noli foras ire*" (Augustine, *De vera reilgione* I, 39, n. 72 [PL 34:154]). The treasure lies under your house, close the windows and the eyes; "this is you, O *Śvetaketu*"(*Chāndogya-upaniṣad* VI, 8, 7, etc.). This Me is not an abstraction; it has a recognizable face. The lover discovers the beloved.

> *Búscate en Mí* ("Seek yourself in Me"). But this is nothing but the entrance. Seek for yourself, you must seek yourself, you are obliged to seek yourself, to know who you are. But you must do this outside yourself (this is why you are seeking), without leaving yourself—otherwise you will not find yourself but another, you will alienate yourself.

The adage γνῶθι σεαυτόν, *(a)gnosce te ipsum*, "know yourself," is an imperative of human nature. We cannot, however, know ourselves as objects, because we are not objects. We should know ourselves as subjects, although full self-consciousness is impossible: the one that is known is not the one who knows.

> You cannot seek yourself in things. They are not you; should you find yourself among them you would simply be a thing. Neither can you seek yourself in a transcendent God because this is not possible for you, and even if it were, God would no longer be transcendent or you would no longer be you—that is, your I. You must therefore seek yourself in *Me*, and this will allow you to be what you are. You must seek yourself by seeking *Me*.

This leads us to the second moment: what we seek cannot be elsewhere than in ourselves.

Búscame en ti

Here too we may distinguish three stages:

1. "Seek me in thyself[12]—as your deepest thou."

It is the pilgrimage toward the *ātman* (Śaṅkara), the search for Being (Parmenides), the journey to the promised land (Moses).

> But in the beginning thou wilt not find anything that resembles Me. In thyself thou wilt find only egoism, littleness, limitation. And what if this were not thee? Hast thou forgotten that thou art "beautiful, graceful, painted in my heart"? If thou seekest Me in thee, thou wilt find this goodness, beauty, and truth that are in thee; thou wilt discover thy dignity and have trust in thyself. How can thou believe in Me unless thou believest in thyself, who is the subject of thy believing?

> Human honor, the honor that in Teresa's Spain was so powerful, is neither prestige nor fame, as Aristotle, Cicero, and Aquinas believed, nor social reputation, however important that may be; it is the honor of the person herself, the dignity of each one of us. If we lose this self-esteem, this trust in ourselves, we will find it difficult to esteem others or to have faith in "God." It is for this reason that "seek me" comes after the "seek yourself." We cannot seek "God" unless we have trust in the one who is seeking. The "death of God" is the result of the death of the subject for whom God could be God. The crisis of our age is, above all, the crisis of man, whom we have reduced to an economic factor in the great cogwheel of competitiveness. Although the "races" in St. Paul's 1 Corinthians 9:24-27 are not ours, we are still dealing with his somewhat infelicitous metaphor. After all, even in other Pauline texts, the victor is not the one who runs the fastest (Romans 9:16). In order to search for the pearl, the kingdom of God, beauty, justice, truth, in us, we must have that self-esteem that makes it possible to believe that there is something good in us.

2. "Seek me in thyself—as thy thou."

It is difficult to be convinced of our dignity even if we succeed in reaching this profound level: not everything is pure inside us. Mysticism runs the risk of idealizing man and of forgetting the human condition. Our search for "him" in us must not ignore the danger of a mirage.

---

[12] Editor's Note: We use here and several places in the following paragraphs the archaic forms of the second person pronoun "thou" to indicate conversion to consciousness of the personal depth dimension in oneself and God when we move to levels deeper than daily superficiality, in which we often treat God and both ourselves and others as "its."

Seek me, seek me then as thou art; it is thee who seek me and thee who find me not as another but as a thou in the intimacy of your being. Thou discover me and speak to me as a friend, a beloved— that is, as a thou who is in relation with thee. Only after thou hast made this discovery wilt thou realize that the silence of this thou reveals something unsuspected. Thou hast conquered dualism because thou experience this thou as thy thou. But thou hast not overcome monism. I am not thee.

Neither monism nor dualism, reality is *advitīyan*, nondualist, as *Chāndogya-upaniṣad* (VI, 2) proclaims. Dialogue is a διὰ τὸν λόγον, a passing through the *logos,* in the Spirit. If we seek the I in us, we can find it only in connection with ourselves, not detached from us—that is, as a "you." We discover it as our "you." We open ourselves to a life of prayer: we turn to "him" as a thou. We pray to "him" as a you, we call him "thou." The personification of what we seek and love is inherent in human nature. To speak to him as a you gives us a great sense of trust and security, as the literature of the world attests. But this you seldom answer us, and almost never directly. The first innocence is lost and a fear arises that everything is a projection of our unsatisfied desires. Influenced by too much psychology or depressed by "the dark night of the soul," many become discouraged or turn back (Luke 9:62).

3. "Seek me in thyself—as your I."

Seek me in thy thou because you will not find me outside of thee. It is I who say that thou must seek me in yourself. You have discovered me as a thou, but it is precisely this thou that turns to thee as its thou. Inasmuch as "I am" so "thou art," *tat tvam asi*! Thou art mine, not so much as the property of a master or a creator God, but as thou art—precisely, my thou, and I call thee thou. Thou art dear to me, as the *Gītā* says. Thou art my daughter, as the Gospel says. Seek me, not as another, not as Two, not as One, but as the *I who I am*—who makes it possible that thou art—a thou, my thou. It is "thou" who art "thee," not "I."

We must make a mental leap: "he" is not another and cannot be such if I seek him in me. The other is alienating, discouraging. The great danger is to abandon the urge to seek and to stop. This stopping is fatal. We stop when we renounce the journey, because if God is the Other, the goal is unreachable. This is dualism. But must the creature resign itself to being always a creature? Shall we never be God? Must we resign ourselves to live like Sisyphus?

Are we condemned to be no more than rational animals who must accept things as they are? Man rebels because he wants more. The serpent's echo, "You shall be like Gods," echoes today in our ears, and that aspiration has never been appeased in human nature. The second Adam, however, offers us an experience that is extraordinarily bold: "Thou wilt not be *like* God unless thou art called to be a son of God himself, to be one with him, to be totally divinized."

Dualism transforms this aspiration into a nightmare. The abyss cannot be crossed. Man thus becomes discouraged, weary of the pilgrimage that fails to satisfy his restlessness. Abandoning God, he throws himself into the things of this world in order to establish the "human city," build a better world, dream about a lost paradise, and project his frustrated hopes onto the future. But this future never arrives, and life is short. It is marxism, perhaps, that has situated the last messianic dream in a historical future. Capitalism does not promise that future to everybody, but only to the winners in the wars of competition.

Insofar as God has withdrawn into transcendence, then, and abandoned him, man consecrates himself to working on things, turning himself into a master and becoming the lord of all those things. This accounts for the rise of the powerful world of technoscience. At least a tower of Babel might have been built, a world government and other such things—while, of course, everything remains under our control. Finally, however, the human project, too, seems to collapse, just like the divine design of a Creator. The clamor of the winners does not stifle the cries of the slaves, the oppressed, and of all the holocausts of history.

Restlessmess is intrinsic to human nature, and ever since antiquity those who believe themselves the best, in order to avoid the Carybdis of linear time are caught up in the whirlpools of Scylla and engulfed by the abyss of a divinity that negates the world, an abyss one can never leave. It is the monism into which the person falls who seeks to liberate himself by his own power, in which case the world is illusory, or at least provisional, and personality is an enigma. The *unum, ekam,* ἕν, is everything. Our pilgrimage would then be that of "the alone toward the alone" (Plotinus, *Enneads*, V, 1, 6; VI, 9, 11). The "terrestrial city" is abandoned, but no residence in the "celestial city" is established. This is disincarnate, acosmic spirituality.

In both cases, the dynamism and the search have ended. And as the *seek me* ceases, so does life. In the first case, man searches for himself only insofar as he is man, and succeeds only by becoming a *good* man. Ethics is turned into religion. In the second case, man turns into God and consoles himself with the belief that no "Consoler" is necessary now because he has already transformed himself into God.

This tension pierces the whole history of spirituality: either Man or God, either the humanistic and atheistic epiphany or the dehumanizing and monotheistic theophany. What is lacking is a mediator, a christophany that is, at one and the same time, human and divine. Neither is man the measure of all things (Protagoras, *Fragment* 1, b) nor God the *metron* ("measure") of everything (Plato, *Laws* 716c; cf. *Cratylus* 385a 6 and *Theaetetus* 152 a 2-4). It is, rather, the Trinity that is the measure, the *metron* of all things—

as the Pythagoreans understood and Ficino, in his own day, recalled (*De amore*, I, 1).

The *seek me* cannot be divided from the *seek thyself*, for the *me* and the *thou* are correlative. The *metron* is human and divine, theandric—indeed, cosmotheandric. This is the third stage, the discovery of the I. Here the Trinity or *advaita* is central.

> Thou art not I. "You" are a "thou" who is in Me, a "thou" that the I releases—by loving. Seeking me in thyself, thou discoverest that it is I who propel thee to search in order to give thy Life in the seeking itself. Thou discoverest the I by being thyself, by being *thy* self, by being the *thou* of the I. It is the I and the I alone that can say *ahambrahmāsmi* (I am *brahman*), Yahwe ("I am who I am"); but thou canst say something much more than "thou art *brahman*," thou canst do something greater than pray to me as a thou, as thy thou. Thou canst unite thyself to me and, without ceasing to be thyself, experience the fact that *thou art* because I say "I am thee," even if thou cannot say "(I) am thee." At most, you could say "thou art I [the I]," but the "thou art" is not the "I am."

Then the mortal jump occurs. God is not the thou, my thou, my possession—as in so many forms of exaggerated, barely sane spirituality. I am not I, "my" I. God is the I. I discover myself as "thou," God's thou. God is the I, and I am God's thou. It is the I who speaks and to whom we listen—not as slaves, not as creatures but as children (children of the Son) in the Spirit. This is the trinitarian life; this is the christophanic experience: neither the mere dualism of creatureliness, the worldly, nor the monistic simplification of divinization.

What or who this Christ *is* who has spoken to Teresa is the focal point of this book.

Part 2

The Mysticism of Jesus the Christ
The Experience of Jesus

Τοῦτο φρονεῖτε ἐν ὑμῖν
ὃ καὶ ἐν Χριστῷ Ἰησοῦ

Have in yourselves the same sentiments
[a consciously lived experience]
that is yours in Christ Jesus.
(Philippians 2:5)

1

The Approach

> That which was from the beginnng,
> which we have heard,
> which we have seen with our eyes
> which we have looked upon and
> touched with our hands,
> concerning the word of life —
> the life was made manifest
> (ἐφανερώθη),
> and we saw it,
> and testify to it,
> and proclaim to you the eternal life
> which was with the Father
> and was made manifest (ἐφανερώθη)
> to us.
>
> (1 John 1:1-2)

This passionate testimony introduces us directly to our theme. Twice its author speaks to us of christophany, in both cases homologized with Life, "the Life that was in him and was the light of men" (John 1:18). Acceptance of this christophany gives us the power to become "children of God" (John 1:12), and if children, we too can "hear," "see," observe," and "touch" the "Word of Life."

It is a question of an experience that gives us the power of discovering ourselves and verifying what others say. Dionysius the Areopagite speaks to us of "the power of discerning odors" (*Coelestis Hierarchia*, XV, 3).

If we take John to be the author of our text, christophany invites us not only to understand his testimony but also to have the same experience, so that his words may echo in us as well. After all, John's words are themselves the fruit of a meditation—the meditation of his eyes and hands. Many others have seen and touched that "manifestation" and have given the same testimony. This means that our situation is not entirely different from that of the early Christians. Faith in Christ does not depend on the latest papyri found at the Dead Sea. Like John, we too can "hear," "see," "observe," and "touch" the Word of Life. Christian thought, whether

Latin or modern, has dwelt too little on the taboric light, a light that is neither a hallucination nor an intellectual projection but the vision of an aspect of reality that still engages us today (See Matthew 17:1ff.; Mark 9:2ff.; Luke 9:28ff.; 2 Peter 1:16f.). The "transfiguration" transforms the observer as well.

We shall try to describe this existential approach.

The Problem

Prologomena

First of all, I should explain the sense in which I am using some key words. By *mysticism* I mean all that which pertains to the ultimate experience of reality. The ultimate experience of reality is the locus of mystical experience.[1]

Reality is used here as the most comprehensive word that embraces all that which, in some way, enters into our consciousness—even the incomprehensible, the ineffable, the non-being, and so on. By *ultimate* I mean that which is irreducible to the intellect. Something is ultimate when it cannot be reduced to anything ulterior, when the sequence of ideas cannot be deduced from one more general or certain, or when the intuition does not go beyond it. Plato would define it as "the principle without an ulterior foundation" (ἀρχὴ ἀνυπόθετος [*archē anypothetos*] in the *Republic* 510b). Abhinavagupta would call it *anuttaram*, that which cannot be transcended (*Parātrīśikā-vivaraṇai,* 1). But this does not mean that what is ultimate for a given individual or group need be ultimate for all the others (contrary to Plato, who in *Republic* 511b defines ἀνυπόθετος as "the principle of all"— τοῦ παντὸς ἀρχή [*tou pantos archē*]). One of the most fascinating discoveries of the dialogue's praxis lies in the fact that what for me is indubitable and evident, which is to say ultimate, for my interlocutor may be disputable and not at all ultimate. What I take for granted may not agree with the myth of my interlocutor.

By *experience* I mean a conscious immediacy—that is, the consciousness of something immediately present. In experience there is neither intermediator nor mediation. We might say that experience is rooted in the *turīya* described in the *Māṇḍūkya-upaniṣad*, from which as prime matter all states of consciousness are derived. Experience lies at the root of all cognitive phenomena, the senses, the intellect, or any other organ by which we enter into contact with reality—without specifying whether and to what extent reality is capable of existing as degrees of being or whether it is we who construct them. In this sense, any experience whatsoever is ultimate.

---

[1] For a brief but excellent synthesis of mystical phenomena, see Dupré (1987). For recent studies of Christian mysticism see Ruh (1990) and McGinn (1992).

Insofar as it is experience it cannot be derived from anything else or deduced from any other instance. The experience that I may have in touching a stick (which my eyes will see as broken if I submerge it in water in an oblique way) does not represent an ultimate experience for my mind inasmuch as that mind may interpret the entire phenomenon in a different way and ascribe it to various levels of reality or appearance. Is the snake that I see with my imagination on my evening walk—to use the classical example of vedanta—truly a snake, or is it perhaps a rope that my mind reveals to me? Or is that which I believe to be a rope perhaps but a divine manifestation and not a rope at all?

The *ultimate reality* is therefore a reality that I cannot deduce from anything else or reduce to anything else. *Mystical experience*, therefore, means the experience of that which reveals to us ultimate reality as we have described it. But this is only a formal description; nor could it be anything else because it claims validity beyond any actual and possible interpretations. Let us leave open the question of what this ultimate reality might actually be; that is a postexperiential question. After all, ultimacy itself is relative to the journey we undertake in order to reach it. We are accustomed to speaking of "union with the divine"—through love or knowledge—or "contact with the sacred." Even if we share most of these descriptions within their respective contexts, we cannot limit mystical experience to either a theistic or deistic notion of reality, or to a religious phenomenon in the confessional sense of the word. In any event, the field of mysticism has little to do with paranormal or parapsychological phenomena.

One problem we must first resolve is whether it is possible to speak of such experience. Every word must remain silent and dissolve itself, along with the mind that thinks it, says the vedic tradition (see *Taittirīya-upaniṣad* II, 9, 1). Or, as the Christian and many other traditions declare, "In the beginning was the word," although the Beginning is not the word. The Beginning is Silence—that is, the Father from whom the Word springs forth, as the martyr St. Ignatius of Antioch wrote at the end of the first century (*Ad Magnesians* VIII, 1 [PG 5:669]): "The one God manifested himself through his Son Jesus Christ, who is his Word coming out of the Silence (Εἷς θεός ἐστιν, ὁ φανερώσας ἑαυτὸν διὰ Ἰησοῦ Χριστοῦ τοῦ Υἱοῦ αὐτοῦ, ὅς ἐστιν αὐτοῦς Λόγος ἀπὸ σιγῆς προελθών)."

In any case, we shall speak of this as we speak of silence.[2]

The field of consciousness is much more comprehensive than that of intelligibility. "Intelligence is nothing other than consciousness covered by the veil of ignorance" (*Tripura Rahasya*, 21). We take account of the fact that, even though we do not understand it, the unintelligible does exist.

A second problem is whether it is truly possible to compare such different experiences—a problem that is complex precisely because the very

---

[2] See Baldini and Zucal (1989), with an ample bibliography.

contexts themselves differ. A "diatopic hermeneutic" is necessary—that is, an interpretation that transcends not only the temporal difference (diachronic hermeneutic) but likewise the difference in places (*topoi*), which have had no direct contact with each other, so that common presuppositions cannot be assumed a priori.

Since the time of Brahamabandhav Upadhyaya, and more recently Abhiṣiktānanda, the question has been asked, for example, in the Christian sphere in India, as to what the relationship might be between the Christian and the *advaita* religious experience.[3] It is therefore necessary, above all, to describe the two experiences in their respective contexts: personal/non-personal, historical/non-historical, biblical/upanishadic, dualistic/monistic.[4] We need to accept the fact that no comparison is possible between two ultimate experiences.[5] Every question engages the person who poses it, and the answer is conditioned not only by the question but also by the questioner's parameters. Must we therefore abandon every effort at intercultural understanding? Not necessarily, so long as we remain conscious of the limits intrinsic to such efforts in their entirety. It is as if in every so-called experience we find ourselves in front of a cord with four threads: we are able to distinguish but not separate one thread from another. We touch one through the other, while at the same time we are in a position to identify but not isolate them. In fact, in every experience what we have is *pure experience*, that mysterious, spontaneous, atemporal and nonreflective act by which we enter into immediate contact with reality. This experience is the fount from which all the successive activities of our spirit originate.

In the second place we have the memory of this experience, which allows us to turn it into an object of description, analysis, and other acts. Here we see the appearance of the temporal. Memory makes pure experience present to our mind and, in a certain sense, enriches it, joining it with past experience and intensifying our consciousness of it. Memory allows us to speak of experience even though we cannot give it any meaning (2 Corinthians 12:2-4 is a good example).

In the third place, there is the *interpretation*, the thought, the conscious analysis of the experience that memory mediates. This interpretation occurs in the light of the categories at our disposal. It is clear that at the moment in which we speak and reflect we are conditioned by our education, our idiosyncrasies, and our culture. We often tend to attribute to our interpretation a universal validity equal to that of experience itself.

In the fourth place, our interpretation is not exclusively our own; we are not alone but integrated within the complex context of an entire cul-

---

[3] See Dupuis ([1989] 1991) 71-73.

[4] See the illuminating chapter in Gort (1992), which analyzes in general (and sometimes in particular) the possibility of sharing the religious experience—though the case of Christ is not mentioned.

[5] See Smith's polemic (1992) with Steven Katz, and the relevant bibliographical references.

ture. We are intrinsically dependent on the space and time that have been given to us to live in. Our interpretations are traceable not only to the memory of our experience but also to the entire baggage of past experiences and corresponding ideas we have inherited from our personal and collective past, which may be said to act almost as feedback. The interpretations of others influence, willy-nilly, the understanding of our own interpretation. We may define all of this as the *reception* of our experience in the complex of the kinds of knowledge in which we ourselves are included.

In brief, where *E* is the *complete* experience and *e* is the totality of *our* experience, *m* is our memory of it, *I* is our interpretation of experience, and *r* is our reception in the cultural sphere of our time and place, *E= e.m.i.r.*

What are we asking, for example, when we posit the question of the identity or nonidentity of *Christian* experience and *advaita* experience?

We possess sufficient data about *m, i, e*, and *r*, but we still cannot say much about *E* unless we know *e*, the first and most important variable. We know that even in the face of simple empirical experience, our descriptions can vary considerably.

In our case we can say that the traditional interpretations of the Christian and the *advaita* "fact" certainly differ in the respective ways in which they are received. On the other hand, however, those who believe they have had the two experiences within their respective traditions discover that they are equivalent in a homomorphic sense. In both cases we "see" that reality is reducible to neither unity (monism, docetism) nor duality (dualism, humanism). The divine and the human are neither one nor two.

In any case, our task consists not in comparing experiences but in studying the asserted or possible mystical experience of Jesus the Christ. In order to know the experience of someone, inasmuch as it is experience, we must participate in that experience. But how can we know we are doing this? We can know the different cultural environments; we can also discover that we have similar interpretations and even suspect that our memories reveal a certain correspondence; but can we go any further? Nobody can have an experience by proxy; it would not be an experience. Experience is personal.[6] But might not faith be precisely this participation in the ultimate experience? Might not the person be community more than individuality? Is not divinity infinite Life in eternal participation more than a supreme individual Being? If we intend to describe Christ's experience, we cannot ignore these great questions.

The Environment

The first draft of this text appeared on the occasion of a seminar in Rajpur in 1990 held in an ashram at the foot of the Himalayas. Christian

---

[6] "The Supreme Experience," in Panikkar (1983) 291-327.

and shivaitic experts in the knowledge and practice of their respective mystical traditions were present. I remember having noted at the time that, in preparing for the seminar, entitled "Shivaitic and Christian Mysticism," one indispensable paper was missing. I maintained that it was one on the mysticism of Jesus Christ. In my judgment, I said, there could be two reasons for the omission.

The first is positive and consists in a desire to respect a certain parallelism and safeguard a regime of parity: Christianity and shivaism are two great ancient traditions that should be treated on the same level. Any kind of a priori prejudice that favors one or the other should be avoided. It would have been strange to present a paper on the mysticism of Shiva as God. Attention was deliberately centered on the experiences of his faithful, just as attention was focused on the mysticism of the disciples of Jesus Christ. If, however, the attempt to speak of Shiva's self-consciousness would make no sense, to try to describe Jesus's self-consciousness, however difficult, was not altogether out of place.

There is no doubt that Christian mysticism is rooted, directly or indirectly, in Jesus's personal experience—something that cannot be said of Shiva's mysticism. The homeomorphic equivalence of Christ here would not be Shiva but his *śakti* ("energy, power").

The second reason was rather negative. It explained that the absence of any study concerning the mysticism of Christ could be derived from the prejudice—on the whole, unconscious—of Christians. Their conviction that Jesus Christ stands above everybody and beyond any possible comparison makes them feel that it is better not to involve him in any attempt at "comparative mysticism." Since the seminar was not specifically Christian, there was no a priori reason to consider Jesus in a way different from the great shivait mystic Abhinavaguptācarya, inasmuch as both are historical figures. Considering Jesus as God, an anthropological or psychological analysis makes no sense, but since Jesus was also man we do not see why we should not study him as such, as we would study any other man. It is for a good reason that it has been said that "Jesus, preacher of the message, has become Jesus the message preached."[7] Indeed, most christologies deal with the message and are based on Jesus's impact on the earliest Christian communities.[8]

---

[7] McGinn (1992) 62. The same observation is in Swidler (1988) 10-19.

[8] "The only knowledge we have of the Christ-event reaches us through the concrete experience of the first local communities of Christians" (Schillebeeckx). This simply means that the problem is displaced, inasmuch as we find the same difficulty in understanding how the first Christians appropriated that experience. If we do not know the experience of Jesus, we cannot even know the experience of Peter, Paul, and the first Christians. This only means that the problem has been displaced onto a second plane, which undoubtedly presents the same difficulty as the search to penetrate the experience of the first Christians. If we cannot know the experience of Jesus, we can even less know that of Peter, Paul, and other contemporaries. See Thompson (1985), who honors the subtitle of his book—*The Jesus Debate: A Survey and Synthesis*—which is centered, in any case, in "the Jesus event."

But is it possible to understand the message without understanding the messenger? We "read" what he said and study how others have understood him. Perhaps this is the reason why Christian theology, except for the mystics, has emphasized personal experience so little. In this case, however, theology becomes only exegesis and interpretation.

Can we, or at least do we have the right to try to, relive—to a certain extent—Christ's experience so that our understanding will not be only an arbitrary subjective perception but also a reactualization of the original experience? St. Augustine, in *De utilitate credendi* (V, 11), had already asked himself how we might discover the intention and meaning of an absent or dead author. This part of my work is, then, a Christian approach in silent dialogue with the mind and heart of the shivaitic tradition. It is a Christian text that intends to make sense in a shivaitic context, even though, writing in a Western language, we cannot ignore the Western Christian sensibility.[9] In fact, the Christian reader is the first interlocutor of this study.

A Christian reflection in an Indian context cannot neglect either the religious or the sociopolitical situation of contemporary India. A comparison may be useful. The christology of Latin America meditated and practiced by the so-called *theology of liberation*, "cannot fail to give rise to certain suspicions," writes one of its leading exponents. "For some reason or other it has been possible for some Christians, in the name of Christ, to ignore or even contradict the fundamental principles and values that Jesus of Nazareth preached and actualized."[10]

This study's Indian background is similar in part to that of Latin America. India's social structures and historical situation are perhaps even worse. The condition of *dalits* (the "oppressed") sums up what I mean, and this is a reminder that the problem is not exclusively Christian, though no Christian reflection can ignore it.[11] A christophany in India cannot ignore the fact of the *dalit* because of their special theological relevance.[12] Oppression and exploitation are world phenomena that no christophany can ignore without contradicting itself. The problem of the *dalit* is all the more urgent because—not unique in history but important on the sociological plane—until today it has had a pseudo-religious justification. Though the vedantic ideas of the world as non-real and of karma as a fatalistic chain constitute subtleties or aberrations within Hinduism itself, a certain mentality has been widely diffused among the peoples of the Indic[13] subcontinent, which increases the degree of tolerance on the part of both the oppressed and the oppressive system. We must not be scandalized by this, because even though Christ calls money mammon and tells us to love our

---

[9] For the acts of the congress see Baümer (1997, 1976).

[10] Sobrino (1978), preface.

[11] See Alegre (1995) and González-Faus (1995).

[12] See Pieris (1988) and Wilfred (1992).

[13] We use the adjective *indic* to refer to the culture of the subcontinent of Southeast Asia in order to distinguish it from *Indian*, the adjective that reflects the modernization of India.

neighbor as ourselves, the current Western Christian mentality experiences little guilt in enjoying a standard of living that is heavily responsible for many structural injustices.[14]

To sum up, the environment not only refers to the bucolic coziness of the cultivated and peaceful inhabitants of an ashram but also includes a population more numerous than that of the whole of Europe, whose greater part live on less than a dollar a day and are giving signs of losing hope. And I implore the reader not to consider this reference a digression, even if it may give the impression of moving into a different sphere. Christophany, after all, intends to join heaven and earth.

The Starting Point

The Text

Although most works on christology ignore the topic, we intend to explore the mysticism of Jesus Christ.[15] We are attempting to enter into the most sacred recess of the human and propose to reach an understanding of a being whose nature is fundamentally self-understanding. Since human beings are different from all other objects of consciousness, we cannot understand them unless we understand how they understand themselves. Man is a self-conscious being, and Jesus Christ was also a man, one who seems to have appropriated for himself and for others the phrase of Psalm 82:6, "You are gods" in John 10:34 in order that all "may participate in divine nature" (2 Peter 1:4). In this light, the words of St. Paul in Ephesians 3:2 acquire a new meaning in comparison with the usual one. There "the stewardship of God's grace" consists in the fact that "the Gentiles are fellow heirs, members of the same body, and partakers of the promise in Christ Jesus through the Gospel" (Ephesians 3:6). In fact, this has been the most natural and intimate aspiration of every Christian—indeed of all people. For the desire to become infinite ("like Gods," Genesis 3:5) seems connatural to man.[16] Despite the real differences [between the two systems of

---

[14] From time to time the West produces books that alarm the general public, such as Fanon (1963) or, more recently, Forrester (1996). Nevertheless, the great powers seem incapable of "dismounting from the tiger."

[15] See Renwart (1993), who analyzes some fifteen contemporary works on christology, though none of them deals with our problem. Kuschel (1990) presented an important work in narrative theology.

[16] Recall the subtle and vast polemic, half a century ago, concerning the so-called *desiderium naturale videndi Deum* ("the natural desire to see God"). On one hand, all theologians agreed that God is the end of every being; still, on the other hand, there was a fear of evacuating the meaning and role of sanctifying grace—and thus of the whole of Christianity, should the mere natural desire carry us to a vision of God.

interpretation], Jesus was not the only one to reveal to us the abyss of the *ahambrahmāsmi* ("I am *brahman*").

How are we to proceed? Does a method exist that would be more or less adequate? To know how a person understands himself, should we not perhaps be that very person? *Individuum ineffabile* ("The individual is ineffable") said the ancients. First of all, we do have a text, or better, a series of texts that have been scrupulously analyzed. One might say that no other historical personage has been subjected to such scrutiny. Of course, this inquiry aims high because our interest is directed not at a text but at a person whom, nevertheless, we may come to know through a series of texts. Or is it possible to gain access to the mystery of the person in other ways? One thing is certain. Although texts are not sufficient, perhaps, for understanding and knowing the author, we cannot set them aside.

It would be wise for a scrupulous exegete to meditate on the liberating power of St. Thomas's sentence *Omnis veritas quae, salva litterae circumstantia, potest divinae scripturae aptari, est eius sensus* ("Every truth which, without violating the literal meaning of words can be adapted to sacred scripture, also constitutes its meaning" [*De potentia Dei*, q. 4, a1]).

Even if we cannot at this time resolve the entire problem, we must mention it in order to overcome the nominalistic temptation to resolve human problems by reducing them to abstract parameters. However helpful it may be in some areas, algebra is not a discipline appropriate for anthropology or for a philosophy that is faithful to its name.

The traces of Jesus are clear enough: some thirty years of private life, and about three years—or perhaps only one—of intense public activity. We have the four Gospels as well as a limited number of canonical and noncanonical documents, and other events recorded in subsequent literature.[17] We know, moreover, that Jesus's impact over the past twenty centuries has excited exalted apologetics and furious attacks—and a wide range of intermediate interpretations, as well as novels, films, and many works of art. All of this constitutes part of Jesus's image.

We know some of his words, many expressions that have been attributed to him, several of his actions, and we can reasonably advance some conjectures concerning his more important goals. What emerges from all of this is a portrait that we can sum up briefly. Jesus was a man of Galilee who lived in a restless area in a small part of the world, marginal in terms of the political standards of the period. He belonged to a proud people with a millennial history that perceived an imminent catastrophe generated by an internal crisis, and especially by the domination of a powerful foreign

---

[17] For the canonical sources of the New Testament, as well as for the noncanonical, such as the Apocrypha, see (among a host of studies) Orbe (1985) and the subsequent volumes in the same series. See also Crossan's useful "Inventory of the Jesus Tradition by Chronological Stratification and Independent Attestation" (1991) 427-50, with its 552 items.

empire. Whether he was Jewish fully or only on his mother's side,[18] Jesus supported neither the conservatism of the Sadduccees nor the extremism of the Zealots, nor the middle way of the Pharisees, nor that of the more esoteric Essenes. He stayed alone and experienced an immense compassion for the *ʿam haʾaretz*, the simple people deprived of education and among whom he excited enthusiasm for a certain time. He was followed, without being much understood, by only a small group of men and women of different social strata, mostly of humble origin. All this happened almost two thousand years ago. He was then crucified by the Romans, at the instigation of some of his own people. At that time thousands of other men were crucified because they did not conform to the political status quo. Today almost all of them have been forgotten, except for the singular and fascinating person of Joshua, son of Miriam.

As to his activity, it may be said that he limited himself to doing good to simple people, healing their bodies and souls, and preaching the forgiveness of sins. Only occasionally did he have discussions with cultured people; most of the time he preached to the humble. His most remembered words, the so-called Beatitudes, which seem to have been pronounced on different occasions on a mountain or a plain of his country, seemed beautiful even if a little ingenuous. To his more intimate friends, as he called them, he transmitted a more profound message that gave special emphasis to unity and intimacy with him. He seemed to follow the rituals of his own tradition, even though he did so, it seems, with a certain degree of freedom.

The greater part of his doctrines remained within the range of Hebrew tradition, placing great emphasis on the love of God and neighbor, peace and freedom. These noble teachings may also be found in many other human traditions. Some have nevertheless judged him to be timid, a liar, a man who aroused expectations and promised spiritual rewards while knowing he would never be able to satisfy them. Jesus, the son of Mary, has aroused hatred and love in both ancient and modern times. There are those who assert that he was Mary Magdalen's lover, the secret father of John the Evangelist, a subtle hypocrite, and an astute scoundrel who had a secret political plan to overthrow both Romans and Jews and establish his fundamentalist messianic kingdom. Others say that he was only a fanatical Jew, whose plans evaporated because Judas, the Sanhedrin, or someone else thwarted his actions.[19] Perhaps now we understand Jesus better through the fruits his followers have left. But even these fruits are ambivalent: we find both saints and sinners among his followers. We cannot, therefore, exclude a priori any possible interpretation, even though we are now

---

[18] Rosenberg (1986) 27ff. and *passim*.

[19] See Haven-Smith's recent arguments (1997). It is surprising that, in his passionate and violent attack against Christianity, Deschner (1990) barely mentions the figure of Christ, but simply quotes Goethe's phrase: "Among so many crosses and christs, they have hidden the true Christ and his cross."

defending our own thesis a posteriori by presenting a convincing picture of his personality.

The Context

The traces of Jesus's life were not left suspended in air but were impressed on Jewish soil at the time of the Romans, within a Semitic context of ways of thinking and confronting the world. The people he addressed did not come from Africa, Greece, India, China, Europe, Egypt, Babylonia, or Sumeria.[20] Jesus knew how to read and probably even to write, but he did not seem to have much knowledge of the vast world or of cultures other than his own. There are occasional echoes that may be traced to other traditions but could also be no more than factors common to human experience. As to his travels outside the country when he was young, every hypothesis is possible, yet besides the fact of there being no proof, it is difficult to find clear traces of other cultures either in his words or his behavior.[21] Despite this, his words and actions display both a non-Jewish and non-orthodox current. In fact, the evangelists several times suggest a certain detachment from the Jewish atmosphere and the customs of the people who gave him birth. The more we make Jesus a Jew—as a certain contemporary current wishes to do for the commendable reason of eradicating the Christian shame of anti-Semitism—the more clearly does his distancing himself from Jewish orthodoxy emerge.[22]

It is surely a positive sign of our time that Christians, starting with the pope, seek forgiveness for Christian anti-Semitism and that the Jewish roots of Christianity are underscored, but it is not enough to repeat the same syndrome of blaming others and to consider Pilate guilty and the Romans responsible. It seems that Christians are in no position to seek the forgiveness of "pagans" and those of other religions. I believe that this movement toward reconciliation with Judaism should constitute only a first step toward greater harmony with other religions as well.

In any case, Jesus cannot be understood without placing him in his Jewish background, which was "popular" in the sense that there are no

---

[20] "Jesus did not show any signs of hellenistic influence" (Maisch and Vögtle 1969, 176). Several passages in *Sacramentum Mundi* (Rahner 1969, 3:174-209, with a rich bibliography) are worth consulting, as well as Crossan's descriptions (1991).

[21] Consult four different yet correlative descriptions of the man Jesus: Ben-Chorin (1967), who describes Jesus as *der Nazarener in jüdischer Sicht* (and, incidentally, does not quote any of the expressions of Jesus we are about to examine); Swidler (1988), who makes the Jew Jeshua "the measure of what it means to be Christian," a Jesus who is, of course, both "radical and feminist"; Rosenberg (1986), who liberates Jesus from his descent from the Old Testament and presents him literally as *barnasha* (Son of Man); and Augstein (1972), who shows the incongruities of all the theologies and churches that build on the unstable foundation of a heterogeneous Jesus of Nazareth.

[22] See Vermes (1973), in addition to the other authors cited.

traces of erudition in it. He was neither a Gamaliel nor even a Paul of Tarsus, neither an Akiba nor one of the intellectual giants of his own tradition. Whatever "the quest of the historical Jesus" has meant in the Christian theology of the past two centuries, and whatever tension there might be between that quest and the "Christ of faith," it is impossible to understand the personality of Jesus the Christ if the concrete traits of a Jew who lived and died no more than sixty generations ago are negated or minimized. These sixty generations, however, have made a weighty contribution to both clarifying and obscuring the understanding of Jesus. Perhaps no other figure in history has been presented in more variegated forms.[23] I am referring not just to the so-called lives of Jesus but also to all the epistemologies that have been advanced as the basis for every kind of theology, christology, and ecclesiology.[24] Is it possible to extricate ourselves from such a jungle?[25] This context forms the thick texture in which the figure of Jesus appears. In any event, we cannot trace an image of Christ capable of establishing some kind of consensus. It is precisely this impossibility, however, that allows us to discover some traits in the "personality profile" of Jesus of Nazareth that transcend historical contingencies. Let me explain this by an example.

We can maintain that such a Jesus said, "I and the Father are one." We do not affirm either his divinity or madness, or even his irresponsibility. We say only that the traces of the historical or mythical Jesus, as they come down to us, bear witness to this assertion and that this affirmation discloses an experience that is central to human life.

The Pretext

Knowledge of context is necessary for understanding any text, and this is an important factor in the diatopic hermeneutic insofar as the interpretations of contexts are governed by principles different from those that regulate the understanding of texts. We know, however, that inasmuch as every text is also a pretext to say something, it is necessary to study its structure in order to discover the pretext that stands above and beyond the context. It is important to understand the pretexts insofar as they constitute an existential question that transcends the purely conceptual understanding of a text.

Confessing the existence of the pretext is even more delicate for the hermeneutic of the text and knowledge of the context. This is so because,

---

[23] See Pelikan (1987) for a fascinating description of Western history in terms of Jesus's positive impact on the world.

[24] See the sad and ironic description of a brilliant Indian exegete who died in an accident in 1995: "How many of the 1500 articles and books published on the Gospels every year really touch on problems that interest people?" (Soares-Prabhu 1981, 320).

[25] Notice the principal methodological question of *Bṛhadāraṇyaka-upaniṣad* III, 4ff., according to which it is not enough to know an idea in order to know its author.

on the one hand, it implicates us too, and, on the other hand, the pretexts very often remain unconscious, veiled by interests, even by the interest of truth—a truth, however, that we more or less "intuit." What has been the pretext that has spurred Christians to interpret the man of Nazareth as they have?

Our inquiry must acknowledge that our personal eyeglasses have delineated the form of the Jesus that we see, while our being conscious that we wear glasses and have an idea of how they both form and deform the image allows us to attribute to our description the necessary qualities of uncertainty and variability. This may permit us to create a concrete picture that might convince a certain number of those for whom the name of Jesus is no light matter.

Our question was whether we are capable of penetrating into the deepest recesses of another person or whether we must content ourselves with acting as an investigator who simply reconstructs a past event? The ultimate question is whether Christian faith is based exclusively on the trust placed in those theologians and investigators who reconstruct the traces of the historical "founder" of Christianity, or whether it might originate from another source as well. Is Christian faith founded on a historical book or on a personal experience? The fundamental issue is whether it is something like grace or simply the proper conclusion of a syllogism.

I would not like to be misunderstood by Western Christians who believe in the myth of history. It cannot be denied that Jesus was a historical individual who lived two millennia ago, although it serves no purpose to ignore the fact that in many parts of the world, and for the next Christian millennium, the figure of Christ could make sense also if seen under another light. Using traditional Christian expressions, it could be said that, if Jesus was a Jew, the resurrected Jesus—that is, the Christ—is neither Gentile nor Greek nor Jew. I do not wish to engage in theological controversy; I simply intend to understand the figure of Christ in a context wider than the Semitic and the historical. Is a circumcision of the mind necessary in order to understand the man of Galilee when his closest followers had already rejected the circumcision of the body? (Acts 15:1-28).[26]

I would like to reassure Christians that they will lose nothing of the profundity of the Christian tradition by renouncing a certain monopoly of Christ. My interpretation is orthodox—unless one identifies orthodoxy with microdoxy. I would also like to assure those who do not participate in the Christian creed that no profundity of their respective traditions would be lost by considering the figure of Christ as a homeomorphic equivalent to "that which" other cultures express and understand in a different way. The great difficulty, philosophically speaking, derives from the substantialization of *this* "that which." Homeomorphic equivalence certainly does not signify religious equivalence.

---

[26] See Panikkar (1992).

One may object that inasmuch as the context proper to Jesus was the Hebraic world, we are not allowed to extrapolate from it. However, the first generations of Christians, starting perhaps with John and culminating in the Councils of Ephesus and Chalcedon, already transplanted the context into the hellenistic world. The possibility of a further intercultural transplantation, therefore, should not be excluded. It may be objected that we are no longer in the same situation as that of those more formative periods. I would answer simply: "Jesus Christ is the same yesterday, today, and throughout the centuries" (Hebrews 13:8). In other words, I am neither denying history nor indulging in a "gnostic" interpretation of Christ. It is precisely because history is very important that it must not be reduced to the past.[27] I am not presenting a complete christology but simply a non-docetic realistic christophany.

Here then is our pretext, which our confession of faith makes more open and flexible. We have believed in Christ through many and necessary mediations and would now like to describe this experience by returning critically to those very mediations. The Christian tradition is neither merely doctrinal nor exclusively historical. The history of Christians, and thus of Christianity, is rich with both light and darkness. It is true that a lotus flower may be born of a quagmire, but it is also true that we can be pricked by a splendid rose.

The principal question, therefore, remains suspended. Although we surely cannot do without the text, are we able to penetrate it without remaining imprisoned, as Buddhists would say, in sterile subtleties or pernicious opinions?[28] How can we find an orientation in the complexity of contexts?

The Christian answer is clear. The orientation is found in tradition, which furnishes us with the pretext that provides the interpretative key. To use consecrated terms, tradition, along with the scriptures, is an indispensable hermeneutic instrument even though, like the scriptures themselves, it is polysemic as well as fluid and alive. The *pretext* is never purely objective.

Too often tradition is considered a complex of doctrines that have been crystallized into dogmatic formulas which interpret the scriptural texts. We

---

[27] Dupuis (1994) comes very close to our problem since he presents a christology both centered on the person of Christ and open to the other religions of the world. He criticizes dogmatic and genetic methods as deductive and finds a hermenutical triangle "in the mutual interaction between text, context, and interpretation" (p. 9). This allows us to "turn to many diversified theologies and christologies" (p. 10) so as to prepare "the way to a christology of religions."

[28] This study does not intend to be a repudiation of biblical criticism. However, although we must become familiar with Christian exegesis, it is also necessary to heed the observation of Soares-Prabhu (1981) 318: "For it is precisely this use of an historical method to interpret a religious text that explains the failure to reveal the true meaning of the Gospels, while providing an infinite amount of information about them. . . . A specific method is used to obtain exact information for the purpose of interpreting a text that aims at personal transformation. The method is inadequate for the intention of the text."

then find ourselves with a kind of doctrinal Christianity, almost an ideology, patched together on the basis of some historical facts that successive generations have interpreted. The result is a body of doctrines, a system of beliefs similar to the constitution of a state or the rules of an institution, directed at promoting cohesion, discipline, and efficiency. But can religion be nothing but an organization? Is faith no more than the correct interpretation of doctrine?

Clearly, tradition means much more than this. The "transmission" (*tradere*) of tradition is not limited to producing a version of scriptures that is correct, in proper form, and up-to-date. What tradition transmits is life, faith, a sense of belonging to a community, an orientation of life, a participation in a common destiny. Christian tradition is not doctrine alone; it is also *ekklēsia* in the deepest sense of the word. It has to do not only with what Jesus said and did but with who he was and who we are.

Tradition is more than an authoritative or normative hermeneutics. It offers more than a text or interpretation. It transmits a word that is living and therefore spoken. The intention and even the nature of our texts go far beyond what a historical-critical method succeeds in extracting from them. But how do we know this? A certain kind of exegesis governed by apologetical pretexts (which is not our case) has sought to convince us that the texts themselves bear witness to their own intention and nature. But if the text validates itself, we fall into a vicious circle and the testimony is not valid. The pretext can never serve as foundation: it would not be reliable. The text itself must therefore be founded elsewhere. But the general acknowledgment of the hermeneutic circle (according to which we need a particular precomprehension) cannot satisfy us since we are already familiar with other kinds of pre-comprehension that are of equal value and that challenge our interpretations. In brief, we need something different, something that precedes all the scriptural texts.[29]

In order not to lose the thread of our argument, we shall not pause to deal with the "hermeneutic circle" and its complement, the "hermeneutic center" that every circle presupposes, nor on that hermenutical modification that is called "hermetic."[30]

It is certain that no book can constitute the ultimate foundation of any faith, since it is precisely faith that is needed in order to give the book the value of witness. It will be said that the book does not mean scripture but

---

[29] At an international congress I asked a well-known exegete how, with his purely analytical premises, he explained the fact that he was more interested in Jesus than Socrates or Buddha, or even Copernicus, Hannibal, or Napoleon. The only real answer was "the reason of State—that is, the politics or power and its influence." If we eliminate the personal and mystical fact that we find something else in Jesus—which must also pass the test of critical reflection—no reason is left for justifying our interest in Jesus more than in any other "hero."

[30] See Klostermaier (1997), who cites Rombach (1991). It is not by chance that Klostermaier derives his "inspiration" from a profound knowledge of Indian traditions that opens him to dialogue and interculturality.

what scripture says. In that case, we must ask: Who tells us what scripture really says? The teachers, many traditions answer. But how do they know it? And how are we to recognize the genuine teachers?

Άνάγκη στῆναι, the Greeks would say, "It is necessary to stop," to find a foundation. which in fact is the Word: "God was the Word" (John 1:11), as is said in many traditions. On this point, incidentally, vedic exegesis could be helpful. The Vedas, in fact, constitute the *primordial word*. There is no one to tell us the meaning of the primordial words because we would then have to use other words or signs *ad infinitum*. This is the meaning of the traditional *apauruṣeyatva*. That is why *mīmāṃsā* is considered atheistic. The word is primordial: "In the beginning is the Word. The Word was with [i.e., "near"] him" (*Tāṇḍa-mahā-brāmaṇa* XX, 14, 2). "The Word is *brahman*" (*Bṛhadāraṇyaka-upaniṣad* I, 3, 21). The Palestinian Targum also renders Genesis 1:1 with an almost trinitarian phrase: "From the beginning, the *mēmrā* ('word') of YHWH created and finished the heavens and the earth with *wisdom*."

But this word, *vāc*, this *logos, mēmrā,* must be listened to: "Faith comes from hearing" (Romans 10:17). This hearing entails a reception in the heart and mind that assimilates the word. Such a listening to the word unleashes experience, the experience of faith. Let us not forget that the Word is the ecstasy of Silence.

We may perhaps simplify this idea by affirming that, although the Word is not scripture, it can act as its vehicle.[31] The Word is not reducible to scripture nor even to interpretation. This suggests that the "apostolic succession," to invoke a traditional term, is more than a transmission of doctrines. In brief, the *pretext* is a transmission of life. The purpose of studying philosophy, Indic wisdom says, is salvation, liberation; it is not only the end but likewise the means. We must aspire to liberation (*mumukṣu*) and undertake our journey toward it with a conscious and attentive eye.

Three Anthropologies

Let me ask our question again. About 2000 years ago there was a man who, in comparison with other great figures of history, was not particularly extraordinary. He was an honest and just man who did not let himself be dragged into any extreme position, either political or religious. Nevertheless, this man died young because he outraged those who held power because of his inflexible attitude against hypocrisy and his transgression of the religious laws of his people. Finally, he was condemned to death.

---

[31] As von Balthasar (1961b) I:28 puts it, *Die Schrift [ist] nicht das Wort, sondern das Zeugnis des Geistes vom Wort* ("Scripture is not the word but, rather, the testimony that the Spirit gives the word").

In the two millennia that have passed since his death—or, as many prefer to say, his resurrection—he has inspired millions of people, has been a central reference point, and has affected the course of history as no one else. He did not write a single word, but only spoke and acted, and a handful of simple men and women gathered in his memory to commemorate his death and life. What did this man think of himself? Is it not perhaps blasphemous to dare to enter into a person's most intimate sanctuary? Yet if he has been the central symbol for so many people of so many different backgrounds for so long a time, we should have the right to ask why, and to seek to penetrate his mystery.[32] For this reason, we must ask ourselves who this man is.

If Jesus Christ signifies something for the Christian tradition, it is because, in one way or another, Christians sense (John 6:68) that he spoke "words of eternal life," and did not simply make correct assertions about the state of the world. It is therefore imperative for us to understand the man.

"What do the people say of 'me'?" Jesus asked. Note that if we translate the Greek original literally, we avoid the ungrammatical "I" (Luke 9:18; see Mark 8:27 and Matthew 16:15).

Before the predicates of the famous response of Peter ("Messiah," "Son of God") we find the genuine subject—σύ, "you" ("You are . . ."). We need to open our eyes and ears to the mystery of the "thou." He asks about his "me," and the response says, "Thou."

To be understood, this "thou" requires a vision of the man. Let us approach the problem in the light of a threefold anthropological paradigm: Man as individual, Man as person, Man as image of the divine—even if this threefold distinction is not the only one possible.

Above all, we shall describe Jesus within the modern individualistic framework. Second, we shall offer some reflections within a wider Western thought structure. Third, we shall mention the Indian reception of this problem, one that recovers, it seems to me, a vision that is in wide agreement with the original Christian intuition.

The Individualistic Approach

That Jesus was an historical person is undeniable, even though some passages in scripture and some traditions refer to Christ as a generic man, a second Adam in whom the whole of human nature is assumed.[33] But

---

[32] It is not surprising that Adolf von Harnack, a theologian whom many keep at a distance, wrote that "the important thing is not to evoke in ourselves the same sentiments as Christ but, rather, to grasp Christ himself" (quoted in Kuschel 1990, I, 2, 2).

[33] Eckhart offers an example of a discussion that was very much alive in his time: *Deus verbum assumpsit naturam, non personam hominis* ("God the Word assumed the nature, not the person of men"; *In Johannem*, LW III, § 289), and immediately adds: *Natura est nobis omnibus aequaliter communis cum Christo univoce* ("Nature is equally common as an univocal form, between all of us and Christ").

what is an individual—an isolated substance? Today's dominant culture, especially that of Western origin, presents man as an individual entity. Since individualism is one of the most profoundly rooted myths in contemporary consciousness, it is extremely difficult to challenge. In some cultural backgrounds individualism has become taboo.

Within the ambit of an individualistic anthropology we find a unique access to the holy of holies, to the mystery of individuality: although we cannot cross the threshold, we can surely observe the traces that the person in question leaves when he breaks out of his atomistic monad. These traces are discovered by an inevitable though inseparable threefold mediation: *What* do these traces *in se* and *per se* reveal about this person? *How* do these traces present themselves where they are found? And *what kind* of form do they assume if they are examined through our personal lenses? We consider then:

a. the words and works of the individual as indices of the person himself;
b. words and works that are said and done within a concrete context (which confer meaning and value on them) ; and
c. our interpretation of the above by means of our particular vision, which in turn is influenced by a series of propositions without which we cannot confront the investigations of the traces.

Here we confront three obstacles that must be overcome. These formidable dragons defend the intimate castle of private individuality—or, as individualists will say, "the sacred nature of man."

The prospect does not seem very promising. The traces, which the Latins called *vestigia*, are ambiguous and ambivalent, as their immense variety indicates. The traces are not the image. In order to recognize something as image, it is necessary in a certain way to "know" the original, although the original remains enclosed within the fortress of its individuality. We can therefore readily understand the desire to conquer this fortress. The undertaking, however, is formidable.

Even if we should succeed in lowering the drawbridge that gives access to the castle of individuality, nobody would believe us unless we are able to present credentials that can be verified only if we prove we have penetrated to the heart of that castle. Such credibility can be guaranteed, however, by the moral and intellectual qualities of the witness, as a Christian "apologetic" has amply demonstrated and Indic philosophy has studied in a thematic way.[34]

But something more is required. It is necessary that we understand in some way the language of the testimony, that it speak to us in a human

---

[34] Consider the category of the "trustworthy witness," so widely studied and discussed in Indic philosophy.

tongue. To continue my analogy, the castle cannot remain the private property of any individual but should be accessible to all of us as well, so that we may "verify" the testimony. In short, our hearts must burn with the same fire (see Luke 24:32), or confess that we believe "because we ourselves have heard and understand" (John 4:42). It is only within ourselves that we can meet—and perhaps understand—the mystery of someone else's identity.[35] Even if we should succeed in lowering the drawbridge that allows us access to the castle of individuality, I can know the identity of another only as I share his identity.[36] Everything else is nothing but bureaucratic identification, not true identity, as we shall see again in Part 3 of this book.

Identification consists in placing the other within a system of coordinates in order to avoid confusion with any other being. Every being is thus defined in a univocal way. In our case we could define Jesus of Nazareth as the Jew, the son of Mary, born most probably in Bethlehem in 4 B.C., who after a few years of activity in his own country, died on a Roman cross in Jerusalem under Pontius Pilate. Such identification at least leaves no doubt about whom we are talking. But are we sure we have succeeded in reaching that individual's identity? Have we succeeded in really knowing him? Have we penetrated his personal intimacy, his self-consciousness, what he really thinks of himself? Identification is not identity. In order to approach someone's identity, we must appeal to another type of approach that goes above and beyond the first. We need a knowledge impregnated with love; otherwise we touch no more than the *what* and not the *who* of the person.[37]

In phenomenological terms, love is a nondualistic experience.[38] This is the reason why it is only with great difficulty that love enters into any Husserlian *noēma* ("understanding"). Love is neither equality nor otherness, neither one nor two. Love requires differentiation without separation; it is a "going" toward "the other" that rebounds in a genuine "entering" into oneself by accepting the other within one's bosom.

Without love we may be capable of "identifying" an object to a certain extent, of localizing it, of describing its aspects and foreseeing its behavior. This is so-called scientific knowledge—which is not knowledge in the classical sense. In our case, however, we aim not at an identification of the object but at knowledge of a "thou" who is himself a knowing subject. In order to accomplish this end, I must know myself in such a way that there

---

[35] See two important theological works on which we cannot comment here: Chatterjee (1963) asserts that without the previous condition of intersubjectivity "there can be neither the concept of 'my' self nor of the 'other' self" (217); Ricoeur (1990) distinguishes between *identité-idem* ("same" or *gleich*) and *identité-ipse* ("self" or *Selbst*) (13 and *passim*).

[36] See Panikkar (1977).

[37] See Panikkar (1972b and 1972c).

[38] See Panikkar (1983) 277-89.

is space in me for "the other," so that the other is not only someone "out-side" but a certain "other-than-me," an "other self"—who perhaps, like me, participates in a unique "Self." In any event, in order truly to know the "other," the movement must be reciprocal—a meeting must take place. I must be loved by the other so that I may be enabled to see him in the mir-ror in which the love of the other has transformed my very self. Christian scripture says, "If one loves God, one is known by God" (1 Corinthians 8:3); "I will then understand fully in the same way in which I am under-stood" (1 Corinthians 13:12).

Virtually all human traditions have insisted on purity of heart as an essential requirement for knowledge and for leading an authentic life.[39] Only a *sahṛdaya* ("man-with-heart") is capable of grasping the power of a certain phrase, as Indian poetry says.[40] Only the pure in heart will be capa-ble of truly seeing the "other," the "others," the "Other," God. "Blessed are the pure in heart, for they shall see God" (Matthew 5:8). This is what John says too: "And by this we may be sure that we know him, if we keep his commandments" (1 John 2:3; see vv. 4-14). If our praxis is correct, our theory finds the right path. In the same part of his letter John repeats: "I write to you, my children, because you have known the Father" (1 John 2:13-14). Therefore we too can know him. The heart of orthodoxy is orthopraxis.

But is this really possible? Can we really cross that drawbridge? Can we open the innermost chamber of our selves to make room for another "self"? Can the "fusion of horizons" that Gadamer speaks of (1972, 289ff.) as indispensable for an authentic understanding bring about a fusion of many selves without generating confusion? Or must we remain respectably on the threshold of the self-consciousness of others and content ourselves, like Job's friends, with listening and looking? Christian mystics have spoken of the necessity of becoming an *alter Christus* ("another Christ"). In proposing here to arrive at the *ipse Christus* ("Christ him-self"), we are encouraged by St. Paul's exclamation: "It is no longer I who live [i.e., my ego], but Christ lives in me" (Galatians 2:20).

For an individualistic anthropology to dare to enter the "other" and penetrate into his intimacy would be a violation of the individual's dignity.

Once we have banished love from knowledge, the other becomes an object, a stranger, a thing. This leads to Sartre's extreme formulation, *l'enfer sont les autres*—or, more benevolently, to considering them as an obstacle or an enemy. To escape this difficulty, a distinction is usually made between the *aliud* (the *id*) and the *alter* (the "other"). The *alter* is not another *thing* but another *I*. In the face of this "other" we enjoy rights and

---

[39] It should be enough to mention the upanishadic requirement for studying the sacred word; for just one example, see Śaṅkara, *Vivekacūḍamaṇi*, 16-37.

[40] See Gispert-Sauch (1974) 39, for a brief but important study of biblical exegesis from an Indic perspective.

obligations. We must love the neighbor as an "other," as another I, not as a thing. To this end we need, above all, to overcome an ethics of exteriority—a civilization founded on law. Metaphysics becomes irrelevant, and ethics its substitute.[41]

For our purposes, then, we must abandon the idea of "knowing" the "other" and learn to respect him. Alienation is born as the *aliud* swallows us up, because we have not known how to acknowledge the *alter* with the human face who stands before us. We cannot go beyond this; entry is forbidden.

Loving knowledge, on the other hand, discovers the you, not the other. If Jesus is another and not a you for the I who seeks to know him, it is impossible and blasphemous to try to penetrate his feelings, as Paul invites us to do (Philippians 2:5).

A brief critique could say that the problem of the "other" is not so much that of the "other" as it is of the self, of the ego. In order to appease our bad conscience, which is always preoccupied with the ego and not the other, we maintain that the other is an other individual for whom we acknowledge the right to have an "I."

Here an elementary respect for grammar could help. I cannot say "I" unless I refer to myself. What we call an "other I" is, strictly speaking, an abstraction. For me he is not an I but a he or she or an it. Yet I cannot say you without abdicating my I. I cannot call the I of the other "I"—it is not my "I," it is not another "I," none of them is "I." The others have their rights (which are not mine); I must love each of them as an *other* myself but not as if he were myself. As the adage we cited above puts it, *Individuum ineffabile* ("The individual is ineffable"). In that case, everyone would then become a competitor against everyone else.

The old saying that Plautus reported in *Asinaria* 495 and afterward explained by other philosophers has it that *homo homini lupus* ("Man is a wolf to another man") is neither simply immoral nor socially pernicious; it is a thought that is erroneous in both an anthropological and metaphysical sense. We are not wolves that have evolved, even though we may have instincts that are called "animalistic," inasmuch as when we act on them we have in fact lost our humanity. Completely other is the classical wisdom that we find in Erasmus without any further comments, *homo homini deus* ("Man is God to another man," *Adagia* I, 1, 69).

To ask how we can know another individual, therefore, or even dare to penetrate the "holy of holies" of another human being's intimacy, constitutes a false question. Or better, there is an inner contradiction between *being* an individual—*indivisum a se, ab aliis vero distinctum* ("an individual undivided from oneself and distinct from others")—and *knowing* another individual as such. I would cease to be the individual that I am if I should truly come to know another individual *as* individual, and vice versa.

---

[41] See the work of Unamuno, Sartre, Lévinas, and Aranguren, among recent moderns.

The individual who knows or inserts himself into the other would destroy the individuality of the individual known and would then cease to be the individual he is. This "knowledge" of the other (which is obviously a "knowledge" without love) destroys the other and alienates the knower. We are talking about the true knowledge of another I, not of our capacity to predict behavior and control events. We are referring to the knowledge that achieves a certain identity with the object known; we are talking not about knowledge of so-called inanimate entities but about the knowledge of an "other."

To sum up, what I am saying is that if each of us is no more than an individual, it makes no sense to pretend to penetrate another's ego.

Until now we have presented the problem in the light of the modern Western dogma of individualism. But we are not saying that this notion should be understood as asserting that each of us is a windowless monad. After all, we could be monads who stand in relation with other individuals, although such a relation would be external. Since every monad is but a number, the most practical rule would be to respect the group that is the most numerous, so that the majority, driven by a desire for peace, will dictate a judicial system of behavior. Nothing is higher than an individual except a larger number of individuals. We are all enclosed within our own castles; the *individuum ineffabile* is supreme, a little God. The monotheistic God becomes fragmented into small Gods. Could this be the origin of democracy?

This myth does not in fact represent a universal conviction. Even Western thought has begun to entertain serious criticism of this interpretation. Each of us, to be sure, has an individuality, yet we are more than individual entities. The dominant contemporary culture, Western in origin, seems to have exhausted the advantages of individualism, and some who belong to this very culture have begun to discover that such a position leads to a philosophical solipsism, sociological atomism, a political quantification of the human being, and therefore to isolation, to consumerism, and to an undeclared war of all against all: *Homo homini competitor.*

It is in this climate that we find modern reflection on the *humanum*, a reflection whose most positive achievement consists in the new emphasis on the person rather than the individual.

The Personalist Approach

Our intention is to share Jesus of Nazareth's self-consciousness, a particular case of the general problem of achieving the "interpenetration of consciousnesses," as suggested in the first part of this book describing the christophanic experience. Are we so certain that every individual consciousness is an unassailable fortress? Will not the true *cogito* ("I think") be a *cogitamus* ("We think") and the *sum* ("I am") a *sumus* ("We are")? And again: is it really certain that Being is something dead or that the idea of reality as mystical body or *dharma-kāya* is no more than a way of speaking? Is not Being rather an activity, an act? Are we really convinced that consciousness is just an individual epiphemomenon, a completely private property?

We are not even sure that the problem of how to know *an other* has been correctly presented. Here we touch on one of the principal philosophical questions of our times. One could adduce the example of the subject–object separation at either the epistemological or ontological level. Even the vision of the *anima mundi*, with all its related political and ecological consequences, is connected with the same question. It is the problem of personalism and an animistic vision of the world.[42]

We may describe the person as a knot in a web of relations. In such a perspective individuality is no more than the abstract knot cut away from all the threads that contribute to make it up. The knot without the thread is nothing, and the threads without the knot could not subsist. Knots serve a very practical function; they provide effective ways for referring to human activity, from identification cards to the human rights of the individual. But a knot is a knot because it is made up of threads tied together with other knots by means of a network of threads. Although the knots are not unreal, neither are the threads. The network constitutes one great whole. However spatial and material this analogy is, it does show that no such thing as an individual knot exists and that all knots entail one another while retaining their unity. Reality is the net, and the net is relational.

The analogy also emphasizes another human intuition, Eastern and Western: in a certain sense all other beings are reflected, included, and represented in all other beings. Because through all its threads it is in communion with the whole net, every knot in a certain way reflects all other knots. Anaxagoras's ἐν παντὶ πάντα ("all in all"), shivaism's *sarvam-sarvātmakam*, Neoplatonism's *speculation*, Aristotle's microcosm/macrocosm, Buddhism's *pratītyasamutpāda*, Christianity's (and Anaxagoras's) *perichōrēsis*, and the mirror (*speculum*) nature of a certain philosophy, as well as the law of karma, the theories concerning the mystical body in so many religions, the *intellectus agens* of Muslim scholasticism, the Enlightenment's universal reason, as well as modern scientific morphogenetics, magnetic fields, and Gaia theory—all seem to suggest a vision of the world

---

[42] The reader may at times hear the echo of a great number of contemporary philosophers. Although I cite some in the bibliography, the list is not complete—Berdyaev, Bergson, Blondel, Buber, Bulgakov, Bultmann, Cullmann, Ebner, Gilson, Guardini, Heidegger, Marcel, Maritain, Mounier, Nédoncelle, Ortega y Gasset, Rahner, Scheler, Schweitzer, Zubiri. I omit some thinkers who are still alive as well as those of earlier times. I do not include Indian thinkers here because the problems they deal with are quite different.

that is less individualistic and in which our metaphorical castle does not have to be defended from so many dragons.[43]

I have already noted that every cosmovision entails a conscious reception of the world or, rather, is the impact that the *kosmos*, understood as total reality, exercises on our conscious being. A vision of the animistic world would consider the nature of reality as living, as in a certain sense personal. "Being is personal" could constitute a summary formula. The person then would constitute the original level of Being, not just a traditional epiphenomenon of reality, a kind of accident of Being. Too often ontology discusses Being as if it were an entity without any life or consciousness. An equivalent formula would be "Being is relational." This second approach understands reality as "person," *anthrōpos*, as that irreducible dimension of reality under which we experience it. The person is the *satpuruṣa*, the true man—the whole reality, one might say, with reference to the *puruṣasūkta* of the *Ṛg-veda* (X, 90, although the expression is not used there).

In contrast to a personalist ontology, this dead ontology of Western individualism may be seen as the originating cause of a certain discrediting of metaphysical speculation.[44] It should be added that the Christian fear of pantheism led the scholastics to effect a radical separation between *ens realissimum* (God) and *ens commune*, clearly an abstraction.[45] Discussions on "ontologism," should also be mentioned; they reappear in a different form at a later time: at this level all problems are interwoven.

Our question concerns knowledge of the "other." Can my ego meet, and therefore know, an other ego? It is obvious that if "person" means that we are the exclusive owners of our own being, *Selbstgehörigkeit*,[46] it will be impossible to transcend individual boundaries. We must respect, even

---

[43] Among many witnesses, I cite the following: "The aristotelian *nous* is a supra-individual faculty, like the Buddha of Indian speculation or the ʾaql of Islamic doctrine. This faculty of the eastern traditions is super-individual, though essentially personal. . . . The whole framework of the discussion in the west is derived from the incompleteness of Greek metaphysics which limits itself to the individual ego and has never arrived at the profound personal *suppositum* or *hypostasis* (*ātman*). The psyche is no substitute for the *pneuma*, just as the Buddhist *ātman* is no substitute for the Hindu *ātman*" (Mascarenhas 1953, 163).

[44] Nédoncelle (1970) 41-47. Although the title of the first half of the book is "Être et personne," Nédoncelle does not develop the problem mentioned here.

[45] This was the fear of Garrigou-Lagrange, the Dominican who dominated Roman Catholic theology for decades, a great expert on mysticism who could not deny that the incarnation seemed to obscure the absolute nature of God. "L'acte pur est irreçu et irreceptif, irreceptus et irreceptivus. S'il était reçu dans une puissance, il serait participé et limité, s'il recevait une perfection nouvelle, il serait une puissance par rapport à elle, et ne serait plus Acte pur" ("Pure act is neither received nor receivable. If it were received in a potentiality, it would be participated and limited; if it should receive a new perfection, it would be in potency with respect to it and would no longer be pure Act" [1953, 345]). But we have already said that ontological monism leaves no space for the Christian Incarnation, despite Aquinas's *distinguo*. "Pure act" cannot be incarnated, since then it would not be pure.

[46] Guardini (1963) 99ff., actually published in 1927.

tolerate one another, but nothing more.[47] Intimacy, understood as an unassailable fortress, bears an ultimate status, and privacy becomes a virtually supreme value. This sublimation of individuality has led to the deleterious notion of God conceived of as the Supreme Individual, the Other par excellence, as the One who scrutinizes our innermost self and interferes with our identity, as an alienating stranger who dehumanizes us.[48]

We have seen how the distinction between the *alius* and the *alter* throws a certain light on our problem, while leaving the myth of individualism intact. From this perspective we can appreciate the extraordinary "progress" in exegesis and the demythologization and demystification of evangelical and biblical events. *Felix culpa*!

Yet the problem of the other that remains is, in substance, the problem of the One. Once defined in its incommensurability and imprisoned in its subjective solipsism, the individual can either open her windows to meet the other or remain the prisoner of her isolation. It is the ultimate problem concerning the human mind, at least since the Upanishads: *ekam advitīyam* ("one without a second"), and Plato's ἓν καὶ πολλά ("the one and the many")—that is, the problem of the seesaw between monism and dualism. And the difficulty in understanding that the oscillation is possible because a nondualistic fulcrum lies *in between* the two extremes.[49]

What we want to say is that the great contemporary openings on the *alius* that still operate within the myth of individualism are chiefly dualistic theories, even the person is seen by some as a great individual.

If, in the wake of German idealism, we divide reality into the I and the non-I—which simply retranslates the Cartesian dichotomy between *res cogitans* and *res extensa*—if we begin with the great separation between spirit and matter, we shall end in an atomistic vision not only of matter but of spirit as well. From this kind of separationist thinking Leibniz draws a philosophical consequence, while modern individualism develops its sociological implications. It is clear that the non-I cannot merge into the I without destroying it or itself. The principle of noncontradiction cannot be dethroned by any *dictio*. Strictly speaking, the *alius* does not exist. The other does not exist as "other" but as itself. The other exists only for me,

---

[47] Ortega y Gasset, *Autopresencialidad*, would say, echoing St. Thomas, that "the soul is present to itself (*est sibi praesens*; *De veritate*, q. x, a. 8) as the essence of the person (*sui ipsius et sui juris*, in juridical language).

[48] To criticize this image of God is one of the principal objectives of Schoonenberg's theology, responding to the atheism of Sartre, Camus, and others. God "does not dehumanize us but makes us fully human, and finally, through his Word made man . . . our divinization becomes our humanization" (1971). Romano Guardini had already focused on this problem a half century earlier.

[49] We underscore *in between* with reference to the Buddhist *mādhyamika*, the Indian *bedhābheda*, Buber's *Dazwischen* (*das Zwischenmenschliche*), and the *in between* of the Kyoto school. "The kingdom of God is also in between" (ἐντός, Luke 17:21).

for the others. The other is not other for itself. It is our egocentric perspective that calls it an other.

Reality is not formed by I and non-I. It is not reality that is dialectical; it is reason. The thou belongs to reality as well and is neither contradictory nor foreign to the I. The thou is neither I nor non-I. Relation is advaitic.

The relation I/thou is not dualistic like a relation between two substances, between two "things." The reality I/thou is a relation that constitutes reality itself. There is no I without a you, and vice versa. But neither is the relation monistic; in that case it would not be real. I and you are neither identical nor reducible to I (alone) or you (alone) nor to a higher individual (of a higher unity). To discover myself as a thou is to discover the deepest identity in myself, neither in the face of "an other" nor within a narcissistic mirror. It is rather equivalent to discovering my dynamic *ipse*, as being myself — *tat tvam asi*! The *tvam* belongs inseparably to the *tat*.

"This thou art"; a thou who responds to the calling of the I that constitutes it as a thou, who in turn "allows" the I to be I. The person is the complex of all the personal pronouns: a relation. We are aware that the word "person" has a long history and translates improperly two fundamental hellenistic concepts in the elaboration of the trinitarian doctrinal language as *prosōpon* and *hypostasis*. We also know that discussion regarding the so-called personality of God defended by Abrahamic monotheisms, as well as the "divine impersonality" attributed to Eastern religions, rests on misunderstandings on the one side and reciprocal "ignorance" on the other. The recent philosophy of personalism also exhibits many nuances.[50]

In any event, we will use the word "person" to express the second anthropological conception.

The person is neither an individual nor an undifferentiated existence. Precisely insofar as it is something ultimate, the person escapes every definition. Person is relation because Being is relation. Being is a verb, a communitarian—that is, personalist—action: *esse est coesse—et coesse est actus essendi* ("to be is to-be-together—and to-be-together is the act of being").[51] A person is a knot that is conscious—that possesses a human consciousness—of being a knot, a consciousness that could be called self-consciousness or a knowing oneself to be an I. Person is that being that *says* I. But this I is not the subjectivity of the individual I, who erupts with the Reformation, even though it traces itself to Augustine and continues up to Kierkegaard and our own times.[52]

Not only is a person capable of communicating but the person is com-

[50] See Pavan and Milano (1987) for an illuminating study of the contemporary theologic-philosophical problem.

[51] This leaves open one of the most fundamental intercultural problems. Is the category of "Being" the most suitable for expressing "reality"? The discussion is inextricably bound to language, and there are languages that lack the concept of being.

[52] See Milano (1987) 68, who cites Maritain and Moltmann.

munication itself. An isolated person, completely individual, is a contradiction in terms. Since the person is neither singular nor plural, six persons cannot be killed so as to save sixty: quantification in this case is not applicable. Every person is an end in himself or herself; their dignity is inviolable. The political consequences that derive from this condition should unsettle the various contemporary systems. "Human rights" are the rights of Man, not of the individual; Man is a person.

Insofar as human knowledge is personal, it engages the whole—the whole of us and the world—even if imperfectly: it must therefore be distinguished from mere calculation. To know is to participate in the known and thus widen the reality of being a person. The constitutive nature of the person, we would like to stress, is to be relation, and thus capable of knowing. But a person is not only capable of communicating; he is communion itself. I am person insofar as I am communion. Communion is not possession, nor does it mean that other beings (objects or other subjects) belong to me. It is not a question of either the property of objects or domination over subjects. Communion means the belonging (one to the "other") as subjects, not simply as objects of a higher subject. Communion does not mean that one possesses a you (or a you an I), but that both belong to one another, that one does not exist without the other, and vice versa. Neither is the I prior to the you nor the you to the I. The relationship is not causal because their being is a *coesse*, a *Mitsein*. *Ser es estar (juntos)*—"Being is a being (together)."

This implies that I cannot know another subject if I treat her as if she were an object. I can, in this case, identify her but cannot discover her identity. "Nobody can say that Jesus is Lord if not in the Holy Spirit" (1 Corinthians 12:3). This assertion would seem rather absurd if "say" meant uttering terms and not really knowing—that is, becoming that which one knows.

It is significant for us to remember that scholastic philosophy, at least since St. Ambrose,[53] and probably since St. Justin,[54] believed that any truth that anyone asserted originated from the Holy Spirit. Aquinas enjoyed repeating this idea in saying, *Omne verum a quocumque dicatur, a Spiritu Sancto est* ("Everything true, by whomever it is said, is from the Holy Spirit"; *Summa theologiae* Ia-II, q. 109, a. 1; *In Joannem* VIII, lect. 6, etc.).

The question of Christ's personal consciousness did not constitute a great problem after the acceptance of the dogmas proclaimed at the Council of Chalcedon: from then on, the person of Christ is the divine person who works through the two natures as its "organs."[55] On the other hand,

---

[53] See Ambrose, *Glossa Lombardi* (PL 191:1651) and *Glossa Ordinaria* (PL 114:540), as well as Ambrosiaster on 1 Corinthians 12:3 (PL 17:245 and 258b).

[54] See Mouroux (1952) for additional commentaries.

[55] See John Damascene, *De fide orthodoxa* III, 15 (PG 94:1060), with which Thomas Aquinas agrees. See *De veritate*, q. 27, a 4: *Humana natura in Christo erat velut quoddam organum divinitatis.*

with the birth of psychoanalysis, the direct impact of modernism and the more indirect influence of the whole Enlightenment mentality, a lively controversy developed toward the beginning of the twentieth century with regard to the so-called "I of Christ."[56] This was already the question at the beginning of the twelfth century,[57] with the dawn of "Christian humanism": to attribute a human personality to Jesus seemed to deprive him of his divinity. The problem, as often happens, lies in the failure to deepen the premises. In order to ensure the unity of Jesus Christ, the first Christian councils agreed in declaring that in Christ there was one person alone (the second person of the Trinity) and two natures (the human and the divine)— which naturally requires two wills so as to safeguard human freedom. The moment that Christ's humanity was emphasized, however, and his autonomy acknowledged (otherwise, he could not be considered a man), problems became complicated. If Christ's I is in fact the divine person and at the same time Jesus enjoyed a full human consciousness, how could an omniscient divine consciousness coexist with his human consciousness? The subtleties of such a theology are fascinating and amusing.[58] Nevertheless, we shall not enter into them here.

It is interesting to note precisely when the question of Christ's human consciousness became a problem. Within an apersonalistic scholastic ontology the question was not troublesome. With the birth of individualism, however, and the philosophies elaborated since Descartes and Kant, the question became philosophically insoluble. If Christ was a human individual, he could not at the same time be a divine one. The only response was *sola fide*. But the intellectual apartheid of such a *fides* (which ironically was called *sola*) could not last long, and the question became a burning one: Who is this Christ? Post-Enlightenment theology displaces the question about Jesus from "Who do the people say is the Son of man?" (Matthew 16:13) to "Who do you yourself say you are?"

To sum up: if we are all persons and not individuals, participation in the self-consciousness of the other is not impossible, although it does have limits. The I understands the other to the extent that the other is a you; and this other becomes ever more a you to the extent to which the I knows and loves it. What we are saying is related to the ancient *disciplina arcani,* which the initiate alone could understand (as a consequence of participating in the ritual). For the same reason, Christian faith was traditionally

---

[56] See Xiberta (1954); Galtier (1939, 1947, and 1954); and Parente (1951 and 1952).

[57] Cf. Santiago-Ortero (1970).

[58] See as corollary the theological discussion concerning "Christ's faith" (Hebrews 11:2) or whether he also had faith. Cf. Kendall and O'Collins (1992). The question concerns whether we are representing an objective or subjective genitive—that is, whether we may say that Jesus Christ might not have had any faith because he experienced the beatific vision or that he did in fact find faith. See also the chapter "Jesus's faith" in Schoonenberg (1971), 146: "Belief is an act or attitude of the whole person" and is not simply an acknowledgment of abstract truth.

required of those who began the study of theology. The study of the Vedas and of Buddhism also had to be preceded by an initiation that would open the way to a certain knowledge, made possible only through love and con-naturality.

Those for whom Jesus Christ has become a you can to a certain extent participate in what Christian scripture calls the Spirit of Christ (John 14:26; 16:13) and so can possess a certain knowledge of Jesus Christ (see 1 Corinthians 2:16; 1 John 5:20). This knowledge contains dangers of its own that should not be ignored, hallucinations and pathological fantasies of all sorts. We must also keep its limits in mind: the you participates in consciousness in the same way as the I, yet the two remain distinct and can-not be reduced to one. The relation is *advaita*, a-dualistic. The history of mysticism is full of examples of false and unhealthy confusions. The I and the thou are not only interdependent but *inter independent,* as in the Trin-ity. We are able to know the thou, although we will never completely pen-etrate an other consciousness, precisely because each one of us participates in that same consciousness in a unique manner.

This is our problem. I shall now examine a third perspective.

The Ādhyātmic (Pneumatic) Approach

We desire to know Jesus. At the beginning we said that there was only one door for penetrating the innermost recesses of a being: to examine the traces left by his words and deeds. This method is legitimate only on two conditions: that we be conscious of what we are doing and ask permission for a similar incursion. This was the approach of our first type of anthro-pology, which is dangerously similar to a scientific experiment (experimen-tal psychology).

We also said, in the light of our second perspective, that to force the door is out of the question, because personal consciousness is not an enclosed space but a common *agora*, where human beings find their com-munion only by staying together and interacting. What we therefore need is to share the same ideals and, above all, to love, for it is this that will allow us to establish a certain communion insofar as we already participate in the very personal structure of reality. In a significant sense this second approach is similar to the kind of observation that psychoanalysis prac-tices.

But there is also a third approach, which consists in sharing not only ideas and ideals but Being itself. Scripture and Christian tradition insist that not only do we share Christ's very feelings, but we are one with him and transformed in him. This is the way of *experience*—the mystical method. Mystical experience, of course, can eliminate neither reason nor the senses. The *oculi fidei, mentis et sensus* ("the eyes of faith, mind, and sense") are interrelated—a kind of integration, I would add, that represents an inescapable task for contemporary philosophy. This threefold approach must be integrated from an intercultural perspective as well. Our study constitutes an endeavor in this direction.

We deliberately use the adjective *ādhyātmic*, as well as other words taken from a culture that has remained to this very day foreign to the Judeo-Christian tradition, because it is not only cultures but religions too that suffer when they remain enclosed within themselves. I am not using *ādhyātmika* in the sense of *sānkhya* (as a third, interior, type of suffering) but in the *vedānta* sense, that is, "in relation to the Self" (*ātman*), with respect to an integral anthropology in which the real man is considered in all his dimensions, as *sat-puruṣa*.

If the first approach is individualistic with respect to the person, the second is so in relation to the whole of reality. Man is neither a separate "individual" nor a "person" isolated from the rest of the universe, including the divine. Neither is humanity a being in itself: the whole of reality is constitutively interconnected.

By introducing the adjective *ādhyātmic* I wish to give a fresh voice to the tripartite anthropology of early Judeo-Christianity as well as ancient hellenic Christianity.[59] In this sense I could have entitled the present chapter "the pneumatic approach."[60] In fact, the first Christian centuries saw man in intimate relationship with matter through his *body*, in constitutive relation with all living beings (especially other people), through the *soul*, and in a particular bond with the divine world through his *spirit*.

I introduce this word "spirit" for a second reason as well: to contribute to a revaluation of this tripartite anthropology that has been so forgotten within the Christian tradition as to cause the prevalence of the Platonic division between soul and body.[61] Perhaps an Indian perspective could serve as an external stimulus to deepen this "Pauline" anthropology. In a living tradition nothing is definitive.[62]

Let us attempt to take a short step in the process of deepening our understanding.

If we human beings are formed of spirit, soul, and body (πνεῦμα, ψυχή, σῶμα—*pneuma, psychē, sōma*—in 1 Thessalonians 5:23), we are not just animals, but contain within us a spark, a spirit, something else; and it is this that makes us divinizable in a way that is very different from all other beings. The tradition of Vishnu finds no difficulty in admitting that an ani-

---

[59] See de Lubac (1979) 59-117, for an illuminating study that shows how the Pauline intuition of 1 Thessalonians 5:23 has been neglected or minimized by many modern theologians.

[60] See Daniélou (1961) as an example.

[61] "This anthropology—of the Greek rather than the Latin fathers—has remained very foreign to Western thought" (Congar 1958, 312).

[62] Even though we share the defense of this tripartite anthropology, it seems to be an exaggeration to say that the "definitive formula of biblical and Christian anthropology" is found in this vision of man. See Louis Bouyer, in de Lubac (1979) 70.

mal is God's *avatāra* because, as we have said, the *avatāra* possesses an exclusively divine reality. "Those who are ignorant do not recognize my nature when I assume human form," says the *Gītā* (IX, 11). Thousands of pages of Christian scholasticism debated the question whether it was possible for God to be incarnated in an animal or even a thing, although, apart from lucubrations concerning the *de potentia Dei absoluta*, such an incarnation would not bear the meaning the incarnation has for Christians. While acknowledging divine power to be absolute, St. Thomas clearly states that *sola natura humana sit assumptibilis* ("only human nature is assummable," *Summa theologiae*, III, q. 4, a. 1) because the *creatura irrationalis non habet congruitiatem* ("an irrational creature does not have 'congruency' [with the divine]" in *ad 3*). However this may be, our interest is concentrated on the different conceptions of man according to which knowledge of the other is either possible or impossible.

We began by asking ourselves how we can know another individual or person. Our implicit presupposition was that knowledge is that innermost act of ours through which we arrive at knowing others. But what if knowledge did not belong to us as a merely private activity? If, on the contrary, it were something in which we only participate? In the latter case, knowing would not mean I am conscious that my ego knows but that I participate in knowing, that knowing is given to me and that I am conscious of it. The first question was concerned with whether "we" can know another individual, the second turned on the problem of acknowledging the you of our person; the third extends to the problem of knowledge as such—neither "objective knowledge" nor that which is merely "formal," but the knowledge that "identifies" and therefore saves.

Commenting on scripture and expressing a belief common to different traditions, Richard of St. Victor writes that love stands at the origin of consciousness and that, once we become conscious of something, contemplation springs forth, whence knowledge originates.[63]

Millennia earlier, this intuition constituted the epitome of many civilizations. Know "thy 'self,'" Greek wisdom said, and the Christian mystical tradition echoed this.[64] "Know your 'Self,'" the Indic tradition repeats

---

[63] See John 14:21: "He who receives my precepts and follows them loves me; he who loves me will be loved by my Father; and I will love and manifest (ἐμφανίσω) myself to him." This saying seems to make praxis, and therefore love, preeminent. Richard of St. Victor comments: *Ex dilectione itaque manifestatio et ex manifestatione contemplatio et ex contemplatione cognitio* ("From love springs manifestation, from manifestation contemplation, and from contemplation knowledge"; *De Trinitate, Prologo*, PL 196:888C). Knowledge certainly is a *cognitio ad vitam aeternam* ("knowledge for eternal life," according to John 17:3). Richard's text continues: *Sed sicut in fide totius boni inchoatio, sic in cognitione totius boni consummatio atque perfectio* ("as every good thing originates in faith, so in knowledge we find the fullness and perfection of every good thing"; PL 196:889A/B).

[64] Cf. Haas (1971) for a detailed description of this aphorism. *E caelo descendit,* γνῶθι σεαυτόν ("from heaven descended *gnōthi seauton*") Juvenal writes (XI, 27), as cited by Erasmus (*Adagia* I, 6, 95).

emphatically, meaning the Self that is the true Self and not "your" own ego (see Matthew 16:24; Luke 9:23). Only when it ceases to be your ego will it emerge as the Self that is, indubitably, thy Self. To know God and Christ constitutes eternal life, scripture says (John 17:3), emphasizing that "intelligence (διάνοια) has been given to us so that we may know the true [God]" (1 John 5:20). Our third question, therefore, impels us to shift knowledge of the "other" to knowledge of God. A Spanish saying expresses this idea in poetic form: *el camino más corto pasa por las estrellas* ("The shortest way [between two persons, two hearts] passes through the stars"). It is in this sense that I would interpret a cryptic upanishadic text: "He revealed himself in a threefold way": *sa tredhā ātmānaṃ vyakuruta* (*Bṛhadā-raṇyaka-upaniṣad* I, 2, 3). Plato suggests, and Plotinus confirms, that true self-consciousness is one and the same as knowledge of God.

The first question, consequently, does not concern knowledge of the "other" but knowledge of our selves. *Ko' ham?* "Who (am) I?" (*Aitareya-upaniṣad* I, 3, 11). One day a scientist objected to an Eastern sage who showed a certain skepticism with regard to technological civilization: "But we westerners have succeeded in sending a man to the moon!"

"That is true," the sage conceded, "but you do not know *who* you have sent!" In order to know ourselves, we must know *who* it is in us that knows. To know the *who*, the Self, the vedānta will say, constitutes realization, salvation.

Here we face a danger that must be immediately avoided: gnosticism, understood as a spirit/matter dualism and rejection of the body as a prison for the spirit. If knowledge is no more than epistemic, this presumed salvific knowledge excludes the body, and thus the world, and so falls into either a dualism or an idealism that denies any reality outside the "idea." But we have already pointed out that knowledge consists in growth of the whole being and that the third eye sees the other dimension of the real. The French *connaître*, to be born together, succeeds in making the sense of "knowing" more immediate.[65]

This means that self-consciousness does not consist in the knowledge of any object: we are subjects, not objects. If we transform Jesus into an object of our knowledge, we may indeed reach a certain objective knowledge about an individual named Jesus, but we shall not succeed in knowing Jesus, who did not know himself as object. Nor will we share in his self-consciousness. And if a man is characterized by his self-consciousness, we will not have known him until we share his self-consciousness. "You cannot know the knower of consciousness," says an Indic text (*Bṛhadā-raṇyaka-upaniṣad* III, 4, 2). "In what way will the knower be able to be known?" the same text asks (II, 4, 14). "He, the *ātman*, is not this and is

---

[65] Discussion continues concerning the relation between γιγνώσκω (*gignōskō*, "know") and γίγνομαι (*gignomai*, "to generate"), words that do not belong to the same hypothetical root.

not that. . . . But in what way will the knower be able to be known?" we are asked a little later (IV, 5, 15).

The Upanishads assert that if we undertake a search for an object, we shall never find it because our object will be split progressively into more objects, and specialization will develop endlessly. The Upanishads alert us by asserting that this objective knowledge is not "that by which everything is known." The question then arises: "How can it be known?" (*Bṛhadā-raṇyaka-upaniṣad* II, 4, 14). The answer cannot come from Descartes' *Regulae* nor from any kind of objective method because, even if it is conceded that we may succeed in knowing the knower, for that very reason we would not know the knower because he would then become the known—known by us. We would have reified the subject and thereby transformed it into an object; but our question was about the subject.

There is, however, a way of knowing the knower, to become the knower. This becoming is true (salvific) knowledge. Jesus too tells his disciples to abandon all fear and become what he is: "Be myself, feed on me, remain in me."

Tat tvam asi is the ultimate upanishadic intuition: "This thou art." Discover yourself as a thou, as the one who feels and understands the *aham-brahmāsmi*: "I am *brahman*." This can be said truly only after we have realized that *ātman* (is) *brahman*, so that it is *brahman* which says that it is (am) *brahman*, and not my ego. The three personal pronouns come into play here; all are necessary for a complete realization (of the self).[66]

Knowledge of the other is not presented here as knowledge of "an other." It is simply knowledge, the knowledge that arises when one becomes what one knows, that which one must know: "That is the *ātman* in you that is found in every thing," concludes a text already cited (*Bṛhadā-raṇyaka-upaniṣad* III, 4, 2). It is no longer a question of invading intimacy or objectifying the hypothetical "other." The "other" has become your Self. Has it not been written: "Love your neighbor as your self" (*thy*self)?[67] This is what I was referring to when I criticized a certain kind of epistemology that is detached from anthropology (and ontology) and spoke of knowing as a growth in being—of our being.

I am saying what, in one form or other, virtually all mystical schools have underscored. Full knowledge is synonymous with a participation that allows us to achieve identity with the known, something that constitutes more than a simple epistemic activity. To achieve knowledge of Jesus is not to obtain information about Mary's son, nor even about the meaning of the expression "son of God" (in this respect Harnack was right). To achieve knowledge of Jesus Christ is a mystical act, an act that constitutes the

---

[66] See Panikkar (1977) 696ff.

[67] See the Archimandrite Sophrony (1978), ch. 2: "One prays for the whole world as if it were one's self."

human spirit's highest understanding precisely because it means knowing the icon of the whole of reality (Colossians 1:15-20).

In brief, if we share a human nature, and this nature exhibits an intellectual aspect, then consciousness of self is not only knowledge of our respective egos but also a participation in knowledge (knowledge of Self—as subjective genitive, that is, of the knowing Self). A strictly monotheistic world vision will maintain that this consciousness of self is the privilege of a supreme Being and will allow us only an asymptotic and analogical cognitive process. In a trinitarian vision, however, there is room for both identity and difference. The other can be known to the extent to which it shares the same reality with us, but we shall never lose our unicity, our identity, because in the trinitarian vision reality is irreducible to an indistinctive unity. In this experience, obviously, the other is not an *aliud*, but the *thee* in a polar relation to the *I*. "Nobody knows the Son if not the Father; nobody knows the Father if not the Son, and those to whom the Son chooses to reveal him" (Matthew 11:27).

We know him thanks to the illumination that, in the last analysis, "descends from the Father of lights" (James 1:17). James's spiritual insight was taken up by a spiritual tradition that began with St. Augustine and St. Bonaventure and continues, though with notable variations, until the ontologism of the last century.

We have characterized man as a self-conscious being, although a total self-consciousness is impossible—as Socrates had already noted (*Phaedrus* 229e). The *autos* would cease to be *autos*. And so it is that, once again, we need the Trinity. *Brahman* is *brahman,* a certain vedantic system says, but does not know that it is *brahman*. It is Īśvara, the same as *brahman*, that knows it is *brahman*, that recognizes itself as *brahman*.

In other words, "I cannot be absolutely identical with my self." I cannot find my absolute identity, not only because I live in the temporal, which is a constant otherness (the "I am" who says so or thinks it is already an "I was" remembered, or an "I shall be" projected), but also because no predicate exists that is capable of saying who the subject is without having transformed it into a predicate. Reason tells us that I cannot know totally who that I is who says "I am" or asks himself "Who am I?" I cannot think by means of an "absolute reflection," although perhaps I can be it without knowing or thinking it. What meaning does it have, however, if I can neither say nor think it? We cannot say that "it cannot be it" although we can surely assert that I would not be "I," I would not be an "I am" but an "am" that does not belong to me. Yahweh is the only one who can say "I am"—that is, pronounce his own name.

Hence there is no absolute consciousness of self. The I known is not the I knowing. The I knows itself in recognizing the you "equal" to the I. The complete *noēsis noēseos* (Aristotle, *Metaphysics*, XII, 9, 1074 b, 33ff.) leads to absolute idealism or solipsism. If the I knew itself totally, the I would be pure knowledge without any space for a you. And if this Being were real, its knowledge would then be identical with reality. If God were this absolute I without a you who knows itself in total identity, Being would be completely intelligible and reality pure intelligibility. The unintelligible would not be real. That, however, is pure idealism.

The egotistic consciousness of the I, on the other hand, is a consciousness of the you. These yous manifest an ontological gradation that ranges from a pure consciousness of the trinitarian thou to our empirical consciousness of material things.

But there is more. The "strict" consciousness of the you (subjective genitive) is, from the perspective of the you, exhaustive. From the perspective of the I, on the other hand, the you is simply the consciousness of the I (objective genitive) that the I has of its self as object (of its self-consciousness). But this you leaves an "empty space" for the I which "is" not consciousness alone (precisely because there is no absolute egotistic consciousness—the I's total self-identity). The I has consciousness of its self as a you which, though it is not the I, identifies itself with the I. This "empty space" is the Spirit. Certainly the Logos is "equal" to the Father, the Logos is but the Logos of the Father, and the Father is "equal" to the Son he has generated. But precisely because there is no absolute egotistic consciousness but only consciousness of the thou, the I (whom we call Father) leaves "space" to the Spirit as hiatus, as a space between the Father and the Son. The Spirit represents the *advaita*, the nondualism between the Father and the Son—hence they are neither two nor one.

If only the Father and Son existed in absolute equality, the duality would collapse into monism—and there would be no "space" for us. The Spirit obstructs, so to speak, the "short circuit." The Spirit is the dynamism of Life—in which we exist.[68]

Even from a less metaphysical point of view, we may ask ourselves: Where is our true I? Within or without, in contemplation or in activity? Is it the way of entasis or ecstasy? In brief, the *ādhyātmic* approach does not ask, What is man?—as the first approach does. Nor does it ask, Who is man?—as personalist anthropology does. Rather, it asks, Who am I? The first method allows us to ask, What is Jesus? The second asks him, Who are you? The third wishes to penetrate into the Who am I? and finds itself bounced back into the trinitarian *perichōrēsis*.

Let us not lose the thread of our argument. It should be clear by now that our enterprise is not a problem to be solved but a life to be lived.

To sum up, we desire to know the self experience of the man Jesus— that is, to speak of the mysticism of Jesus Christ. If he is simply a historical individual who lived in Palestine two thousand years ago, we must follow the current exegetical method, which will be very useful in tracing

---

[68] See a text of Meister Eckhart on which we will not comment: . . . *in spiritu sancto sunt omnia, ut deus non sit in nobis nec nos sumus in deo nisi in spiritu sancto* ("All things are in the Holy Spirit so that God is neither in us nor we in God, but rather, in the Holy Spirit"; *Sermo* IV, *Lateinische Werke* IV, 25).

the context in which he lived and will constitute a needed corrective to prevent us from projecting our hypotheses onto a nonexisting background. We must, however, respect the appropriate geographical and historical distance: Jesus remains a fascinating and unsettling unknown—a *he*. We may or may not discover that "*he* is the Way"—a doctrine.

If in our consciousness we discover ourselves to be persons—that is, the polarity I–you, the reality of the you will reveal itself (the you itself) ever more and more to the extent to which our intimacy becomes illuminated by a loving intellect: Jesus, living and mysterious companion—the *thou*. We may or may not discover that "*Thou* art Truth"—a personal encounter.

If in the process directed at knowing our selves we should discover the innermost Self in which our ego has been transformed—that is, if we should become or realize this Self—we would discover in it precisely that figure toward which our inquiry aims: Christ, symbol of that Self with whom—perhaps without that Jesus—we would not have dared identify ourselves, the *I*. We may or may not discover that "*Thou* art Life"—a mystical experience.

The three negations—"or may not"—constitute neither an anticlimax nor the expression of a personal fear. They fulfill a threefold function. First, these considerations do not offer an apodictic conclusion. They are not syllogisms: there remains room for freedom. Second, this reading is not the only possible one: there is room for other interpretations. Third, despite all our good will this study may have gone astray. There is an opening for corrections.

This long meditation tells us that not only are the three methods legitimate but that they are also relative to their respective visions of the world. Once we become conscious of this pluralism, we can attempt to show how the three methods complement one another.

Existential Inquiry

The Status Quaestionis

In a discussion such as ours the inquirer is involved not just marginally but in depth. The problem seizes us completely. This vital interest, however, does not imply that we must defend any particular "party line." Our inquiry is directed at nothing other than what we experience as true: "It is by experience that men arrive at science and art."[69] The expressions of our experience are not infallible, however, and must therefore remain open to criticism and dialogue.

---

[69] See Aristotle, *Metaphysics* I, 1, 981 a: ἀποβαίνει δ' ἐπιστήμη καὶ τέχνη διὰ τῆς ἐμπειρίας τοῖς ἀνθρώποις (*Hominibus autem scientia et ars per experientiam evenit*).

Our involvement is total inasmuch as we are raising in a critical way the question of the ultimate meaning of life,[70] a question that is the homeomorphic equivalent to the problem concerning the identity of Jesus Christ. We ask who Jesus Christ is and expect an answer that will reveal to us much more than the pure biographical data concerning a given individual. Who Akbar or Montezuma might be is surely an important question but we do not relate them directly to the ultimate purpose of life, as we do with the drive that sustains the question concerning Jesus Christ. Although the answer may be disillusioning or different from what we had expected, the question is charged with that expectation, one that entails no preconception, however, because the question is critical and we must be prepared for any answer. If one asks why an inquiry about Akbar or Montezuma could not have produced the same impact as an inquiry about Jesus, the answer is that it could have done so, but in fact has not. Christian imperialism? Possibly, and in fact this has frequently been the case. The question is legitimate and also realistic. We must, however, call attention to three cautions.

First, to raise questions about any person whatsoever ultimately becomes an inquiry into the mystery of man and reality. In this respect, an inquiry about Jesus is but one example of the inquiry into the mystery of a person. In fact, from Homer to Einstein, from Caesar to Mao, there have been many icons of this kind: Jesus is only one of these—central for some, irrelevant for others.

Second, it is a fact that the historical relevance in time, space, and events (with respect to good and evil) of Jesus Christ's impact on human life is, if not unique, surely quite exceptional. Besides, in the overall climate of Western culture, Christian or not, history bears its own importance. The essential role of history is probably a pre-Christian idea that owes much to the Semitic mentality, but Christians, as qualified heirs of the abrahamic tradition, have elaborated a complete *Heilsgeschichte* which maintains that history culminates in a "history of salvation." In any event, due in great part to how this Jesus Christ has been interpreted, history has become the principle for judging reality and includes the Western method of calculating time. In this sense, the question concerning Jesus Christ differs from the one about Aśoka—to cite another famous name. It is necessary to remember, however, that the importance of the historical Christ, dependent as it is on the central role of history, is not the same as the importance of Christ for the peoples of the world who do not live in the myth of history.

Third, if the question about Jesus originates from a legitimate curiosity about this person, it does not differ from the one about Aśoka, although

---

[70] As Bellet (1990, 23) says, "Christ seems to escape every attempt at neutrality and hence objectivity. . . . He is, in a certain way, the never-ending total of all the interpretations or perceptions of Christ that mankind is capable of crafting." The entire book should be read as a "Fifth gospel that rests on texts but with a support that does not act as a support because the word is always granted its necessary freedom" (ibid., 60).

the question about Christ carries much greater weight insofar as the claim that Christ is the Savior does not permit neutrality: indifference itself already constitutes a position (Matthew 12:30).

It should be clear that the question about Jesus is important for our life. Although we cannot abandon our prejudices completely, we should be conscious of them and ready to eliminate them should they become an obstacle to the discovery of truth. It is undeniable, however, that the interest of many readers in the mystical experience of the man of Galilee, is due not to a simple curiosity about a certain individual (unique as each person is) but to the fact that this man involves us (and many others) in a special way. We suppose or believe that his experience is of capital—not to say unique—importance for most of humanity. It is not a question of mere curiosity.

I have already said that personal involvement does not imply a commitment to defend a priori any particular opinion or attitude. We may remain disappointed or abandon Jesus, either because he does not offer us any "words of eternal life" or because the very expression "eternal life" has lost all meaning, or even seems to us to be an outright lie. Nevertheless, the question concerning Jesus Christ's identity claims to be an ultimate question. We ask ourselves who such a being might be because he has exercised a considerable impact on the history of human life on earth and still holds a central meaning for many. We should therefore examine critically whether these expectations are justified; to ignore them would not do justice to the question itself, which, for some, is charged with twenty centuries of history. The context of such a long history is important—although for the Jews it is a question of four millennia (Abraham), and for still others it embraces the entire context of human history since the beginning of the universe (*sānatana dharma*, and so forth). The questions about Jesus are certainly no small matter—nor are those about the Buddha, Durgā, Viracocha, or Krishna. To the question of Jesus as to who men say he is corresponds our question as to what Jesus says man is.

This consciousness makes it impossible to neglect any methodological reference to the person who poses the question. We can neither deny nor repress our convictions, which implies that our approach can be a synthesis of three methods insofar as we grant each of them a certain validity. Our study does not renounce form criticism, historical criticism, the knowledge of canonical and apocryphal texts, orthodox and heterodoxical interpretations, nor does it adopt the "epistemology of the hunter"—that is, of those inquirers who imagine that they are immune from any presuppositions and shoot at whatever moves. Neither does our study proceed in a pietistic way nor start from a sentimental vision of Jesus—nor from a unilateral evaluation of history. Christian history is not free of contradictions.

The question about Jesus is neither pure speculation nor an abstract *theologoumenon*. If a Christian is a person who has been baptized and received the eucharist, this should signify that she has met Christ personally, even though this experience has usually not reached its fullness (Matthew 13:3ff.). The authentic Christian is not so much the follower of an ideology or a person who believes in the beliefs of others as one who has experienced the reality of Christ.[71] Without this personal encounter, everything remains nothing more than superstructure. Let us not forget that the grace of Christ is Christ himself and that the *opus operatum* (i.e., [as a result of the sacramental] "work having been performed") of Catholic theology is not magic but *opus operantis Christi* (that is, [as a result] "of Christ performing the work").

This meeting is and remains pure imagination or a mere convergence of ideas or ideals unless it is above all a meeting of persons, a meeting in the innermost center of our existence, a meeting that embraces our whole being. Many mystics define it as a falling in love, others as an actual touching. All this would remain an illusion, however, unless this meeting could actually take place; otherwise Christ remains no more than a figure of the past or a construction of our imagination or, in the best of cases, the memory of someone who no longer is. The meeting is not with the "Messiah" or any other attribute but with the "thou" of this ineffable mystery which Christians call Christ.

In short, this meeting is possible if the communication and communion unfold within the innermost center of our being: the person. Perhaps the very idea we have of person is such because we ourselves have experienced this personal encounter. In any case, this meeting is personal because the person does in fact constitute this kind of relation. An isolated individual (if such existed) would not be a person. The person is our innermost, most mysterious reality, incommunicable because she is already communion. The individual is the unknown who is encountered on the street; the person is someone who is received in our heart.

It is crucial to make my thought as precise as possible, in order to avoid a pietistic or sentimental interpretation, as well as a cerebral or rational one. It is not a question of meeting someone in the way we encounter a friend; this would be a product of pure imagination, since Jesus lived twenty centuries ago. Nor is it a question of meeting my own inwardness or my ego, although this might in fact entail a concrete discovery. Perhaps the word "encounter" does not express the idea adequately. Once again, it is not a question of dualism. Christ is not only the friend or the spouse, though human language is virtually compelled to draw on such metaphors. Christ is not an other. Nor is it a question of monism—I am not Christ. We are neither one nor two. This is the nondual relation of the person, the experience of *advaita* that we tried to describe earlier.

---

[71] See Frei (1975) for an analysis of this presence of Christ in a postmodernist and post-deconstructionist analysis of how a person becomes "present" in the consciousness of another.

At this point I must apply the theory of *pisteuma* to myself. It is not possible to speak of this matter in the third person. I cannot, for example, explain the meaning of Durgā unless I myself reach the *pisteuma* of the believer (in Durgā), which may differ from the *noēma* of the nonbeliever. Likewise, I will not be able to furnish an adequate description of Jesus Christ if I put my faith in this symbol into parentheses (*epochē*). In confessing my belief I will avoid every possible absolutization—as those who believe in reason are often inclined to do when they speak of "pure" reason. I shall constantly remember that this is my belief but I cannot set it aside. The methodological doubt about truth and certitude already implies an ontological fracture that provokes the doubt. The methodological doubt appears along with the pretension that something exists that is absolutely indubitable, while in fact we cannot pretend not to believe that which we do believe, and vice versa. The critical imperative is the relativization of the *pisteuma*.

Personal Experience

Having said all this, we must now take the final step. It is no longer a question of an intellectual exercise nor of an act of will but of an empirical and existential plunge into the abyss of reality, into what Paul defines as the depths, the abyss of divinity (Romans 8:39; Ephesians 3:18; 1 Corinthians 2:9-10). It is a question of the Christian mystical experience.

Christ's experience was his personal experience. I can receive it only in my own personal experience, the experience of my own identity. As I seek to express it, I will perhaps undergo the influence of what I have learned and use a Christian vocabulary or that of Jesus Christ himself—and for this reason I will give the impression of reporting his experience rather than my own.

On one hand, meditation on his words and actions may give form to my experience or provide a framework in which to express it; on the other hand, the personal experience of my own identity may have found for itself in the example of Jesus Christ an image and perhaps even a model.

One could say, echoing what Newton once wrote, *Hypotheses non fingo* ("I do not fashion hypotheses"). To this, inspired by Gadamer, one could add, neither will I fashion *Erfahrungsverschmelzungen* ("fusion of experiences").[72] Having recognized this inextricable relation and setting aside for the moment the question whether I would be capable of expressing my personal experience even in different language, or whether other traditions have given form to it, I shall try to describe it as a hermeneutical suggestion for understanding the experience of Christ.

---

[72] As we have noted above, Gadamer (1972) 289 and *passim* speaks of the act of understanding as a "fusion of horizons."

As I awaken to reality, or simply to consciousness, I find in myself a desire to know all things, though I discover them as veils. Those veils reveal to me their apparent form while at the same time they conceal what they are. Since I do not find their "essence," I turn to my inner self. I begin the conscious pilgrimage to the center of my being but even here I do not find any foundation or any refuge, neither in myself nor in anything present to my consciousness. I cannot identify myself with my body or my mind or with what I am today, was yesterday, or will be tomorrow. I experience myself as alive, below or beyond or simply different from anything of which I might be conscious. My foundation seems simply to be an abyss, an *Abgrund* (or, even, *Ungrund*). I neither find nor discover myself. But is it precisely this "myself" that asks, Who (am) I? *Ko'ham?*

Reason tells me that, since I do not come from my self, I must come from some other source. To conclude that I am a "creature" may be logical and legitimate, but it does not constitute an experience. My experience is simpler; I find it in myself. What I experience is contingency and this experience is neither that of the "sinner" launched into the world nor that of the "just" called by heaven. The experience of contingency is tangential (as the word suggests), neither immanent nor transcendent. That which touches me tangentially (*tangere*), that makes me touch (*cum-tangere*) is neither transcendence (untouchable) nor immanence—which cannot be touched either. We can experience neither transcendence, "No one has seen God" (John 1:18), nor immanence. There is no space to have such experience.

In the experience of contingency I discover the tangential touch between immanence and transcendence. Touch requires that somebody touch something, but in the touch itself we find neither duality nor unity; we find instead a nondual union—*advaita*. In the experience of contingency I do not experience myself as "creation" (of somebody else) because I touch the infinite, nor do I experience myself as the "creator" (of myself) because this touch is actualized in a point that has no dimensions. I realize that I participate, that I am an integral part of that very flux we call reality, although the word "participate" does not express the experience adequately.

What I truly am cannot be something that I am not. I am neither matter nor spirit, neither devil nor angel, neither earth nor heaven, neither World nor God. I am the point of the tangent in which those two poles meet: I stand in between. Everything that I *have*, I have received—from parents, ancestors, culture, earth, from an evolutionary past, karma, God, or anything else whatsoever. What I *have* may be called creature but what I *am* is certainly not identical with what I *have*. The *me* I have, and with it I have

everything else. The *I* I do not have, (that) I am. What I am is neither creature nor creator. I do not know what I am. I know that,
although limited, I have already in some way transcended the limits: consciousness that I am finite shows me the infinite. I am neither finite because I know I am such, nor infinite because I am
conscious that I am finite.

I must admit that perhaps I would not have thought of asking myself,
"Who am I?" unless others had urged me to do so—and thereby incited me
to search for an answer.

Ever since I was young I heard it said that it was God who created
"me," but since then, though I was in no position to explain this
until later, I had the experience that this "me" was not really I. Yes,
I do *have* a "me" but I am not identical with that me. "My" *I*
seems to be found beyond that "me." But about this "I," which in
a certain sense is inseparable from my "me," I can say nothing—
except, perhaps, that though it does "remain" me, it is not *me*, as
one Eastern text among others seems to confirm:

> All beings subsist in me,
> but I do not subsist in them,
> nor even do beings subsist in me.
> (*Bhagavad-gītā* IX, 4-5)[73]

I felt responsible for everything that the "me" did but not completely responsible for everything that it was (or is). Everything has
been given to "me"—my ideas, my ability to achieve intelligibility,
along with time, space, birth, inclinations, and so on. No scientific
answer is exhaustive. Everything may be the fruit of the global evolution of the human species that has arrived at me, but nothing
achieves or discovers the I. The I is not "me" even if the "me" uses,
abuses, and at times usurps the I. I have long meditated on a passage in the *Ṛg-veda* I, 164, 37):

> What I am I do not know.
> I roam around alone, under the weight of the mind.
> When the Firstborn of Truth reaches me
> it has been granted me to participate in that same Word.

---

[73] Zaehner translates this, "And (yet) contingent beings do not subsist in me." S. Piano
renders it, "Nor are beings in me." Here is the meaning of contingency: to subsist and not
subsist; to be and not to be; a touch that does not touch, detached (*āsaktam*; *Bhagavad-gītā*
XIII, 14).

We are confronted with a paradox. The more my "me" acts, so much less is the I active; and the more the I is active, so much less does the "me" intervene. The explanation seems obvious: I cannot say or know *who I am* inasmuch as the variety of predicates possible cannot be identified as such with the subject. My consciousness of self cannot be completely objectified. The I is prior and higher than knowing who or what I am. In brief:

> I have succeeded in experiencing the "me" as the *you* of the I. The I moves me as a you, the you is the *agora*, the *kṣetra*, the field of the I. My task was to listen more than to speak. I was also able to notice that my so-called prayer was a letting myself be guided more than a request for help, an answer or response to a solicitation to which I was subject more than a request addressed to another. To call God a thou, it seemed to me, with all due respect, was not very convincing—and also egocentric. God is the I, if anything, and "I" the you. Yet, in moments of difficulty, suffering, and testing in my life, I was led spontaneously to invoke thee, Father, Divinity—and even more frequently, Christ, my *Iṣṭadevatā*.[74]

> Later the roles seem to have been inverted—the *interior intimo meo* of Augustine, Ibn Arabī, Thomas, Eckhart, Calvin, the Upanishads and many others began to become real.[75] My small *I* was neither relevant nor ultimate. We find an echo in Paul's scriptural sentence: "It is not my 'me' that counts: I do not consider my life precious for me" (Acts 20:24). The I was becoming elusive while a more real self appeared that was neither my ego nor a divine I. My true self could be neither a simple rational animal nor a divine being. A *mesitēs* ("mediator," 1 Timothy 2:5) was emerging within, a mediator (not an intermediary) between the infinite (whose traditional name is God, transcendence, the absolute I) and my ego, my "me." Naturally, what came to my mind were all the texts that describe Christ's dwelling in the deepest center of our being, as well as similar affirmations that a great many spiritual masters of other traditions have made.

---

[74] *Iṣṭadevatā* is not the deity we have chosen or arbitrarily preferred; it is rather the icon of the deity that allows everyone an intimate and personal relation while knowing that it is only an icon. The *iṣṭadevatā* is that form of the divine that corresponds most closely to our culture, idiosyncrasy, and personal circumstances; it is the concrete name we find to express our experience of this ultimate Mystery that many call God. In Egyptian religion the notion of *netjar* existed in the same sense—that is, the God (a God, the Supreme God, "my" God) with whom I feel directly related. The *iṣṭadevatā* is neither objective nor subjective; it is relational. The "my God" of a sincere prayer is truly "my God."

[75] *Tu autem eras interior intimo meo et superior summo meo* ("And you were more deeply in me than my innermost part, and higher than my highest part"), writes Augustine in the *Confessions*, III, 6, 11. See Panikkar (1966) 248ff. for other texts.

I could also personally relive the four adverbs of the Council of Chalcedon,[76] the theanthropy of Bulgakov and the *theōsis* of many church fathers. Is this not perhaps the experience of divine immanence? It could also be called the *advaita* experience. The mediator mentioned is the *anthrōpos* Jesus Christ—as the second Adam in which human nature as a whole is represented (1 Corinthians 15:22 and *Denzinger* 624). Perhaps I was discovering myself simply as man.

> I experienced the "inner energy," the "grace," the "power" that was my most innermost self, and which made me do things that are otherwise inexplicable (though psychology can always intervene by offering two-dimensional explanations). I was discovering Christ.
>
> But I speak of "memory" and already concede too much to "interpretation."

"Thinking to myself I no longer say I, nor do I say you when I think of another," wrote Yunus Emré, a turkish dervish of the fourteenth century.[77] "My I is God, I do not know others outside of my very God," St. Catherine of Genoa wrote (*Vita*, XIV).[78]

If a simple man like me (and many others) is able to live such experiences, it becomes easier to believe that the "man Jesus Christ" could have lived them, in a much higher manner. One recalls Thomas Aquinas's dictum, *Omnis cognitio est per aliquam similitudinem* ("All knowledge occurs through a certain likeness"; *Summa theologiae*, I, q. 14, a. 11, ad 3). Aristotle and Kant affirm the same idea.

To sum up: where there is a more or less objective rational "arena" in which various forms of rationality may be found, a meeting place also exists between the different experiences, which can only be the *agora* of the same experience. If I am to enter into contact with the experience of Jesus, the meeting must take place within the sphere of a common experience— *minutis minuendis*.

The Search for Credibility

What we have said had to be clarified from the very beginning because it justifies and relativizes our selection of texts.[79] We could defend this by

---

[76] The human relation with the divine, even without hypostatic union, is qualified by four adverbs: *inconfuse, immutabiliter, indivise, inseparabiliter*.

[77] Vannucci (1978) 149.

[78] Panikkar (1966) 249.

[79] See C. H. Dodd's (1970) excellent chapter on Jesus's "Personal Traits," where he describes rather effectively just a few of Jesus's observations on things and persons but not the utterances about himself. See Kahlefeld (1981): *Christentum ist eine Beziehung auf die konkrete Gestalt Jesu Christi* ("Christianity is a relation with the concrete figure of Jesus

asserting that Christian tradition has retained such texts as central. But again, this understanding of tradition depends on a choice, even if it follows that of the idea of the *ecclesia magna,* which has become a standard historical narrative. We are sufficiently aware of obscure historical aspects and of the machinations of this church, such that they weaken this standard narrative. The texts that we shall cite are not, of course, the only ones that could be selected, but they do allow us to furnish a certain picture of the mystical experience "the man Jesus Christ" might have had.

My comments may still be valid even if the historical Jesus did not pronounce the words cited literally, or were not the second person of the Trinity. In any case, I maintain that he is a prototype of the human condition. It should be clear, at this point, that if I speak of an experience and meeting with Christ, it is not a question of evoking or imagining the past but rather of a meeting with someone alive.

In saying this, we do not intend to ignore the achievements of exegetical analysis or the context of traditional orthodoxies. Nor do we seek to place Jesus Christ in an African context (Christ the proto-ancestor, the healer, the chief)[80] or in an Asian context, saying, for example, that he is the *sadguru,* or the *jīvanmukta,* the supreme *satyāgraha, advaitin,* or *yogi,* the Prajāpati incarnate, *cit,* the highest *avatāra, ādi-puruṣa,* divine *śakti,* the tempieternal *Aum,* or some other.[81] Neither do we confront Christ with the key figures of other religions.[82] Although all these problems are important, we are now engaged in a much humbler, though even riskier, effort—a personal exercise in what the ancients defined as *fides quaerens intellectum,* because I am convinced that faith is man's life (Romans 1:17; Galatians 3:11; Hebrews 10:38) and that faith is the way to liberation (*Upadeśasā-hasrī* 1, 1).[83] "Unless you believe, you will not live"—or "not understand," as another interpretation of an ancient Hebrew text says (Isaiah 7:9).

We quickly discover that we are not alone in this enterprise.[84] In fact, the greater part of genuinely mystical interpretations of Christ point to the same direction. There is also a significant similarity between the affirmations of many other philosophers and sages of different traditions—without claiming that they all say "the same thing" (as if such a thing existed as a Kantian "thing in itself").

Christ"). See also Felder (1953) and Graham (1947), which, though a little dated, still have value. Both have a chapter on "The Personality of Jesus," while Felder has a paragraph on "The Interior Life of Jesus."

[80] See Evers (1993) 175ff.

[81] See Sugirtharajah (1993).

[82] As examples, see Robinson (1979), Fries (1981), Venkatesananda (1983), Koyama (1984), Knitter (1985), Thomas (1987), Vempeny (1988), Dupuis (1989), Keenan (1989), Schreiter (1991), Moran (1992), and Lefebure (1993).

[83] See the important affirmations about *śraddhā* ("faith") in *Bhagavad-gītā* III, 31; VI, 37, 47; VII, 21-22; IX, 23; XVI, 1-17; etc.

[84] See Amaladoss (1981). Other non-Western christologies have emerged in recent years, some of which are included in the bibliography.

It is worth singling out the fact that, although Christianity asserts that it bases itself on the person of Jesus—with the exception of some interpretations during the first few centuries—a great part of Christian self-understanding rests on the historical narratives of Jesus's words and works rather than on one's own personal consciousness. We should remember once again that, according to the virtually unanimous tradition of most religions, faith or initiation is required for the authentic study of the "sacred doctrines." "Teacher of the initiation" is an accepted title for both African and Oceanic christology.[85] In the modern Western Christian tradition a strong wind of objectivity has swept away the mystical consciousness, pushing it to the margins of Christian life. Christic faith, which began as "religiosity of the Word," has continued to evolve, sociologically speaking, into a "religion of the Book." The *colloquium salutis* that a certain theology aims at, between the divine Word and the human word, is above all a colloquium between two "words," not just the reading of a text.

Whoever that young rabbi might have been or whatever consciousness of self he might have had, the important and decisive thing was thought to be faith in what had been written about him, not only in the first documents (canonical) but likewise in subsequent writings (conciliar—and even, for some, papal). Despite several different ideas, we undoubtedly find a certain consensus in acknowledging what he has said and done. For a certain period of time it seemed that all problems were resolved by admitting that he was the son of God or, in any case, an extraordinary prophet, an instrument of divinity who played both a cosmic and a historic role. In other words, it seemed that what really counted was his function, his doctrine, his example. "Christian faith" became virtually synonymous with the acknowledgment of a complex of facts and doctrines. The living figure of Jesus Christ was protected by a heavy doctrinal mantle, just like the traditional madonnas of southern Europe, virtually buried under heavy clothes, jewels, and flowers. I am not challenging either the legitimacy or truth content of these systems of belief. I am only undertaking a different pilgrimage, or simply seeking to become travel companions on the human path, this time with a lighter knapsack.

Today one hears talk of a christology "from above" in opposition to a christology "from below."[86] Here we must be careful. Although labels have practical value, they always impose limitations on reality, which, like the rainbow, shows no boundaries between colors. If someone were to classify this study, she might define it as a christology "from within." After all, we do know that the "kingdom of the heavens" *is* (ἐντός) neither "between" nor "within," but in the same intimate relation with the whole of creation—because reality as a whole is "triune." That is why we must always

---

85 See Evers (1993) 179 and May (1990), both of which have large bibliographies.

86 See Bordoni (1991) 247-49, who also speaks of an implicit christology and an explicit one.

subject our experiences to the dialogue and criticism of the "we," the "you" of the community.

There was no reason to be very curious about Jesus the man since he was considered to be fundamentally a divine being—an understandable attitude as long as the Christian emphasis was placed on theocentrism. Within this framework Jesus continued to be simply an instrument of God, who resurrected him from death, inspired what he had to say and do, and was by his side when he performed miracles. After all, Jesus had asserted that he had come to do the Father's will, and to say only what the Father wanted him to say. In listening to him, therefore, the Christian is obeying God's will. What more could we want? Is it perhaps only morbid curiosity to go beyond what he simply said and did and examine what the man Jesus felt and experienced?

Some might feel it necessary to psychoanalyze Jesus of Nazareth. They are surely free to do so. But although such a project is legitimate, we should, in that case, speak not of his mystical consciousness but of his psychological disposition. This is always an appropriate caution because the interest in psychology, the weakening of a certain image of God, and the growing fascination regarding the figure of Christ outside ecclesiastical circles seem to justify this desire to learn more about the man Jesus and what inspired him to say and do what he said and did.[87] Who did he think he was?

But we might also leave Jesus tranquil on the analyst's couch and simply walk by his side and ask him *where* he lives (John 1:38), and from where he speaks. I am following this second approach as a way that differs from both experimental psychology and deductive theology. It is obvious, however, that in this respect he was rather elusive.[88] If biographies of Jesus continue to be produced today, is it because of curiosity, literary fashion, or because his figure still inspires, in good and evil? Jesus remains a personality who does not leave us at peace.[89]

The Western Christian and post-Christian tradition could be interested in such approaches, as many modern novels on Jesus prove; nor should we neglect the importance of the "feminist christologies" that are emerging today. They offer a sorely needed corrective to patriarchal (or "kyriocentric") interpretations and constitute an essential complement to christo-

---

[87] A reference to Drewermann seems obligatory at this point (1984-85, and 1987-88). The importance of the theological controversy regarding his ideas should not be minimized. See Benedikt and Sobel (1992).

[88] "I truly believe that now we can know almost nothing about Jesus's life or personality" (Bultmann 1958a, 8). "This statement is often badly misinterpreted. It should not be taken as an assertion that Bultmann denies any knowledge about the historical Jesus. What we cannot know is the most intimate life, the heroic struggle that so fascinated the early interpreters" (Baird 1977, 39).

[89] I have already mentioned the interest in Christ in a wider context. See Stöckli (1991) for a Steinerian approach; Schiwy (1990) for a serious presentation in a New Age direction; and Massa (1995) for a brief contribution to a mystical understanding of Christ.

logical studies. I, however, am seeking to approach the figure of Christ neither out of psychological curiosity nor for apologetical purposes, but from an Indic perspective. Almost unconsciously, it asks: What kind of person "intoxicated with the divine," or what kind of religious hero was this historical figure who has given life to one of the most important movements of the last two millennia?[90]

We know more or less what Jesus did. We have also heard what he might have said; what has sprung out of all this stands before our eyes. Is it not legitimate, therefore, simply to ask ourselves once again who Jesus might be? We know what Christians have said.[91] But he himself, who did he think he was? How did he experience his human consciousness?[92] He asked: Who do people say is the "Son of man"? Here we turn the question around and address him: "You, what do you say of yourself? Who do you think you are?" Or should we content ourselves with the elusive answer given to John the Baptist? (Matthew 11:2-6)[93] Is it perhaps blasphemous to dare penetrate into the personal intimacy of this Christ?

Before continuing to consider Jesus the Christ's possible intuitions, let me try to exemplify my logical journey and analyze another phrase which a man like us might have pronounced, "I am an elephant that flies in the skies."

At first sight I cannot understand a statement of this kind. I cannot prove that I am a flying elephant—that a human being is an elephant that flies. I must admit that for me the statement is incomprehensible. To understand a phrase correctly means to discover that it is intelligible, and thus to

---

[90] Geiselmann's thirty-two-page article (1962) ends as follows: "We should not delude ourselves: what we have in front of us is only the specifically Western interpretation of Jesus Christ. Tomorrow, perhaps, when the Eastern Asian sensibility and mind will attempt to investigate the mystery of Christ, other aspects of Christ will be disclosed, depths until now inaccessible to the West" (p. 770). This text may be complemented by a phrase of Keshub Chandra Sen, so often repeated in India in the nineteenth century: "It seems that the Christ that has come to us is an Englishman."

[91] Artists often exhibit a more profound intuition: "Whoever he might or might not be, whoever he might be convinced that he was, he was surely a man, independently of whatever else he might have been. And he had the face of a man, a human face" (Büchner 1974). This statement is at the beginning of Büchner's book, which has splendid illustrations that span many centuries and cultures.

[92] *Sed primum quod tunc (ad primum usum rationis) homini cogitandum occurrit, est deliberare de se ipso* ("The first thing that happens to man [when he first reaches the use of reason] is to inquire about himself"; Thomas Aquinas, *Summa theologiae* I-II, q. 89, a. 6). Again: *Primum quod occurrit homini discretionem habenti est quod de se ipso cogitet, ad quem alia ordinet sicut ad finem* ("The first thing that happens to man when he reaches [the power of] discernment is to reflect on himself and direct all other things to this as an end"; ibid., ad 3). Could Jesus be an exception to this?

[93] See the excellent christologies of Kasper (1974), Sobrino (1976), Rovira Belloso (1984), and González-Faus (1984), which, however, do not take into sufficient consideration—as Dupuis does (1994, 1997, 2002)—the fact that christologies could be important for other cultures and religions too.

become convinced that what is understood is true.[94] I am therefore compelled to limit myself to assert that a certain human individual, who is apparently sane, has made such an assertion, which I find incomprehensible. I nevertheless trust the other person and believe that for him the phrase holds a meaning that escapes me.

If I still want to decipher what that person might wish to express by that assertion, I may arrive at certain conclusions. Though I must confess that I myself have not reached such a state of consciousness, I have studied totemism, shamanism, and other analogous phenomena: I can therefore more or less imagine that a human being might succeed in identifying herself with an elephant. Those who have experienced the feelings and intelligence of these pachyderms can agree with me and also be able to achieve a kind of elephantine consciousness and claim with conviction to be an elephant. Widening my empathy to its maximum, I could even go so far as to assert, "I am an elephant." Yet I could not do this without a certain trepidation and some reservation, inasmuch as I have not abandoned my human consciousness.

I must confess, however, that the assertion is not altogether intelligible to me and that I can only give it a partial sense because I am able to empathize with someone I trust who says, "I am an elephant." In short, I can "believe" that the assertion "I am an elephant" could have a certain meaning for a very special human being, even though I myself cannot fully reach this level or grade of consciousness.

The second part of the assertion, however, I do find altogether unacceptable—"that flies in the skies." At this point I have to say that the man is either dreaming or the prey of an hallucination. No real elephant, I object, has ever flown in the skies. My hero here is certainly mistaken when he makes such a claim. The thing makes no sense, and with all my good will and desire to believe him, I must nevertheless conclude that he is either deceiving himself or all of us. Perhaps he is a very special human being endowed with the supernatural power of flying and may identify himself with an elephant—although not with an "elephant that flies" precisely because elephants do not fly.

As I put together the two parts of the assertion, I have the comforting suspicion that the first part too is an illusion. If my *noēma* rejects both parts, my *pisteuma* can at most accept the first part of the assertion, although both the *noēma* and the *pisteuma* compel me to reject the second. We cannot believe in something that is not credible, even though it is based on the authoritative assertion that Christ is God, that the church has a divine "hot line" or that the magisterium possesses a different kind of knowledge, which is higher or better. "If a thousand scriptures assure me that fire does not burn, I will not believe them," the *mīmāṃsaka* said millennia ago.

---

[94] See Panikkar (1975c) for philosophical support for the next paragraphs.

As most religious traditions assert, we must distinguish between ratio-nal and other possible kinds of knowledge. But we cannot contradict our-selves. Belief must be reasonable and reason believable. I can believe what I cannot understand, but I cannot believe what (for me) is not believable. I can believe anything so long as I believe it is credible. Tertullian can defend *credo quia absurdum* because he believes that the impossible can be believ-able—thus unsettling the rational (natural) order. But he cannot say that he believes the unbelievable.[95]

In short, there is no reason to formulate any hypotheses unless we can give them some meaning. We cannot believe "I and the Father are one" if this assertion is for us, a priori, meaningless. And it is in fact meaningless if we are closed to assertions that are based neither on the senses nor deducible from them. And we shall be closed to the meaning of these asser-tions if our life flows along only on sensory or purely rational levels—if, that is, we remain insensible to the third dimension of reality, blind to the mystical consciousness.

At the risk of giving the impression that I wish to project this experi-ence onto Jesus Christ, or believe that this experience might be a shadow of Christ's experience, let us confront what I consider the three *mahāvākyāni* of Jesus Christ.[96]

---

[95] See Schestow (1994) 311, the intelligent defense of Tertullian, with respect to the orig-inal famous phrase, which refers to the crucifixion: *Mortuus est Dei filius prorsus credibile quia ineptum est; et sepultus resurrexit: certum est quia impossibile* ("God's son is dead, fully credible because scandalous; and, buried, he rose: it is certain precisely because impossible"; *De carne Christi*, 5). On this we must renounce the attempt to comment.

[96] From *mahā* (great) and *vākya* (phrase). The vedantic tradition has condensed the teaching of the Upanishad into five great phrases, called *mahāvākyāni*.

2

The Expressions

... ἐὰν οὗτοι σιωπήσουσιν,
οἱ λίθοι κράξουσιν

... *si hi tacuerint,*
lapides clamabunt

... if these should remain silent,
the stones will shout out.
(Luke 19:40; cf. Habakkuk 2:11)

It is almost superfluous for us to ask which of the three utterances we are about to discuss is most relevant. Still, although all are interlinked, we may say that the first is central to the whole enterprise of Christian understanding.[1]

After we have reproduced a few texts we shall offer a brief interpretation and conclude with an experiential comment.

First, let us bear in mind the scholastic distinction between discerning, thinking, and understanding. We find the following in Thomas Aquinas (in *IV Sententias* I, *dist.* 3, q. 4, a. 5, c):

- *Discernere est conoscere rem per differentiam ab aliis.* ("To *discern* is to know a thing by differentiating it from others.")
- *Cogitare autem est considerare rem secudum partes et proprietates suas: unde dicitur quasi coagitare.* ("To *think*, on the other hand, is to consider the thing in its constitutive parts and properties, whence the derivation of *cogitare* from *co-agitare*.")
- *Intelligere autem dicit nihil aliud quam simplicem intuitum intellectus in id quod sibi est praesens intelligibile.* ("To *understand*, however, is nothing but the simple intuition of the intellect in which it makes the intelligible present to itself.")

---

[1] In what follows we reproduce the original Greek only when we think it is important. At times we present more than one translation so as to show different nuances in meaning. In the absence of references the translation is ours.

Thomas refers to a text of St. Augustine (*De utilitate credendi* XI, 25), in which he makes a distinction between *opinari, credere,* and *intelligere.*[2]

Let us remember another distinction, beautiful in its Teresian simplicity:

¡Oh válame Dios cuán diferente cosa es oir estas palabras y creer-las a entender por esta manera cuán verdaderas son! ("Holy heaven, how different it is to hear and believe these words than it is to experience them as true"; *Moradas* VII, 1, 8).[3]

Again, let us reflect on a classic text by Miguel de Molinos, virtually unknown today. He writes in the 1676 introduction of his work *La ciencia mística no es de ingenio, sino de experiencia; no es inventada, sino probada; no leída, sino recibida* ("Mystical knowledge is not the work of the imagination but the fruit of experience; it is not invented but rather lived; not read, but received").[4]

The texts in this section encourage us to speak not on behalf of the stones, those "living stones" so dear to St. Peter (1 Peter 2:4-8), but rather in the name of that "crowd" (πλῆθος,, Luke 19:37) of men and women of our age who are driven by a thirst for words that would express life, not simple recipes for *know-how*—even in spiritual matters.

Abba, Patēr

The Texts

Abba, Father,
for you all things are possible;
take this chalice away from me!
Yet not what I will,
but what you will.
(Mark 14:36; see also Matthew 25:39; Luke 22:42; John 12:27)

What a revealing reiteration! *Abba* means father and (*patēr*) means father.[5] If Jesus spoke in Aramaic, he must have repeated the word. Now

---

[2] The etymology bears its own importance (as truth: ἔτυμος). Today "to think" (*pensare*) does not suggest *cogitare*. As I have written elsewhere, to "think" is to *soppesare* ("to bear") the love that inheres in every "thing" so that it may reach its place in the cosmos (which also means harmony). To *capire* (from *capore,* to "grasp") is more aggressive than *intus-legere* (or *inter-legere*).

[3] Teresa de Jesús (1967) 439.

[4] Molinos (1976) 103.

[5] "Even without wishing to venture into the desperate enterprise of analyzing Jesus's psychology. . . ." Thus Schillebeeckx (1985) begins one of his reflections on *Abba.* Elsewhere he

let us imagine that Mark (and his source, or sources) was pressed to do so in order to convey its ambivalence: on the one hand, "papa," "daddy," biological father, head of family; on the other, the name—however patriarchal—most common for defining the closest and least terrifying aspect of the deity that we find in numerous religions, including the judaic.[6] In the light of many documents of ancient religions, we might ask ourselves if calling God Father and Mother constitutes an anthropomorphism, or, on the contrary, if calling parents Father and Mother might not be a theomorphism. In primordial times the human relation with the Gods seems to be stricter than the purely biological one. The divine world is seen as the model for the human world, and not vice versa. Two-dimensional modern cosmology has lost the three-dimensional cosmovision of the ancients: *Dii nos respiciunt* ("The Gods observe and bless us"), wrote the second-century African slave Publius Terentius (*Phormio* 817), accentuating a popular belief, found also in Eastern texts, for example, *Īśā-upaniṣad* 1.

Abba was probably maintained in first-century Christian liturgies in order to stress the special relationship with the divinity to which the word alluded on Jesus's lips.[7] Although he might have uttered the word frequently, it appears in the texts just once. At other times only πατήρ (*patēr*) appears.[8] In St. John's Gospel we find πατήρ μου (*patēr mou*), "my father," thirty-five times. It is important to note that the only time the Aramaic word appears on Jesus's lips is in the almost desperate prayer in Gethsemane, when Jesus pleads to be spared that "hour," and then adds that God's will be done.[9]

Jesus does not have any doubts, for he is convinced that God is his Father. He speaks of God as "my Father"[10] in a provocative way—Kittel says "disrespectfully"—[11] in the light of his judaic tradition.[12] He turns to

---

concludes that "Christ's experience of *Abba* constitutes the source of his message and praxis" (p. 125).

[6] For a good summary, see Schrenk (1967) especially 949-59, and Quell (1967) 959-82, for the Old Testament. See also Heiler (1961) 464-666; van der Leeuw (1956) §20, 195-201 for a few references.

[7] "The invocation *Abba* is seen here as an experience of singular significance" (Schrenk [1967] 1006).

[8] "*Abba* is undoubtedly the most theologically dense word in the entire New Testament," writes González de Cardedal (1975b) 99, in the chapter "*Abba* and its christological importance" (pp. 97-104), with many bibliographical references. The whole work is a valid contribution to the "Understanding of Christ in the light of the category of meeting" (p. xiii).

[9] See Schrenk (1967) 985. The word "Father" is used 415 times in the New Testament, in most cases referring to God.

[10] We abstain from listing the extraordinary number of studies on this topic. See the bibliography in the few works cited.

[11] Kittel and Friedrich (1964), I:6, whom others follow: "Israel's religious language and the formulas of prayer the *Talmud* has handed down ignore this word as indecorous and absurd . . ." (Bordoni 1991, 539).

[12] See a summary with pre-Semitic and other sources in Botterweck and Ringgren (1973) 1:1-19. Although YHWH is called the father of the people of Israel, Ringgren asserts, "In the

him as Father in the intimacy of prayer: in jubilation (Matthew 11:25; Luke 10:21), on the cross (Luke 23:34-46), in the highest prayer when he finds himself facing death (John 12:27-28), in direct prayer with the Father (John 17:1, 5), and as he calls him "holy" or "just" Father (John 17:25, and elsewhere).

The Aramaic word appears two other times in St. Paul's epistles. The context of these passages is our human invocation of the Father (*Abba* is a vocative), and we are able to pronounce the word in virtue of the Spirit in its relationship of true filiation.

> For all who are moved by the Spirit of God are sons of God. The Spirit you have received is not a spirit of slavery leading you back into a life of fear, but a Spirit that makes us sons (πνεῦμα υἱοθε-σίας, *pneuma huiothesias*) enabling us to cry "Abba! Father!" In that cry the Spirit of God joins with our spirit in testifying that we are God's children (τέκνα, *tekna*); and if children then heirs. We are God's heirs and Christ's fellow-heirs, if we share his sufferings now in order to share his splendor hereafter. (Romans 8:14-17)

When Paul invites us to shout out: "*Abba, Patēr!*" he affirms that, inasmuch as we are God's children, we are authorized to pronounce the word, and he immediately adds that both the divine Spirit and our own bear witness that God is our Father—that is, that we are his children. And it is this testimony of our spirit that prods us to speak of the Spirit of Jesus.[13]

The same experience is described in the third text:

> To prove that you are sons, God has sent into our hearts the Spirit of his Son crying "Abba! Father!" You are therefore no longer a slave but a son, and if a son, then also by God's own act an heir. (Galatians 4:6-7)

Here again we discern a "vital circle," a kind of *perichōrēsis*. It is because we are children that God sends his Spirit, and it is because God sends his Spirit that we are his children. It is Christ that Christian theology has seen as the "cause" of our filiation.

The Interpretation

Two fundamental considerations issue from this text: Jesus calls God his Father and invites us to do the same by virtue of the divine Spirit that dwells in us.

Old Testament YHWH is very rarely called Father" (p. 17), and adds that "God as father does not hold any central position in Israel's faith" (p. 19). Concerning the idea of Son in Israel; see also ibid. 1:668-82.

[13] See the bold and perhaps somewhat neglected phrases of 1 Corinthians 2:10-16, which in the present context are worth meditation.

What does this mean?

The first meaning is to be sought within the Hebraic tradition of the period, which echoes at least one branch of the Semitic tradition that stretches back two millennia. "God is Father"—and Father means he who generates, educates, corrects, protects, governs, loves. This meaning of Father undoubtedly belongs to a patriarchal culture that is, perhaps, open to criticism, although it is precisely for this reason that the word bears an "inclusive meaning" as giver of life (father and mother). Purified of its anthropomorphic bonds, the word may be interpreted as meaning source, origin, foundation—just as the subsequent tradition will understand the word "father" when employed in the trinitarian doctrine. It has nothing to with either genus or sex.[14]

But in the second place, and surprisingly, from the very beginning, as his contemporaries noted, Jesus accentuated the fact that God is *his* father, his daddy, in a manner so intimate that the Christian tradition was led to interpret it literally that Jesus of Nazareth had no other father. Even if we can more or less reconcile this assertion with the existence of another purely human father not in competition with the divine Father, this is something of no concern to us at this time and place. We are only seeking to understand Jesus's experience. Without a shadow of a doubt he seems to have had a very intense experience of a divine filiation.

The numerous texts in which Jesus refers to his Father have been so thoroughly certified and accurately studied that we need not return to that problem. Jesus calls God his Father.

Only one observation seems pertinent here. The relationship of Father to Son is so intimate that we slip into either an anthropomorphic idea of God (God is man's Father) or a theomorphic image of man (man is God's Son). The classical theologies embrace the first—God is man's Father (transcendent); contemporary theologies the second—man is God's son (immanent).[15]

Here again, an intercultural consideration of diatopic hermeneutics may help us build a bridge between these two perspectives. If the divine world is the model of reality—including ourselves—we start with God and must then say he is the Father. If the human world is the model, we start with ourselves and must then say that we are the children.

The last two texts are not reported as Jesus's words, although they do refer to Christ's central message, as one of his disciples understood: if Jesus

---

[14] In conformity with a certain Anglo-Saxon mentality, Lee (1993) writes: "It seems strange that Israel, almost intentionally and for a long time, seems to have avoided calling God its 'Father.'" The reason might be sought in the fear of creating confusion with the fertility gods.

[15] As a very beautiful example we may cite González-Faus (1984). In a comment on John's prologue, in opposition to some theologians, he observes that "John sees no other divinity in Jesus than his being man" (p. 331), and cites several times Leonardo Boff's phrase regarding Jesus, "God alone can be human to such an extent."

really calls God his Father, those who have received the Spirit possess the same power of calling God their Father: they too are children. This happens when we discover that Jesus is our brother: those who have the same father are brothers.

It is almost superfluous to remember that "to call" does not signify the simple act of naming in a purely nominalistic sense. Every calling, active or passive, signifies the bestowal of a mission along with its relative power (Romans 9:12; Hebrews 5:4; 1 Corinthians 1:9, etc.). Modern consciousness has weakened the power of the name and of naming.

There is a difference between Christ's filiation and ours, a difference that seems to constitute a fundamental idea that is important to maintain in Christian self-understanding. Until now this difference has been expressed in the assertion that Jesus is God's natural son and we are adoptive sons. Here we touch on a very delicate point that, once again, an intercultural reflection may help us understand. For a certain kind of mentality, which we could consider the product of Roman civilization, law, loaded as it is with all its juridical categories, is little less than ontologically real. For the people of Israel the relationship with the divine, founded on a pact and a promise, leaves God's transcendence intact. Israel is the people of God, and God is the shepherd, the master. The relationship is not one of kinship; were it so, it would be blasphemy. Christians, in conformity with Jesus's words, and in order to accentuate the difference, assert that while we are adoptive sons, Jesus is the natural one.

This theological proposition presents some difficulties, the first with respect to Jesus. The Word, second person, is certainly God's natural son: in the language of the councils, he possesses the self-same divine nature; while Jesus, on the other hand, also possesses a human nature, like us. We might ask ourselves whether Jesus would then be a natural son through his divine nature alone or also be such through his human nature. If Jesus, as man, is not God's natural son, his incarnation, from God's point of view, is not real—it would constitute thomistic monotheism. If Jesus as man is God's natural son, then nothing would prevent us too from being the same. In order to maintain the distinction, God is said to make an exception for Jesus, while excluding us. This agrees with a moral conception of the incarnation: Christ came upon earth solely because man had sinned—a theme widely discussed in medieval theology and the source of profound division within the schools. The reason: at the heart of the discussions and divisions we find two christologies: Christ redeemer (from sin) and Christ restorer (of creation—to the point of divine plenitude). The first has prevailed in Western churches and in popular devotion. On the other hand, many texts seem to give our sonship a value more real than that of being named heirs to certain rights, as we see developed profoundly in Paul, the great theologian of election and predestination (Romans 8:29-30; 11:1ff.).

To begin, we find the "Petrine" phrase that we "participate in the divine nature" (2 Pet 1:4).[16] This is not an example of the much-feared pantheism.[17] We *become* participants in the divine nature by entering in communion with it (θείας κοινωνοὶ φύσεως, *theias koinōnoi physeōs*). It is more than a participation. It is a *koinōnia* ("communion"). God *is* his very divine nature; it is through his power that we reach (γένησθε, *genēsthe*) it. And it is through the work of the Spirit that we "become *transformed* in that same icon (τὴν αὐτὴν εἰκόνα μεταμορφούμεθα, *tēn autēn eikona meta-morphoumetha*, 2 Corinthians 3:18). This metamorphosis bears the meaning of the whole adventure of creation and constitutes the trinitarian *perichōrēsis*. The Gospel also tells us that Christ is the vine and we the branches (John 15:5). In commenting on these words, St. Augustine does not hesitate to say, *unius quippe naturae sunt vitis et palmites* ("The vine and the branches do in fact constitute the same nature"; *Tractatus* 80), and St. Thomas approved his statement. Paul himself is not afraid to cite a Greek poet to tell us that already in the present, "we are of his race"—that is, of his same ethnic origin (τοῦ γὰρ καὶ γένος ἐσμέν, *tou gar kai genos esmen*; Acts 17:28), as the preceding phrase asserts: "In him we live and move and exist" (we are, ἐσμέν)—and not only in the future (1 Corinthians 15:28). St. Luke reports words of Jesus that link our real sonship with the resurrection (Luke 20:36). All these texts speak to us of a real, not just juridical, filiation.

The other two texts that speak of *Abba* underscore the fact that "if we are children, we are also heirs." We do not wish to discuss now whether τέκνον (*teknon*, "child," but grammatically "neutral" in Greek) and υἱός (*huios*, "son") mean the same thing or whether υἱοθεσία (*huiothesia*, "adoption") in Romans 8:15 means adoption as legal fiction or might have a less legalistic meaning. In any case, the texts tell us that we too can participate in Christ's sonship in relation to the Father. We are not told that we are heirs and thus possess the same rights as the children, but that we are really made children, and consequently also heirs. Sonship comes first. The texts, moreover, show that Christ is "the body's head," the reason for which we too participate in the divine nature.[18]

For a different type of mentality the juridical fiction is not real, and thus an artificial, untrue sonship does not satisfy. Here we encounter once

---

[16] It is significant to note the embarrassment exegetes feel with respect to this passage, even though the epistle is not St. Peter's. See Leaney (1967) 107, who believes in a stoic influence; Hauck, in Kittel (1964 ff.) 5:80, cites it without comment, unlike his treatment of the Pauline texts, although, of course, there are theological monographs on "divinization."

[17] Let us note that today we are rediscovering the doctrine of deification, even in St. Thomas. See Williams (1997), who ends with the following phrase: "The *Summa* does not contain an explicit question on deification because the argument of the last part of the work is (precisely) deification."

[18] Gregory of Nyssa defines Christianity explicitly as τῆς θείας φύσεως μίμησις, *imitatio divinae naturae* ("imitator of the divine nature," in *De professione Christiana* [PG 46:2144]).

again the influence of the monotheistic ideology, which, so as not to weaken God's absoluteness, can see the incarnation only as a miracle that an omnipotent God performs, while making an exception for his own Son.[19] For a trinitarian conception, on the other hand, the Son "equal" to the Father is he through whom "everything has been made" (πάντα δι' αὐτοῦ ἐγένετο, *panta di' autou egeneto*; John 1:3), so that the Only Begotten is also the First Begotten (Colossians 1:18; Revelation 1:5). Our filiation is a real participation in the divine nature that is realized to the extent to which we *become* what, with Christ, we are called to be (Colossians 3:1). Our divinization is as little docetic as the humanization of the Logos.

This is what tradition asserts when it says that through grace we become Christ, while Jesus is what he is by birth—something that also takes place through the work of the Spirit (Luke 1:35). It might seem right to pause a little longer on this point inasmuch as we are meditating on our right—and duty—to exclaim (we too) "*Abba, Patēr!*"

Let us recall once again the patristic saying, "If God becomes man, it is so that man too may become a true God." Here we may apply, in an inverse sense, the patristic fathers' argument against Arius: if Jesus Christ were exclusively man (as Arius maintained), he would be unable to divinize us. Were we to remain "human" alone, not even Christ's divinity would be necessary. A transcendent God has no need of a "God-man" in order to forgive or redeem us. In short, our filiation is real—and not only because it grants us the right to be "heirs."

What then is filiation?

Jesus is the natural son of God in a metaphorical sense. God has no wife, as Muhammad seems to have said ironically. Moreover, what we find here is no more than an analogy—and a very weak one—between human and divine nature, as a frequently cited conciliar text notes (Denzinger, 806). The *primum analogatum* would signify that which generates life and is the source in which we participate: *Natura naturans et naturata*. The Son is he who receives from the *fontanalis plenitudo* ("Fountain of fullness," in Bonaventure's words) precisely that "nature" which makes him son.[20] In

---

[19] See one of the many phrases of that giant whom I have called—ironically, and because of his monotheistic rigor—the greatest *Muslim* theologian, Thomas Aquinas: *Unio [Incarnationis] relatio quaedam temporalis est, quae quidem realiter est in ipsa natura assumpta, sed in Persona assumente secundum rationem tantum, sicut et de aliis relationibus ex tempore de Deo dictis, ut Dominus et huiusmodi dictum est* ("The union [of the incarnatio]) is a certain temporal relation which is real in the very nature assumed [in Jesus] while in the Person who assumes [in the Son] is only a logical relation—that is, not real but only in the created mind; as all the other temporal relations that are attributed to God, as when he is called Lord, and so forth"; *In IV Sententias* I, d. 3; III d. 2, q. 2, a. 2, sol. 3, ad 2). For him the whole of creation is a *relatio quaedam* (*Summa theologiae* I, q. 45, a. 3). Later we shall quote this rigorous monotheistic thought again: Śaṅkara would agree.

[20] According to Aquinas, *In Filio est esse Paternitatis quia in divinis non est nisi unum esse* ("The being of Paternity is in the Son because in the divinity there is but one being alone"). Thus Thomas can say: *Tantus est Pater, quanta [est] tota Trinitas; Summa theologiae,*

order to explain this nature, a whole metaphysics is necessary; we cannot even skim the theme here.[21]

Adoptive son is another metaphor. If the first metaphor is "natural," that is, taken from the "nature" of things, the second is cultural, insofar as it belongs to the juridical order. Filiation is a human *invariant*—all men and women are children. Adoptive filiation is only a cultural *universal* restricted to a certain group of human traditions and thus does not exist at the same level as the first metaphor.

Here a reflection on the "First Begotten" (πρωτότοκος, *prōtotokos*, Romans 8:29; Colossians 1:15, etc.) would be appropriate, above all if Christian language wishes to make itself intelligible to other cultures in terms of so-called interculturation. "He is the first-born" (*pūrvo hi jātaḥ*) says an Upanishad (*Śvetāśvatara-upaniṣad* II, 16). The adoptive son is not a true son. The adoption is a juridical fiction and implies a whole system of human law. The metaphor is not anthropomorphic like the first, but cultural, and makes sense only within a very specific culture—mostly for the regulation of the rights of honor and inheritance for foreigners. We are in a regime of slavery, of the "free and freedmen" (Romans 8:15). We are not God's slaves but the master's children. The slaves and the free possess the same human nature, but it is those who have been "liberated" that inherit the kingdom. This liberation is not our merit but the work of the gratuitous goodness of the Father who has chosen us. All is coherent within a cultural matrix in which the first Christian ferment has inserted itself.[22] This culture is not, however, universal.

To make God a jurist is legitimate, although such an assumption must be taken with a grain of salt. The metaphor would tell us that we are not really God's children but become such only accidentally, by an accidental grace—in order to avoid the pantheism in which we would fall unless we suppress the monotheistic vision.[23]

What we have just said is consistent with a Western juridical conception of grace and is in harmony with the dualism Creator/creature. If, in a strict monotheism, Being is God, then our "participation" in being suffers an ontological degradation. "Taken in itself, the creature is nothing," we read in St. Thomas,[24] who knows St. Augustine's trinitarian cry: *Deus*

I, q. 30, a. 1, ad 4. See also q. 42, where the equality of the divine persons is explained.

[21] See Panikkar (1972a), the first part (written in 1941) of a trilogy (nature, human nature, and the supernatural) that remains *in pectore et in corde*.

[22] The word υἰοθεσία (*huiothesia*) appears only in the Pauline epistles (Romans 8:15, 23; 9:4; Ephesians 1:5; Galatians 4:5) and signifies the gratuitousness of God's act, an act that is certainly real insofar as it bestows a real, not accidental, filiation.

[23] In this juridical conception it is not repugnant to believe that "pagans" are not saved—as a good part of Christianity believed for centuries. See the Athanasian Creed.

[24] *Esse autem non habet creatura nisi ab alio, sibi autem, relicta, in se considerata nihil est; unde prius naturaliter inest sibi nihil quam esse* ("The creature has no being except from another; therefore, by its nature nothingness is more intimate than being," in Panikkar [1972a] 110ff.). Let us also note that creation is nothing but a relation with the Creator,

supra quem nihil, extra quem nihil, sine quo nihil est ("God, above whom there is nothing, outside of whom nothing, without whom nothing exists"; *Soliloquia* I, 4). There is surely no doubt that there is no *ad extra* ("outside") in God, as the trinitarian experience takes into account. And in the mentality pregnant with the Roman genius, juridical adoption constitutes a convincing hypothesis.

Within a monotheistic context we cannot be God's real children. It is important to avoid pantheism while at the same time we do not undervalue our filiation without reducing it to a natural necessity. After all, the subtitle of this book is *The Fullness of Man* not "human fullness"—we are more than "human." Conscious of this reality, theology introduced the concept of the supernatural, an idea that carried with it certain difficulties.[25] The whole philosophical infrastructure must be thought out anew in a trinitarian direction. It is Christ who makes it impossible to sustain both dualism and the abyss man-God.

St. John does not speak of "creation" (Genesis 1) but says, literally, that we were "made," that the Logos generated us (πάντα δι᾽ αὐτοῦ εγένετο, *panta di' autou egeneto*, John 1:3).[26] Unquestionably, our filiation is real. St. Paul employs the metaphor of the body, of which Jesus Christ is the head and we the members, while all participate in the self-same Life. Therein precisely lies the mystery of Jesus Christ, fully human and fully divine, without any confusion yet also without any dichotomy. Christ is thus fully divine even in his corporeal humanity—and we likewise, although we are what we are only *becoming*, or "as in a mirror, in veiled form" (ἐν αἰνίγματι, *en ainigmati*) "in a confused manner" (1 Corinthians 13:12). Although pilgrims, we feel that we are also one with the Father. It is written that we have been given the Spirit (Romans 8:9), which makes us know that we dwell in the Son (John 14:23; 1 John 3:24).[27]

---

because *creatio non est mutatio nisi secundum intelligendi tantum* ("Creation is not the same as change except for way of conceiving," according to the *Summa theologiae* I, q. 45, a. 2, ad 2). We have already quoted Thomas saying, *creatio in creatura non sit (est) nisi relatio quaedam ad creatorem.*

[25] De Lubac (1965).

[26] See some texts in the *Summa theologiae*: *Pater enim, intelligendo se et Filium et Spiritum Sanctum, et omnia alia quae eius scientia continentur, concipit Verbum: ut sic tota Trinitas Verbo dicatur, et etiam omnis creatura* ("The Father, then, understanding himself, the Son, the Holy Spirit, and all the other things which his knowledge contains, understands the Word: thus the whole Trinity is expressed in the Word as well as in every creature"; I, q. 3, a. 1, ad 34). The same thought is repeated with respect to the Son: *R.d.q. in Verbo importatur respectus ad creaturam Deus enim, cognoscendo se, cognoscit omnem creaturam . . . unicum Verbum eius expressivum non solum Patris, set etiam creaturarum* ("I reply by saying that the Word sustains a (direct) relation with creatures because, in knowing himself, God knows every (other) creature . . . his unique Word is the expression not only of the Father but also of all creatures"; I, q. 34, a. 3).

[27] See St. Teresa who comments on this thought in *Moradas* VII, 1 (Teresa de Jesús 1967, 439).

The Johannine formulation expresses the christophanic consecration: "We are called to be and really are God's children . . . we are now God's children, although what we shall be has not been manifested (ἐφανερώθη, *ephanerōthē*) yet. We know that when he will be manifested we shall be like (ὅμοιοι) him" (1 John 3:1-2). The christophanic experience is one and the same as our epiphany (Colossians 3:4). Even Paul states: "When the christophany (Χριστὸς φανερώθη, *Christos phanerōthē*), which is your very life, arrives, then too your epiphany will appear (φανερωθήσεσθε, *phanerōthēsesthe*) with him in glory" (Colossians 3:4).

Vatican Council II itself states that "as children in the Son, we can exclaim in the Spirit: *Abba*, Father!" (*Gaudium et spes* 22). Not even the Latin liturgy seems to be satisfied with a simple adoption; the Collect for the feast of the Transfiguration (August 6), echoing Eastern theology, speaks of our "perfect" (that is, complete) "adoption." In short, if Christ calls God his Father, we too can live this experience through the gift of the Spirit (Romans 8:9). If we both (Christ and us) call God our Father, we can seek to understand what Jesus might have said.

The Experience

I now submit—boldly but reverently—a description that I shall place on Jesus's lips:

> You, divine mystery, whom my people call Father, You are truly the direct origin, he who generates what I am, you are the source from whom I descend. I feel that (your) Life passes through me, that my life does not come from myself but from a fount that not only gives me life in general but also the words, the ideas, the inspiration, and everything that I am. Everything that I say is always something I have "heard."

If Jesus had been born in an *apauruṣeya*[28] tradition, he could also have asserted that his very language is nothing other than the manifestation of the primordial word—the Logos, *vāc* (*Tāṇḍya-mahā-brāhmaṇa* XX:14, 2; *Taittirīya-brāhmaṇa* II, 8, 8, 4; *Śvetāśara-brāhmaṇa* I, 4, 4, 1, etc.). The moment, however, that this word belongs to a monotheistic people, it explicates its experience by saying that, only through things and events, it discovers and reflects the Father's voice and will. It is because Peter intuited this that Jesus blessed him when he said "Thou art," although he felt the necessity of adding some attributes proper to his people's culture, such as "Son of the living God," "the Anointed One," and others still. Because

---

[28] The Vedas are called *apauṛṣeya* (without author) because the mantras themselves do not need any additional reference to tell us what the words mean; otherwise, there would be an endless process.

Peter was too imbued with with judaic culture, Jesus asked him not to make this public.

In the language of the following centuries we could say that Jesus experienced the *continuous creation*, or better, the *constant generation* (by the Father). He felt himself constantly generated, created, sustained, made alive, inspired by that invisible mystery which many people call God and portray in the most diverse ways. This is the *continuous incarnation*, as we will explain later.

"Today you have been generated," "You are my beloved son," as he heard on the banks of the Jordan and on Mount Tabor—and *Son* remains his truest name. The filiation that constitutes it is, in a certain sense, the destiny of every being—whether she knows it or not—and occurs naturally in various degrees. We may sum up its message by saying that we are all children and that all things exist insofar as they participate in that filiation. He feels himself at one and the same time Son and brother. What he teaches is that God is "*Our* Father," not his alone. We are all brothers and sisters inasmuch as we are all children.

What we notice here is a relationship that is indeed intimate and constitutive and yet also hierarchical. God is the Father; Christ is the Son; God is the Source, he is the river of living water that springs from the Father. Without the Father, nothing. He has learned obedience through experience, as Paul (or whoever wrote Hebrews 8:7-9) intuited so well. There is a difference between them, "The Father alone is good" (Luke 18:19), the Son "listens," obeys (*ob-audire*), even when he ignores his "goals" (Matthew 24:36). Jesus is fully conscious of his vocation: to give the world the [Father's] Word (John 17:14) in order to return to the Father. At the end of his short life we could exclaim, "It is consummated" (John 19:30), as he yielded up his spirit into his Father's hands (Luke 23:46).

Does all this make any sense to us? Certainly. If, in one way or another, we cannot relive what these words entail, our discourse about Jesus would constitute a futile exercise in idle speculation. We also—and not we alone—find his words pregnant with "infinite life,"[29] and so we are allowed an analogous experience. Influenced perhaps by his own polemical expressions in reaction to the Hebrews ("you are God" in John 10:34, a text that cites Psalm 82:6), the Christian tradition has often said: "You are Christ"—*alter christus*—or, as I would boldly say, following Paul's teaching, *ipse christus*—"Christ himself." We have already cited his phrase, which is all but impossible to translate: "Let your bearing toward one another rise out of your life in Christ Jesus" (Philippians 2:5). The Greek reads, τοῦτο φρονεῖτε (*touto phroneite*, which is translated *hoc sentite* in the Latin Vulgate). The object of the verb *phroneite* is translated "mind" in

---

[29] It is only in Fridolin Stier that I have found a beautiful translation of "life eternal" (ζωὴ αἰώνιος, *zōē ainōnios*) as *unendliches Leben*, "infinite life." See John 12:50; 17:3; Romans 6:23.

the Authorized Version and the Revised Version, "attitude" in the New American, and "bearings" in the New English Bible. The implication is that one is to participate in the same spiritual experience, the same profound intuition that Jesus Christ had. This experience we are invited to live. For me all of this makes sense, and therefore I feel encouraged to relive and formulate my own experience in his language, the language of the Son:

> *Abba, Patēr!* I do not originate my very being, I am a pure gift. I have received everything that I am, including what I define as "mine." Everything is grace. I experience my contingency because it is not within myself that I find the ground of my being, the "reason" for my existence. Yet this does not signify alienation; it does not mean, that is, that this "reason" resides elsewhere, that it is external to me. Although I am not the ground, neither does that ground exist outside of me. Rather, it exists in the *interior intimo meo* ("in the innermost depths of my being") to cite, once again, the *Confessions* of the great African bishop Augustine (III, 6, 1).

In other words, the *Grund* is not an "other," a non-I, but a "thou," an immanent transcendence in me—which I discover as the *I* (and therefore as my I).

> Not only do I discover my contingency in and through my experience, but I also experience that everything comes from You, mysterious source that many have substantialized as "supreme Being." To call thee "Father" unquestionably signifies a filial relation. It signifies the experience of being generated, of gushing, so to speak, from a source and sharing its nature. It is in that river and in no other water that the source's water flows; nor does this mean that there must be a substance that exists beyond the Father's being. The term itself, "father," is a function, not a substance: the father procreates. My father is not a being who, among many other activities, also generates me. He engages in no other activity than this: generating. You are *my* Father insofar as you generate me. Thou art nothing other than being Father.

I am speaking of this experience of being procreated, generated, produced, given birth, not of the experience of perceiving an "other." I am neither substantializing nor projecting into the past something that, as an experience, can be directed to nothing other than the present. Nor am I "personifying." It is rather a question of experiencing the *this* as the *fons et origo totius divinitatis*, to cite the Councils of Toledo (Denzinger 490; 525; 568); as the *theotēs*, to echo again saint Paul's *hapax legomenon* (Colossians 2:9), or as the "silence" (*sigē*) whence the word springs forth, as St. Irenaeus says. "And we too are conscious of our I both created and uncreated," a traditional theologian asserts.[30] Undoubtedly, at a different time and in a different culture Jesus's experience would rather have evoked the name of Mother, and the metaphor would probably have been more powerful and certainly more immediate.

> I also feel that is not my exclusive privilege. Every being has thee as Father. Every being is generated by thee, font of everything, although it is only conscious beings who can call thee "Father."

We exist because "we are from" (*ex-sistere*), we proceed from this infinite source which is not limited by any name or, in the words of Eckhart, is *sunder Namen* ("without name"), *über all Namen* ("above all names"), *innominabilis* ("unnamable"), and *omninominalibus* ("namable by all [names]")—appellations or non-appellations that are found in a millenarian, apophatic tradition. *Neti, neti* (*Bṛhadāraṇyaka-upaniṣad*, III, 9, 26).

Because words have been eroded and religious power abused, neither Father nor Mother, neither God nor even the Void or Mystery resonates any longer in the minds and hearts of many contemporaries. Why this erosion? Why this abuse? Because, perhaps, the mind as well as the heart has become "mechanized," as Lao Tze had foreseen a long time ago.

Now that I have established that the verbal formulation is relative, let me dedicate a paragraph to show that Jesus's language in uttering *Abba, Patēr!* is appropriate. First of all, the word is a vocative, and the three passages in which it appears present us with extreme situations: a cry, a shout, a prayer, accompanied even by a splattering of blood. It is a spontaneous manifestation of joy, of suffering or hope. It is neither the literary style in the third person nor a tale about others. It is personification alone that satisfies human nature, when, in extreme situations, that same nature experiences the unfathomable life of the creature. We experience a need to personify. An *iṣṭadevatā* is the most human way of carrying us close to this experience. We need to find the divine icon with which we can communicate. Moreover, "Father" does not stand only for source, power, and person. It also signifies protection, especially love—and therefore Mother. In the innermost recesses of our human consciousness we discover within ourselves not only the fact that we love but also that we are capable of loving, precisely insofar as we are loved. Every being has the need of both loving and being loved. Human love is a response. Love has been granted to us. Thinking—characteristic of the human being—is nothing other, as we have said, than to weigh (*soppesare*), the love that every thing has in order to reach its place in the harmonic texture of reality. Thinking is a qualitative more than a quantitative act. The moderator is the person who recognizes the tendency, the *nisus*, by which everything moves toward its place and knows how to direct events and things, without violence, to their ends—an action that cannot be brought to fruition without love. Although we do not

---

[30] Boulgakov (1982) 193.

always identify the source with love, we do perceive love as our tending toward a source, while at the same time we also feel that the love with which we are loved has been, in turn, received.

The source of everything is also the origin of love. Although often on a minor scale, we become conscious of the *perichōrēsis* we have cited so often. At times we do not respond to the same person with the same love with which we are loved but pass it on, so to speak, to a third person. For example, although we might not have reciprocated the love of our parents adequately, we try to bestow that love upon our own children. The "dance" continues. A current of love circulates throughout the three worlds. Love, to be sure, is no mere feeling; it is, rather, the dynamism itself of the real, the force that moves the universe—as so many sacred scriptures and poets say.

In the third place, in a very strict sense, the Father unites power and love, two ultimate "elements" of the universe. The Father is superior to the Son; he is the protector. As we have already said, the symbol father also stands for mother, for the woman who gives life, existence, nourishment, and love, and signifies also sacrifice, sharing, participation in the same adventure, and therefore equality. The son is equal to the father. *Abba, Patēr* means both superiority and equality. In brief, we are capable of reliving the *Abba, Patēr!* We are not orphans: the earth is our Mother, the sky our Father, as so many primordial and ancient traditions assert.

There are at least two ways of experiencing the *Abba, Patēr*—the experience of grace and, in a deeply paradoxical sense, the experience of contingency.

> If I am fully conscious that everything I have and am I have received from the Father, from the Font, I also feel, at one and the same time, that everything is grace, that everything has been given to me, that the initiative itself is a grace that the "Father of lights" (James 1:17) grants. If I am, at the same time, the fruit of grace, if the Origin of my acting and being is not my I, what I discover in myself is my radical contingency. It is not I who sustains myself, who possesses the reason for my own being, for I am contingent. "I can do everything in him who makes me strong" (ἐν τῷ ἐνδυναμοῦντί με, *en tō endynamounti me*)—the one who gives me dynamism, power (Philippinas 4:13). In this experience of my weakness I discover that the ground of my being is much more solid, much stronger than it would be if it were rooted in myself. I cannot sustain myself by myself alone; it is that which supports me that sustains me: *Abba, Patēr!*

I can now read the story of the man of Galilee with a key that unlocks the superb way in which he realized this experience, the extent to which he perceived at one and the same time the closeness and the distance between Father and Son.

If mysticism tells us about the experience of ultimate reality, the experience of Jesus the Christ constitutes the experience of this equality and difference with Him who gives life, with the Source of the universe. *Abba, Patēr!* Every person is a son, a daughter. In this way we can also understand what he said about children and the kingdom of God. Those who have the experience of a father or mother are not, strictly speaking, parents. And when many theologies comment on this passage, they betray—as I myself have done until now—the experience of an adult. It is the child who, in both joy and sorrow, utters "Father"—and here a capital letter is appropriate. It is not a question of feeling dependence or love; it is rather a question of a primordial feeling of belonging. For this reason, today we can say, even better, "Mother"—something that was not possible, perhaps, for the historical Jesus. In order that we live this experience, it is not necessary that we be either saints or Pharisees, cultured or religious; it is sufficient that we have all been children. Not everyone is a father or a mother, although everyone has been a son or a daughter.

And here we arrive at a point in which I detach my experience from the old and venerable expression *Abba, Patēr* and articulate the way many men and women, including children, feel today. Just as children, in the process of growing up, become aware that their parents are not omnipotent, so in the same way the *Abba, Patēr* also matures in a relation in which we no longer depend on an omnipotent father. Scripture calls us συνεργοί (*synergoi, cooperatores* in Latin) (1 Corinthians 3:9), and yet it is with hesitation that I say,

> I can pray and believe in *Abba, Patēr* but I must do so with the same suffering and pain with which, we have been told, thou prayed at Gethsemane.

The word "father" has lost much of its symbolism today. Patriarchalism is bad, but the destruction of the family without offering any substitute is still worse. And we are increasingly aware of the difficulties implicit in a pious speech about a loving and powerful Father who permits the immense tragedies that have occurred in all ages and those even worse tragedies of our technocratic age—worse because they are not grounded in any religious justification. When religious power clearly abused the people's human religious sentiments, social injustices and human tortures were presented and seen as bearing a religious sanction.[31] However perverse this was, victims were able to bear them with less despair than today when secondary causes have become independent of God as the "first cause." Recall our discussion of the *dalit* earlier in the book.

---

[31] Slavery and torture, for example, sought "justification" in the Bible (see Denzinger, 1483). The pariahs belonged to the *karma* and *dharma;* human sacrifices were considered necessary for the life of the world, and so forth.

What a relief when I discover that the old formula *Credo in Deum Patrem omnipotentem* does not correspond to your experience! It is precisely the opposite which you experienced at Gethsemane, and in an excruciating way, on the cross (Matthew 27:46; Mark 15:34). You have experienced the divine fatherhood but not his omnipotence.[32] You have submitted yourself to his will, but not his whims.

How could God's omnipotence allow all this? Every effort to answer by saying that God's designs are inscrutable seems similar to the answer that "God reveals the Trinity precisely to humiliate our intelligence." I cannot believe in all these specious theological explanations (*theologoumena*). *Abba, Patēr!*, on the other hand, is a prayer that can spring only out of a lacerated heart. Yet it cannot be dehumanizing. And there is more.

Perhaps other cultures have shaped my experience. I can readily understand our need for personification but not the anthropomorphism of the individualistic interpretation of the divine figure of the Father. *Abba, Patēr* does not represent to me belief in an Other (as substantialized Being), nor, much less, in a Me. Neither does it signify dualism (God above and we below), nor monism (as a God that absorbs everything). It is here that the expression "My Father" acquires its full meaning. The Father belongs to the "I am" and makes it possible that I too exist. In the light of all this, I go beyond the innocent belief that my Father is almighty—and beyond the other scholarly *aporias* around this belief.

I do not think we will go astray if we see a connection between this experience of filiation and Jesus's third and last temptation, as well as our own—the dizziness one experiences at great heights (Matthew 4:8). From the heights of political, economic, intellectual, and above all spiritual power, we seek the "kingdoms of the earth" and "their glory" (δόξα, *doxa*) and we think that everything can be ours—so that, of course, we dream to make the best use of it. Jesus did not choose "the lesser of evils" by kneeling, in order to become the new "prince of this world"—and bringing it to the Father.

---

[32] The word *omnipotens*, translated "almighty" in English, is used in some of the first creedal confessions to translate the Greek *pantokratōr*. But its real referent was the Lord, the *dominus omnia potens*, which means to say, he who has dominon over everything like a king and in a theocratic sense, not as a absolute being. The *Letter of the Apostles* (from about the year 160), says in the first paragraph, *in patrem dominatorem universi* (Denzinger 1). We also find *Credo in unum Patrem omnium dominatorem* (Denzinger 11, 41-42, 44, 46, 50-51, 60, 64, 71, and elsewhere). The *Vetus Latina*, however, has *omnia potens*. It was St. Jerome who consecrated *omnipotens* in the Vulgate. Trebolle (1995, 147) observes that *pantokratōr* was purely a translation of the divine title of *Yahweh tseva'ot* ("God of the Armies") and was also translated as *kyrios tōn dynameōn* ("Lord of the Powers"). Michaelis explains in Kittel (1964, 3:915) that *pantokratōr* refers to the "supremacy" of God, not to the "power to do all things."

We wish to change the world from a position of power; we wish to dominate politics and economics in order to institute "the kingdom of God"—that kingdom which does not arrive "in ways that can be observed" (Luke 17:20). This is the great temptation of Christendom. Yet neither Francis of Assisi nor John XXIII made use of his power. The *Abba, Patēr* is no pietistic effusion. Man's divinization is not the apotheosis (ἀπο-θέοσις, *apotheosis*) of the individual. Once again the vision is not monotheistic.

However modified by the following text—which underscores the equality of Jesus and his having the same nature as the Father—this first experience is as ineradicable and definitive as the second. As some mystics maintain, even when human consciousness can attain its highest stage and that selfsame consciousness breaks on human shores, it shows an infinite difference from the source. (It is we humans who speak of "infinite knowledge.") This is precisely what the experience of the Trinity is. We know that we are inserted within a cosmotheandric *perichōrēsis*.[33] God is mystery and we too exist within this mystery.

The Father and I Are One

The Texts

Just as the first exclamation was not unique but the expression of a conviction manifested many times in different forms, so this second assertion—of the equality of Jesus with the Father—pervades Jesus's entire message. Yet one must caution that this assertion must be understood in tandem with the many details which the writers of the Gospels or Jesus himself have been able to introduce.

Here we must accentuate the importance that a certain tradition, as well as modern exegesis, attributes to the distinction between the Synoptics and St. John's Gospel.[34] We are interested not in the literal statements of Jesus—the so-called problem of the *ipsissima verba*—but in the complex figure of Christ, as not only the first generations but also Christians of all ages—that is the church—have understood it.[35]

We insist on this point. Either Christians, victims of a collective hallucination, have projected onto the figure of Jesus Christ desires, anxieties, and expectations, transforming them into what they wanted him to be, or

---

[33] We are able to apply the well-known difference between creator and creature (Denzinger, 806) also to the Trinity. Nothing is finite in the Trinity. Father, Son, and Holy Spirit are infinitely diverse.

[34] Massa once again underscores this (1995) 2.

[35] Dupuis (1994) 52 writes that if we are not certain of the *ipsissima verba* ("the very words [of Jesus] themselves"), the *ipsissima intentio* ("the very intention itself") may be confirmed with certainty.

the man truly is what they believe.[36] Even in the first case, the fundamental question remains.

The Buddhist tradition has made the Buddha a *bodhisattva*. The Vishnu tradition has transformed Krishna into a God. The Chinese have transformed Lao Tze into a wise man. All these traditions have advanced such interpretations because there is something in the human being that urges it to do so. A two-dimensional vision fails to satisfy man. Like Śaṅkara and so many others, St. Augustine speaks to us of a restlessness in the human heart. If the divine is not in fact man's ultimate ideal, there is no reason for God to exist for man, for he would then become either useless or diabolical. What we wish to say is clear: unless, in our case, Christ is God's revelation, he is Man's. But let us return to the texts.

Either the phrases we are commenting on make sense to us today, or they are simply words uttered by "an elephant that flies in the skies." Perhaps we could accept a God who spoke incomprehensible phrases, but Christ would then be no more than a divine *avatāra* and not a real man. No man can utter the words as he did if they are completely outside the human range and thus beyond our comprehension.

We choose three out of many possible texts. The first is John 10:30.

Ἐγὼ καὶ ὁ πατὴρ ἕν ἐσμεν (*egō kai ho patēr hen esmen*).

Ego et Pater unum sumus (in the Latin Vulgate).

I and the Father are one.[37]

The immediate context of this *mahāvākya* is illuminating. It reveals a disputation reproduced and reelaborated, I should say, at a later time, but in any case intense. After he uttered this statement, the Jews wanted to stone Jesus, stone him to death: it was a matter of life or death.

We shall not describe the context of the entire passage but will offer only one comment: throughout the entire dispute Jesus does not attenuate his statement. Neither does he minimize his answer; on the contrary, he is exacerbating it as he dares to propose a "blasphemous" exegesis of a Hebrew psalm, "You are Gods" (82:6).[38] All this is summarized at the end

---

[36] It is sufficient to mention Arthur Drews's book *The Christ Myth* (1909; repr., New York: Prometheus Books, 1998), with all the *religionswissenschaftliche* discussions that are still pertinent today.

[37] Let us compare these three with other translations: "I and my Father are one" (Authorized Version); "I and the Father are one" (Revised Standard Version); and "My father and I are one" (New English Bible); *Le Père et moi, nous sommes un* (Bible de Jérusalem); *Ich und der Vater sind eins* (Neuer Jerusalemer Bibel and Rösch); *Jo i el Pare som una sola cosa* (Montserrat); *Jo i el Pare som u* (Mateos/Rius Camps); *Yo y el Padre somos una sola cosa* (Nárcar/Colunga).

[38] See Botterweck and Ringgren (1973) in very many articles (for example, 1:681), and Strack and Billerbeck (1922ff., 2:542ff., and 3:223ff.) for the Hebrew Bible context.

of the disputation when Jesus asserts that his deeds were to manifest the veracity of his words. We are asked to accept the testimony of a life and acknowledge, citing John 10:38, that:

Ἐν ἐμοὶ ὁ πατὴρ κἀγὼ ἐν τῷ πατρί (*En emoi ho patēr kagō en tǭ patri*).

in me est Pater, et ego in Patre (New Vulgate).

Pater in me est, et ego in Patre (the classic Vulgate).

The Father is in me and I in the Father.

In another analogous passage (John 17:21-23) this unity is extended to all who will believe in him: "Because we are all one. As you, Father, are in me, and I in you, may they too be one with us . . . I in them and you in me that they may be perfected in unity." This passage introduces us to our second text, John 14:9:

Ὁ ἑωρακὼς ἐμὲ ἑώρακεν τὸν πατέρα (*Ho heōrakōs eme heōraken ton patera*).

Qui videt me, videt [et] Patrem (Vulgate).[39]

He who has seen me, has seen the Father.[40]

If the first context explodes with danger and dialectical sparks, the second is suffused with grief and sadness, inasmuch as it constitutes part of Jesus's last words, his farewell speech. After hearing Jesus speak so much about the Father, Philip boldly asks Jesus to show him the Father. The answer reveals a certain sadness: "Philip, I have spent so much time with you, and you still don't know me?"

Jesus does not say, "I have already been with you a long time speaking about the Father, and you still do not know *him*." He does not say *him*. Instead, he says *me*. "He who has seen me has seen the Father" (John 14:9). (Thus, "You, then, have not seen me.")

John reports the same idea in a less intimate, more public context during Jesus's last entry into Jerusalem: "Jesus then shouted in a loud voice,

---

[39] Some Greek texts have the word καὶ (*kai*), which also appears in the Vulgate. And in the New Vulgate we read, *Qui vidit me, vidit Patrem*.

[40] There are other translations: "Whoever has seen me, has seen the Father" (New Revised Standard Version and the New American Bible); "He who sees me sees also the Father" (Confraternity/Challoner Rheims Version); *Qui m'a vu a vu le Père* (Bible de Jérusalem); *Wer mich gesehen hat, hat den Vater gesehen* (Neuer Jerusalemer Bibel); *Qui m'ha vist a mi, ha vist el Pare* (Montserrat); *Qui em veu a mi present està veient el Pare* (Mateos/Rius Camps); *El que me ha visto a mi ha visto al Padre* (Martín Nieto).

'He who believes in me does not believe in me but in him who has sent me. The one who sees me sees him who has sent me" (John 12:44-45).

What we would like to underscore is the fact that these statements made sense for Jesus and for those who placed them on Jesus's lips from the beginning—and for innumerable generations since. They do not seem to find the assertion incredible. Perhaps he is saying that he is an elephant (and so, too, are we). Yet this is not as inadmissible as if he were to say that the elephant flies in the sky. What these texts do is to make us revise—and revise radically—our notion of God as separate, inaccessible, and Other.

From another perspective, let us also add John 6:57:

Καθὼς ἀπέστειλέν με ὁ ζῶν πατὴρ κἀγὼ ζῶ διὰ τὸν πατέρα καὶ ὁ τρώγων με κἀκεῖνος ζήσει δι᾽ ἐμέ (*Kathōs apesteilen me ho zōn patēr kagō zō dia ton patera kai ho trōgōn me kakeinos zēsei di᾽ eme*)

Sicut misit me vivens Pater, et ego vivo propter Patrem, [:] et qui manducat me, et ipse vivet propter me (Vulgate and New Vulgate)

As the Father, who is life, has sent me and I live for the Father, so he who eats of me lives for me.[41]

Whether the context concerns the eucharist is disputed. The unity between Jesus and his Father is extended to all who will join in eucharistic union with him. Let us set aside one of the famous ἐγὼ εἰμί (*egō eimi, ego sum*) statements of the Johannine Jesus, John 8:58, which echoes Yahweh's traditional self-description, "I am who am" (Exodus 3:14). We find another polemical "I am" at the climax of Jesus's trial (Luke 22:70). We might also note that the phrases in which Jesus uses "I" have all been carefully analyzed. We also set aside another elusive statement that Jesus uttered when he was openly asked who he was (John 8:25), a text that is difficult to translate. However important the various *egō eimi* statements are, we prefer to forgo any interpretation so as not to lose our guiding thread of thought.[42]

---

[41] "As the living Father sent me, and I live because of the Father, so he who eats me shall live because of me" (New English Bible); "As the living Father hath sent me, and I live by the Father: so he that eateth me, even he shall live by me" (Authorized Version); *De même qu'envoyé par le Père, qui est vivant, moi, je vis par le Père, de même celui qui me mange vivra, lui aussi, par moi* (Bible de Jérusalem); *Wie mich der lebendige Vater gesandt hat und wie ich durch den Vater lebe, so wird jeder, der mich isst, durch mich leben* (Neuer Jerusalemer Bibel); *Així com jo, enviat pel Pare que viu, visc pel Pare, així qui em menja a mi viurà a causa de mi* (Montserrat); *A mi m'ha enviat el Pare, que viu, i jo visc gràcies al Pare; així, també qui em menja a mi viurà gràcies a mi* (Mateos/Rius Camps).

[42] See Stauffer in Kittel (1964), and in general Lamarche (1965) and Liébaert (1965), along with the other parts of vol. 3, all of which are correlated with a rich bibliography.

The Interpretation

Although a more animistic and less individualistic interpretation of these texts could be very helpful, I will merely try to reproduce for the general reader the experience that these words presuppose.

What stands out clearly in these words is the traditional *perichōrēsis*, which is not limited here to the intratrinitarian sphere but extends to the whole of creation. The text seems to say that there exists a current, a Life, that flows from the Father to Christ and all who communicate with him. According to Thomas Aquinas, *Quaecumque sunt a Deo ordinem habent ad invicem et ad ipsum Deum* ("Whatever things come from God are related both among themselves and to God"; *Summa theologiae* I, q. 47, a. 3). This has always been a common belief. According to the most ancient Christian tradition, if Christ is one person of the Trinity, then his material body is also intermeshed in the trinitarian life—just as, in him, we are also enmeshed in the trinity. A modern author echoes this idea in poetic fashion: "And the Father will contemplate the Son and the Son alone; and the Son will love the Father and the Father alone; and both will constitute but one sole joy [the Spirit]."[43]

From a monotheistic point of view, these "blasphemous" confessions seem to threaten the radical separation of the human from the divine. This constituted Jesus's challenge, something the first Christian thinkers well understood. "God becomes man so that man may become God," as we have already noted. What we see here is a bridge, a bridge we are capable of crossing. Jesus seems to be denying that an abyss exists between the human and the divine. And it is precisely for this reason that he eliminated fear and preached love.

The subtleties of St. Thomas are well known: in order to defend the divine absoluteness, he asserted that *omnis relatio quae consideratur inter Deum et creaturam, realiter quidem est in creatura . . . non autem est realiter in Deo* ["every relation between God and creature is real in the creature though not in God"; *Summa theologiae* q. 2, a. 7). Whence, *haec unio [divinae et humanae naturae] non est in Deo realiter, sed solum secundum rationem tantum* ("this union [of divine and human nature] does not exist in God in reality but only in reason"; see ibid., ad 1; see also *Quaestiones de quodlibet* I, a. 2; IX, a. 4).[44]

This is not the time for further comment; we wish only to underscore the fact that the Thomistic system develops out of the monotheism that is Judaic in origin and bears an Aristotelian imprint, even though Aristotle's

---

[43] Turoldo (1996), 210. Let us recall St. Augustine: *Et erit unus Christus amans seipsum* ("And there will be one sole Christ who loves himself").

[44] See n. 16 above.

θεός (*theos*) is quite different from Thomas's *Deus* ("God"). A clear example of this is the reduction of Christ to his historical function as redeemer. In this fashion, if man had not sinned, Christ would not have become incarnate (*Summa theologiae* III, q. 1, a. 3),[45] while acknowledging the opinions of others. Our opinion is trinitarian—as we have explained elsewhere, cosmotheandrian.[46]

In addition to the way some modern traditions offer readings of the first text that invert the order of the phrase and add the possessive in light of the context, we should note how the plural of the verb is used, The text does not say, "I *am* one with the Father," nor does it say "I *am* equal with the Father." Rather, it says, "I and the Father *are the same*"; "we *are* one," one relation. That is to say, there is a definitive "we," an ultimate "we"— *I and the Father*. There is the Father and the Son, and they are different. The Father is Father and the Son is Son. But the Father is Father because he is Father of the Son, because it is *he* who generates. And the Son is Son because he is Son of the Father who generates him. A father without a son would not be father—a son without a father would not be son. The father is father-of-the-son and the son is son-of-the-father. This paternity and filiation constitute their entire "being." They are pure relation. In more philosophical language, their Being is not Substance. Their Being is relational; even grammatically, their being is a verb.

Nothing exists outside the Trinity, nor is the Trinity subordinated to Unity. A *real* divine nature or essence common to the Trinity though distinct from Father, Son, and Spirit would convert the Trinity into a pure modalism. To speak of three essences or natures either makes no sense or would signify tritheism. God is neither one (a substance) nor three (three Gods). God is the ultimate and infinite correlative of reality—"For from him and through him and to him are all things" (Romans 11:36; see also 1 Corinthians 8:6; Colossians 1:16), *Deus ex quo, per quem, in quo omnia*, in the classic Latin phrase.

Let me insist again, both identity and difference exist. Father and Son constitute the difference while identity is this One—ἕν (*hen*), *unum* (a relation). A simple but important observation is now in order. An expression suitable to what we are saying need not have resorted to the current term "difference." Although the Father and Son are certainly not identical, neither are they different. They could be different only on a common plane that would allow a difference between them. If we consider the *Abba-*experience in depth, we would understand that the Father is Father and

---

[45] We should mention St. Thomas's honesty in acknowledging the possibility of other opinions.

[46] Panikkar (1989a and 1993a). See also Sherrard (1992) 10, 147, who uses the term *theoanthropocosmic vision*. I employ the term in a more limited way both because of cacophony and of out of respect for the Greek orthodox tradition that speaks of the "theandric" mystery.

nothing else, and that the Son is nothing except Son. Neither Father nor Son is a substance.[47] Being what we are, we are one.[48]

Father and Son are not different—they are correlative. One implies the other, and one cannot exist without the other. The difficulty in understanding this disappears the moment we explain that both names are nothing but relations. Relation is in fact the category of the Trinity—and *advaita.* The relation between Father and Son denies the duality (Father and Son, and vice versa—one not two: "we are one") without falling into a monistic identity (for the Father is not the Son, and vice versa. Insofar as it is relation, relation is one (the Father does not exist without the Son, and vice versa). Relation is the fundamental category that governs all that is.[49]

The expression "*my* Father" here assumes its most profound meaning. The Pharisees had replied to Jesus, "Our Father is Abraham" (John 8:39). But Jesus refutes them, saying, "If God were your Father, you would then love me" (John 8:42), as if to say, they would understand that power comes from the Father alone (see John 5:19). The expression "My Father" corresponds to the controverted "only-begotten" (μονογενής, *unigenitus* of John 1:14, 18; 3:16, 18; and 1 John 4:9).[50] Here we must refer to the controversy about the word πρωτότοκος (*prōtotokos, primogenitus,* "firstborn" in Romans 8:29; Colossians 1:15, 18; and Revelation 1:5).[51] Actually, Jesus

---

[47] The oblivion of tradition is at times surprising, if not suspect. To give just one illuminating example from Gregory of Nazienzen: Οὔτε οὐσίας ὄνομα ὁ πατήρ . . . οὔτε ἐνεργείας, σχέσεως δὲ καὶ τοῦ πῶς ἔχει πρὸς τὸν υἱὸν ὁ πατήρ, ἢ ὁ υἱὸς πρός τὸν πατέρα (*Oute ousias onoma ho patēr . . . oute energeias, scheseōs de kai tou pōs echei pros ton huion ho patēr ē ho huios pros ton patera.* In Latin, *Nec essentia nomen est Pater, o viri acutissimi, nec actionis, sed relationem eam indicat, quam Pater erga Filum habet, vel Filius erga Patrem. . . . Ut enim in nos haec nomina germanam quandam coniunctionem et necessitudinem declarant, ad eumdem modum, illic quoque genitorem ac genitum eamdem naturam habere significant.* "Father is not the name of a substance [an essence, a thing]; it rather indicates the relation which the Father has toward the Son or the Son toward the Father . . . Just as among us these names indicate a certain homogeneous conjunction and necessity, so with respect to what we have just said, both he who generates and he who is generated possess the same nature" [*Oratio theologica* XXIX, 16; PG 36:96]).

[48] Gregory also writes, "Do you perhaps wish to become a theologian? Respect the commandments!" And he proceeds to advance reasons: "*praxis* is the way to contemplation" (*Oratio theologica* XX, 12; PG 35:1080). This is the reason for my interest as well as suspicion. What is suspect is that a certain theology has lost the contemplative spirit. *Vis theologus aliquando fieri ac divinitate dignus* (τῆς θεότητος ἄξιος). "To be worthy of divinity is the requirement for authentic *theology,* if one is not to utter unworthy words about the ultimate mystery." The following addition is important: Πρᾶξις γὰρ ἐπίβασις θεωρίας (*actio enim gradus est ad contemplationem* ("Praxis is the introduction to contemplation").

[49] See Krempel (1952). I have already indicated my view that this "radical relativity" seems to be a human intuition that is virtually universal.

[50] The New English Bible translation of John 1:18 is "Father's only Son," an expression that does not render well the idea that is still vaguely preserved in "only begotten Son" in the King James Version. The translation of the Italian Episcopal Conference is very clear: "Only begotten" (*unigenito*). The German-language Neuer Jerusalemer Bibel version is ambivalent: *Die Einzige, der Gott ist und am Herzen des Vaters ruht.*"

[51] The New English Bible also avoids the literal translation of the first text: "his is the

never uses either of these expressions; hence we may interpret his condition of Son as exhaustive, not exclusive. Jesus is the only son not in the sense of being the offspring of a father who could have had many other children but in the sense of the sole filiation of a Son who continues to be generated *semper nascens*, always in the process of being born from the Father, as Eckhart would say.[52] In this sense the Son can be one alone inasmuch as the Father constantly generates him. But in this filiation it is we too—and the whole of creation—that exist (Genesis 1:3) as we wait and hope: "Creation itself yearns for the revelation of God's children . . . we too moan within as we wait for God to make us his sons and redeem our whole body" (Romans 8:19-23).[53] It is well known that the word *primogenitus* was eliminated from the creed in order to avoid Arius's interpretation. Arius adopted this term to support the thesis that Jesus was human and only human: the "firstborn among many brethren" (which, interestingly, is exactly how the King James Bible translates Romans 8:29).

It is important to remain conscious of correlations in whose absence we could easily misunderstand this and other texts. In a philosophical sense, the matter is simple. If we do not grasp the relation in itself, we become "victims" of dialectics, assuming that the sole way of grasping differences is to leap from A to B and especially from A to non-A. It is substantialistic thought that sees first A, then B, and afterwards the relation between the two. Only an intellect that does not pretend to *intus-legere* but rather experiences an immediate *inter-legere* is able to grasp relation directly. And this is the same thinking we find in nondualistic *advaita*. Once it has transcended a subject-object individualism, *advaita* becomes conscious of reality such as it presents itself, without engaging in either analysis or synthesis, precisely because it does not begin with an a priori that is ungrounded in reality.

In our case, there is a Fountain, a source of my being, a mysterious Fountain of Being that is neither my ego nor my non-ego. The origin is what it is only insofar as, in fact, it originates. The Father is father because he generates; the Son is son because he is generated. They constitute two poles of the same reality, a "reality," however, that is nothing other than the relation which constitutes both poles.

This relation, in which the whole universe is involved, does not result in a final monism; it is not closed, because it is the Spirit that keeps it open.

---

primacy over all created things" ("born before"). The Authorized Version offers "the first born of every creature." The Italian Bishops' Conference edition has, "Generated before every creature." For an exegesis of the various uses of the word, see Michaelis in Kittel (1964-1974), 6:871-82.

[52] In commenting on John 1:1, Eckhart writes: *et si semper in principio, semper nascitur, semper generatur* ("And if it is always in the beginning, it is always born, already generated"; *Lateinische Werke* III, 9).

[53] Which the Catalan Interconfessional Bible translates: *. . . anhelant de ser plenament fills, quan el nostre cos signi redimit*, which neither the Bible de Jérusalem nor the New Jerusalem Bible, even in the English version, translates.

The Son's return to the Father does not move, so to speak, through the same path that fatherhood does. To be generated is not the same as to generate. To receive is not the same as to give. Passivity is not activity. Here the locus of the Spirit is found also in the doctrine of the *filioque,* even though "through the Son" is a more plausible expression. Bonaventure calls the Son *Persona media Trinitatis,*[54] while Jakob Böhme said that "God is person only in Christ."[55] St. Augustine asserts that God's Son is the "Father's art" (*ars Patris*), and St. Bonaventure argues that "'I and the Father are One,' because, seen as relation, fatherhood and filiation are not two."[56] To repeat, it is only from a substantialist point of view that to start from A is not the same as to start from B. On the contrary, "The way up is the same as the way down," as Heraclitus says (*Fragments* 60).

The Experience

I experience the act of living as a bond with the Father, as a source of life.[57] I feel that this life has not only been granted me but has, in addition, shaped me to be me that I am myself able to say "my Life" as Christ said "my Father." I feel this life flowing in me as a continuous creation and incarnation. "As the Father has life in himself, so he gave (ἔδωκεν, *edōken*) to the Son to have life in himself" (John 5:26).[58] Just as the source and the river share water, so do we share life.[59]

---

[54] See his *Collationes in Hexaemeron* I, n. 14 (*Opera omnia* 5:331-33).

[55] In Hartmann (1890) 88.

[56] Augustine, *De Trinitate*, VI, 10, n. 11; *De reductione artium ad theologium*, n. 20.

[57] Aquinas writes, *Prius vita quam doctrina* ("Life [is] before doctrine"), adding: *Vita enim ducit ad cognitionem veritatis* ("Life in fact leads to a knowledge of truth"—because, as he knew, *Vivere viventibus est esse* ("To live is, for the living, being"; see Aristotle, *De Anima* II, 37 [415b 13]).

[58] St. Augustine has commented in *Tractatus in Joannis Evangelium* XXVI, 19 that, although the Father is greater than he (John 14:28), Jesus can say, *vivo propter Patrem* ("I live for the Father"; John 6:57). We can therefore say that we "live because of Christ," who, despite this (relationship), is greater than us.

[59] St. Augustine expresses this idea, which has perhaps been forgotten by a certain kind of theology, in a concise way: *Quae est ergo doctrina Patris nisi verbum Patris? Ipse ergo Christus doctrina Patris, si verbum Patris. Sed, quia verbum not potest esse nullius sed alicuius; et suam doctrinam dixit, se ipsum; et non suam, quia Patris est Verbum. Quid enim tam tuum est quam tu? et quid tam non tuum quam tu si alicuius es quod es?* ("What is the Father's doctrine if not the Father's Word? Thus, if Christ himself is the Father's Word, he is the Father's teaching. But since the Word cannot be the word of nobody but surely of somebody, in speaking of himself Christ also asserted that he both was and was not his doctrine insofar as he was the Father's Word. What is yours more than yourself? And what is yours more than yourself if what you are is only in respect to another?") See *Tractatus in Joannis Evangelium* XXIX, 3; PL 35:1629. Augustine is commenting on John 7:16: "My teaching is not mine but belongs to him who has sent me."

It is perhaps opportune to return once again to John's words so that we may express this experience and speak of the future rather than the past: we are children and therefore spring from the same water, the same seed, even though what we shall be has not yet been revealed (οὔπω ἐφανερώθη, *oupō ephanerōthē*, 1 John 3:2). Christophany has not yet been fully manifested.

The water must be purified, even though it is already there; the experience of our divine filiation is a human experience. "Not only are we called God's children, but we really are" (1 John 3:1). We are *brahman*, but do not know it.

Is not life itself perhaps the adventure of making one out of two?—*utraque unum*—(Ephesians 2:14), making the two into a One that is no number? Once again, it is the experience of the Trinity. Allow me to say all this in my own words.

> "I and the Father are one" to the extent that my ego disappears, and my ego disappears to the extent that it allows itself to be shared by whosoever comes to me, "feeds" on me or, seeing me, sees not "me" but what I say—sees, that is, what I am. This is what I experience when I possess that transparency which is always more pure the more free I am from my small ego. When my ego imposes itself, others begin to compete and often confront merely their own projections. That is, they face what they already believe and imagine they are. My ego then becomes a wall, and they bounce against it.
>
> When, on the other hand, I am transparent, free of every fear, I am truly myself, my *Self*. Transparency allows a spontaneity that springs from me only when I am pure. It is then that I experience a poverty of spirit. The kingdom of the heavens is mine when nothing belongs to me. "Blessed are the poor in spirit" (Matthew 5:3) has nothing to do with economic questions: it is, rather, an invitation to discover that the whole universe is mine, or rather, is me when it is not a question of a "me"—an ego that interferes with this kind of belonging.[60] This idea entails neither a pantheistic confusion nor a negation of personality. If I am not mine and discover myself as a you, a you of the Father, then I am the whole of reality seen from the small window I shall call mine: "I and the Father are one."

---

[60] See the courageous statement of St. John of the Cross, who says that everything is his: "Mine are the heavens, mine the earth, and peoples . . . God himself is mine because Christ is mine and everything is for me" (*Máximas y sentencias*, 25). The philosophic expression of this experience is man conceived as microcosm. See Plato, *Timaeus* 30 D, 44 D; Aristotle, *Physics* VIII, 2 (252-56; 26-27); Philo, *Qui rerum divinarum heres* XXXI, 155 ("man is a small world and the world a big man"); *De migratione Abrahami* XXXIX, 220 ("the world is a bigger and more perfect man"); *De opificio mundi* xxvii, 82 ("man is a small heaven").

"The pure in heart shall see God" (Matthew 5:8) expresses the same experience. The Beatitudes are neither doctrines nor moral dictates nor categorical imperatives but, rather, externalizations of the most intimate experience: if I do not desire anything for my ego, I am everything and have everything. I am one with the source insofar as I too act as a source by making everything which I have received flow again—just like Jesus.

This is not pride. it is, rather, the experience of the Easter of the resurrection. Christian spirituality ends not with Good Friday but with Resurrection Sunday, which Pentecost makes real to us—a situation that does not divinize by dehumanizing us but, on the contrary, humanizes us by divinizing us. We certainly do not always live at the highest level, though every person thirsts for the infinite and searches for a water that satisfies, howsoever fleeting and hidden it might be.

The person who listens to me surely hears my voice, sees my face, reads my thoughts, suffers from all my limitations. Yet it does sometimes happen that someone hears through my voice, sees through my face, perceives beyond my thoughts, intuits behind my smallness. Those who truly see, I dare say, already see the Father, the mystery, the reality.[61] And this is possible only if this intimate union is neither egotistical nor conserved but rather shared, in service and love. These experiences are perhaps more common than we might believe.

Christ did not come to "teach" doctrines as much as he did to communicate life (John 10:10) and definitely to communicate himself, his own life, the life of the Father—"And his life was the light of men" (John 1:4). Even if we do not deny the fact that Christ did indeed live these experiences to such an extent that our own intuitions seem but pale imitations of that life, we don't have to consider ourselves shallow-minded or sinners just so that Jesus might appear, by contrast, holy and divine: he would probably not have appreciated this attitude. We have, time and again, repeated his words: "I have said, you are gods" (Psalm 82:6; John 10:34). Why should we not feel authorized to speak as Gods? Personal dignity implies this: not only are we one of many rings in a chain of beings (or even of Being) but each one of us is also unique, unsubstitutable precisely because each one of us bears infinite divine value.

---

[61] I discern a homeomorphic equivalent of this mahāyāna intuition that connects *nirvāṇa* to *saṃsāra*. Those who truly experience *saṃsāra* discover *nirvāṇa* (Nāgārjuna, *Madhyamika-kārikā* XXV, 19-20). "On earth as it is in heaven," as the Our Father declares in simple language and the hermetic tradition confirms.

None of these experiences is either extraneous or inaccessible to us. We truly understand what Christ was talking about. What we said at the beginning may now appear more plausible to us. And there is more: if we cannot be sure that the man of Galilee actually did assert this or that phrase, we ourselves nevertheless do feel these experiences in our own hearts. Jesus's message pervades our lives and reveals the supreme experience of the human being. I would now like to quote St. Thomas Aquinas, who is not a sentimental writer: "If Jesus Christ had entrusted his teaching to the written word, people would have imagined that nothing else existed in his teaching other than what was contained in the scriptures."[62]

Inasmuch as I am attempting to describe my experience, I must search in my own heart even as I refer to the scriptures. It is again St. Thomas who tells us that the so-called law of the New Testament is not a written law but, rather, one that is inscribed in our hearts: "The law of the New Testament is inscribed in our heart" (*Summa theologiae* I-II, q. 106, a. 1). Again, when he writes that "The new law is the very grace of the Holy Spirit," St. Thomas is reflecting the whole tradition, while also citing scripture (Hebrews 8:8; Romans 3:27; 7:2).[63]

I must therefore listen to my heart when it is pure and discover therein the Holy Spirit: of course, such listening is not easy to achieve. The holy Job was told, "Listen to me: be silent and I shall teach you wisdom" (Job 33:33). Though not impossible, such a purification of the heart is difficult; it must be practiced continuously. To listen and remain silent so as to learn how to "read" in one's own heart: then it is that we realize we cannot make it on our own. We need others. It is precisely this situation that constitutes the mystery of the human community, the communion (κοινωνία) of the mystical body.

Meditation on Christ's "emptying" throughout the whole life he lived without privileges, as a simple "son of man," leads to all the previous ideas.

---

[62] *Si autem Christus scripto suam doctrinam mandaret, nihil alius de eius doctrina homines existimarent quam quod scriptura contineret* ("If Jesus Christ had entrusted his teaching to the written word, people would have imagined that nothing else existed in his teaching except what was contained in the Scriptures"; *Summa theologiae.* II-II, q. 42, a.4. Thomas reminds us of such texts as John 21:25 and 2 Corinthians 3:3, and cites Pythagoras and Socrates as *excellentissimi doctores*, who did the same thing. We may add Buddha, Mahāvīra and others. Nor did Lao Tze wish to write anything, and the African wise ones, too, do not write but only speak.

[63] Thomas himself quotes Augustine: *Sicut lex factorum scripta fuit in tabulis lapideis . . . ita lex fidei scripta est in cordibus [fidelium]* ("Just as the law of [human] actions is written in stone . . . , so the law of faith was written in the hearts [of believers]"; *De spiritu et littera* XXIV, 41; PL 44:225). It is interesting to observe that Thomas omits a few words of this citation and adds the word *fidelium*. Again: *Quae [Quid] sunt [ergo] leges dei ab ipso Deo scriptae in cordibus, nisi ipsa praesentia Spiritus Sancti?* ("What then are God's laws that God himself has inscribed on hearts but the very presence of the Holy Spirit?"; ibid., XXI, 36). The atmosphere of these citations is far from any kind of legalism.

I am thinking of *kenōsis*.[64] This notion is fundamental for a true meeting with many Asian religions, especially Buddhism, as is just now being discovered.[65] In any event, the death of the I, the *anonadamiento* of Spanish mysticism, constitutes an indispensable condition, as virtually all mystical currents maintain. "In Christ, a new creature" (2 Corinthians 5:17).

Let us repeat: none of this denies the fact that this supreme human experience—the experience of a being who is an empty container yearning to be filled with infinity—may be expressed in different ways by other traditions. Are we not, after all, saying that Jesus Christ is the revelation of the infinite hidden mystery, and so present in the cosmos from eternity (Romans 16:25-26)?

> Even though far from being the eucharistic bread of life for others—and very slow to realize that those who enter in contact with me enter in communication and communion with the source of life itself, which gives Life to me and everyone else, or even though I am so opaque that not all who see me see the Father, I still cannot deny that all these experiences belong to me too and are therefore available to every human being. Might not this be precisely what constitutes "the good news"?

"I and the Father are one." We have already eliminated the fear of pantheism by acknowledging that the difference between the Father and us is infinite—as it is among the "persons" of the Trinity. Our being one with God—our divine aspect, as Christian tradition loves to say—entails neither an indiscriminate fusion nor separation. Insofar as we are one with Christ, we are one with the Father. Although I am not the Source, the Source is neither separated nor separable from me.[66] The toil has not ended: this is time: the temporal "distention" of the cosmos's adventure (1 Corinthians 15:20-28). Since we cannot, now, engage in an exegesis of the text, we should perhaps remain silent.

---

[64] It is enlightening to observe different translations of Philippians 2:7: Emptied himself (New Revised Standard Version, New American Bible, New Jerusalem Bible); made himself nothing (New English Bible, Revised English Bible); *entäuiserte sich* (Neuer Jerusalemer Bibel); *ausgeleert hat er sich selbst* (Stier); *s'anéanti lui-même* (Bible de Jérusalem); *se anonadó* (Nácar-Colunga); *s'anorreà* (Montserrat); *es va fer no res* (Catalan Interconfessional Bible); *es despullà del seu rang* (Mateos/Rius Camps); *spogliò se stesso* (Italian Conference of Bishops).

[65] As an example of this interest I cite a few studies of the Kyoto school: Nishitani (1982); Unno (1989); Ohashi (1990); and in the same spirit Mitchell (1991); Lefebure (1993), and the recent writings of Masao Abe.

[66] After the death of his teacher Nishida, Nishitani wrote in his untranslatable Japanese calligraphy, "Although the source may be exhausted, its water can never be." He was remembering that "to kill the Buddha and the Masters exhibits the highest form of gratitude" (Ohashi 1990, 5). Here we see an example of a different way of thinking. I abstain from any kind of trinitarian comment in the light of the constant dynamism of *perichōrēsis*.

When I refuse to be called "a human being," or when I criticize evolutionistic *thought*, when I claim to be unique and, to that extent, unclassifiable, I am reacting against the invasion of the scientific mentality, which tends to obscure one of the most central of all human experiences: being a unique divine icon of reality, constitutively united with the Source of everything, a microcosm that mirrors the entire macrocosm. In a word, I am one with the Father, infinite, beyond all comparison and never interchangeable. The I is not me. I am not the product of evolution, a speck of dust, or even mind in the midst of an immense universe. Man, the integrally concrete, real man, is not an item in a classification scheme: it is he who does the classifying. This holds for each one of us. I would like to stress that man's dignity lies precisely in his being conscious of the fact that he and the Father *are* one. That is precisely what the Mediator dared to say, *anthrōpos Christos Iēsous* (1 Timothy 2:5). The *ahambrahmāsmi* must be seen in the light of the *tat tvam asi!*

Herein lies the plenitude of man. In the Vulgate, Psalm 25:16 is numbered 24:16 and reads, *Respice in me et miserere mei: quia* unicus *et pauper ego sum* ("Look at me and have pity on me because I am *unique* and poor"). Note, that *unicus* is translated as "alone" in the New Revised Standard Version; and "lonely" in the New American Bible. The Septuagint translates μονογενής as *unicus* and πτωχός as *pauper*; the Hebrew employs terms that correspond to "solitary" and "disgraced," which are more in accord with such contemporary translations as, for example, the New Revised Standard Version.

We must now resume our discussion of the *ādhyātmic* anthropology. After the philological and ontogenetic questions that characterize the primal ecstatic consciousness of humanity—"What are things, other people, and God?"—arises the principal existential question, "Who am I?" I "am" between being and nothingness. Between these two extremes oscillates the story of human consciousness—as the Hebrew psalms cry out.

Who am I? Jesus, like every other man, raised the question. He was concerned to know what others said about him, yet the answers he received did not seem to have convinced him much—except for one that did not come from human lips: "You are my son." This answer, which Jesus heard at the Jordan and again at Tabor, which Peter confessed, the centurion confirmed, the Pharisees denied, and the disciples debated, seems to represent Jesus's central experience: I am not an autonomous I (I only say what I hear—my words are not mine); I am not an I but a thou of the I, the thou of God. Neither autonomy (I am not an individual who exists in himself) nor heteronomy (nor am I a mere instrument that an "Other" or others manipulate). Rather, it is a matter of *ontonomy* (I am joined to Reality, to the Father, in a real relationship of inter-independence).

Strengthened by his experience (that of Jesus), we too can seek to live it with greater trust. We are neither God nor non-God; neither real nor non-real, neither angels nor devils. *Sad-asad-anirvacanīya* (something ineffable, that is neither being nor non-being), says the *vedānta*. Within this historico-religious context, we could perhaps describe Jesus's experience as the answer available to every person. Although perhaps I do not know "who I am," as the *Ṛg-veda* I, 164, 37 says, I surely do know one thing, "I am never completely identical with myself." The subject of the question cannot be identified totally with the predicate of the answer. "How can one see the seen?," St. Augustine asked himself—*Quomodo potest videre videntem?*[67]—thereby reflecting the upanishadic problematic. But in order to discover ourselves as a thou, a *tvam* (*tat tvam asi*), it is necessary that someone, the I, tell us this, and in addition we must be prepared to listen. The Father's "you are my sons" corresponds to Jesus's *Abba, Patēr!*

To become God's children, we must not dehumanize ourselves through a negative asceticism that entails the abandonment of the body and matter, as many forms of Neoplatonic, vedantic, and other forms of spirituality suggest. The Christian *theōsis* resides not in the "flight of the solitary to the Solitary" but in the full realization of the *verbum caro factum est* ("the Word became flesh" of the Creed)—that is, the realization of the incarnation.

It Is Good That I Leave

Our third *mahāvākya* represents the deepest stage of spiritual experience, for many reasons, but especially because it is the most human. The *kenōsis* is an act that continues. The *theōsis* (divinization of man) without the *kenōsis* (divine annihilation) would constitute a diabolical temptation (Genesis 3:5). The Trinity is the fulcrum of Christian experience. The Christ represents both the divinization of Man and the humanization of God. If Christ were God alone or "more" divine than human, his life and "mysteries" could not also represent our destiny—his karma would not be human.

That "meditation on death," which Plato calls μελέτη θανάτου (*meletē thanatou, Phaedo* 81a), represents a comment that is profound in its simplicity. Since ancient times, both in the East and the West, such a meditation has been the counsel that the wise have offered in order to achieve a wise life.

What we have said does not entail any pessimism, since everything falls and dies, and our bodies age and become decomposed. All this should inspire neither anxiety in the face of death nor a more or less morbid desire to die—nor excessive speculation about life after life. It is simply a matter of acknowledging reality and respecting what is, as Jesus taught when he said it is good that stones remain stones (in the temptation narratives of Matthew 4:3-4; Luke 4:4). What we would be wise to acknowledge is this.

---

[67] See Panikkar (1966) 255-56.

Not that I must disappear, not that others are waiting for me elsewhere, not that I am in a rush to leave this earth, nor that I should attach myself to those who have lived with me. Instead, what I must recognize is that our time must arrive, one moment or another, and it is right that it be so because temporal *ex-istence* must be re-born, must enter into tempiternal *sistence* in the Spirit's *manere*. When his disciples ask Jesus to remain and then recognize him, he immediately disappears (Luke 24:29-31). "Life does not die," as a vedic text says (*Chāndogya-upaniṣad* VI, 11, 3). *Vita mutatur, non tollitur,* the ancient Christian liturgy chants—"Life changes, it is not taken away."[68] It is good that time does not stop in us—nor we in time.

The Texts

Ἀλλ᾿ ἐγὼ τὴν ἀλήθειαν λέγω ὑμῖν, συμφέρει ὑμῖν ἵνα ἐγὼ ἀπέλθω ἐὰν γὰρ μὴ ἀπέλθω, ὁ παράκλητος οὐ μὴ ἔλθῃ οὐκ ἐλεύσεται πρὸς ὑμᾶς ἐὰν δὲ πορευθῶ, πέμψω αὐτὸν πρὸς ὑμᾶς.[69]

Sed ego veritatem dico vobis: expedit vobis ut ego vadam. Si ego non abiero, Paraclitus non veniet ad vos; si autem abiero, mittam eum ad vos.

Nevertheless, I tell you the truth: it is to your advantage that I go away because, unless I do, the Paraclete will not come to you; but if I go, I will send him to you.[70]

(John 16:7)

I will not dwell on the scene, even though it is very moving and could have been created a posteriori. We are dealing, nevertheless, with a univer-

---

[68] According to Thomas Aquinas, *Dicitur autem creatura fluvius quia fluit semper de esse ad non-esse per corruptionem, et de non-esse ad esse per generationem* ("Created being is called a river because it always flows from being to non-being through corruption and from non-being to being through generation"). (See *Sermones festivi,* 61.)

[69] In the Greek manuscripts there are some variants that are not substantive.

[70] Again, other translations are interesting: "whereas if I go, I will send him to you" (New English Bible); "It is expedient for you that I go away, for if I do not go away, the Advocate will not come to you" (Authorized Version); "It is expedient for you that I depart. For if I do not go, the Advocate will not come to you" (Confraternity/Challoner/Rheims); *Il vaut mieux pour vous que je parte; car si je ne pars pas, le Paraclet ne viendra pas à vous* (Bible de Jérusalem); *Es ist gut für euch, das ich fortgehe. Denn wenn ich nicht fortgehe, wird der Beistand nich zu euch kommen"* (Neuer Jerusalemer Bibel); *Us convé que me'n vagi; perquè si no me'n vaig no vindrà el vostre valedor a vosaltres* (Mateos/Rius Camps); *Us convé que me'n vagi; perquè si no me'n vaig no vindrà el vostre Defensor a vosaltres* (Catalan Interconfessional Bible); *Os conviene que yo me vaya. Porque si no me fuere el Abogado no vendrá a vosotros* (Nacar-Colunga).

sal human situation: the future does not seem bright, his followers will be persecuted, and the state of mind that has entered into his disciples may be described in this way: the Master is about to leave them at any moment without having finished hardly anything while, at the same time, almost abandoning them. We can understand Judas's frustration and desperation: Jesus's mission is about to end in a total fiasco.

The people have abandoned him because it has become too risky to follow him; the synagogue declares him a heretic, indeed blasphemous; the political representatives despise him; and his "own" do not understand him. He has not left them anything durable, no institution; he has neither baptized nor ordained, much less has he founded anything—though he may have manifested the intention of doing so. He has left both the Spirit and himself as a silent Presence in the eucharistic act. He has sent them as a lamb among wolves and refuses to change tactics even at the end: wolves are still roaming about. He promises his followers only one thing: the Spirit.

This is not the place to examine in depth the meaning of the verb *sympherein*, which is translated as "it is good" or "to your advantage," and which literally means "to put together," "to gather." In this scenario the verb means something profitable, advantageous, opportune, in harmony with the entire situation.

His life is about to reach its end and he is certainly about to go to the Father (John 14:12; 16:17, 28; 20:17, and elsewhere). In any event, he is about to go, despite the fact that he has just reached the fullness of his age. While he consoles his disciples by saying that he has not left them orphans (John 14:18), he also makes them understand that they will not see him again. And the specter of his imminent death weighs constantly on them. He promises them consolation, comfort, an intercessor, a mediator, an advocate, an aid, a Paraclete. In other texts the advocate is described as the Spirit and often called "the Spirit of truth" (e.g., John 14:17, 26; 15:26; 16:13), a reflection perhaps of the language of the Qumran community.[71]

Ὅταν δὲ ἔλθῃ ἐκεῖνος, τὸ πνεῦμα τῆς ἀληθείας,
ὁδηγήσει ὑμᾶς εἰς τὴν ἀλήθειαν πᾶσαν.

Cum autem venerit ille, Spiritus veritatis deducet vos,
in omnem veritatem.

When, however, the Spirit of truth will come,
he will guide you to the whole truth.

(John 16:13)

---

[71] The *Manual of Discipline* of the Qumran community bestows upon the "spirit of truth" the function of "illuminating man's heart, setting it on the path of virtue . . . bestowing understanding and intelligence . . . a spirit of discernment" (1QS IV:2-6).

The text could not be any more explicit. As soon as he leaves, the Spirit of truth will come and introduce us to the truth in its entirety. Is it a matter of the ingenuous faith or blind trust in the Spirit? It is presumed that Jesus also said that it is the Spirit that gives life: *Spiritus est qui vivificat* (John 6:63), although some exegetes tend to contextualize this phrase in eucharistic discussions.

The Spirit is a Spirit of truth, that truth which makes us free (John 8:32; 2 Corinthians 3:17). Although this Spirit will not carry us toward precise formulations or fragments of truth, it will carry us toward truth in its entirety, toward indivisible truth, toward the discovery (ἀλήθεια, *alētheia*) of the recondite nugget of truth.[72] "Consecrate them in the truth" (John 17:17). The Spirit does not make us omniscient but true seekers; it does not lead us to know everything but to be everything—the *totum in parte* ("the whole in the part"), the icon of reality.

Let us remember that the truth Jesus is talking about is not the correspondence (*adaequatio*) between an abstract intellect and an idea; it is rather an *aequatio ad* (from *aequitas*, "equality"), a sort of "equality toward" the order of reality (*rta, dharma,* τάξις [*taxis*], *ordo*).

As we have already said, the way of truth is one and the same as the search for justice—and vice versa. To separate the truth, the truth that makes us free, from its incarnation in life—that is, from justice—represents the rupture of human life into a theoretico-conceptual and a practico-temporal world, a rupture that bears mortal consequences. The justice of the Gospel, the *dikaiosynē* (δικαιοσύνη) is indissoluble insofar as it binds human justice and divine justification. A christophany for our age cannot accept this dichotomy—as liberation theology is trying to tell us.

There is much more. Although truth can perhaps be translated into concepts, it itself is not a concept any more than orthodoxy is a doctrine. As I noted in the dedication, truth itself is "journeying," like a pilgrim. Such a description would make no sense, however, and we would fall into an anarchical relativism, if truth were identified with a conceptual system. Not only is truth a relation; it is also a personal relation. It is not truth that is adored; it is *true* adorers who adore the divine mystery in spirit and truth (John 4:24). Truth is one and the same as the spirit of truth.

Ὁ πιστεύων εἰς ἐμὲ τὰ ἔργα ἃ ἐγὼ ποιῶ κἀκεῖνος ποιήσει καὶ μείζονα τούτων ποιήσει, ὅτι ἐγὼ πρὸς τὸν πατέρα πορεύομαι.

Qui credit in me, opera, quae ego facio, et ipse faciet,
et maiora horum faciet, quia ego ad Patrem vado.

---

[72] The *Gospel of Truth* discovered at Nag Hammadi and marked by Valentinian tendencies says in chapter IV: "Jesus Christ, by means of a hidden mystery, has illuminated those who are in the dark. By drawing them out of oblivion, he has illuminated and shown them a path. This path is the Truth, and it is precisely the Truth that he taught them." Cited in Orbe (1985) 124.

> He who believes in me, will do the works that I do, and will do
> even greater ones because I am going to the Father.[73]
>
> (John 14:12)

Let us recall those traditional theological distinctions which prevent us
from thinking that the disciple is capable of surpassing the teacher, even
though this text seems to assert that such a possibility exists. In any event,
the assertion does suggest that we are only at the beginning of a new manifestation of the Spirit and that our task is to continue it in a creative and
even more admirable way.

It seems important to note the causal connection of the phrase: we shall
do greater things *because* he is going to the Father. He does not leave us
"orphans"—without a Father (John 14:18). He is the mediator (μεσίτης,
mesitēs, 1 Timothy 2:5), not the intermediary (cf. John 14:20). The mediator has accomplished what he had to do (John 17:4). Now it is up to us.
But the bond remains: he returns to the Source from which we too can
drink the living water (John 4:14) that is clearly bound up with the Spirit
(John 7:37-39).

The Interpretation

"It is good that I am leaving you" possesses a profound christological
meaning. It removes the temptation to any kind of panchristism or even
christocentrism. Jesus knew that it was good that he leave, that he had not
come to remain but to remain in us in the most perfect form, not as a more
or less welcome guest foreign to us but in our very being. This is the meaning of the eucharist. This is the work of the Spirit.

"It is good that he is leaving us." Otherwise we would make him
king—that is, an idol—or we would rigidify him into concepts, into intellectual containers. We would turn his teaching into a system, imprison him
within our own categories and suffocate the Spirit.

"It is good that he is leaving you," as he did at Emmaus, at the mountain of Galilee, or as he did when they wanted to kill him or make him
king. The warning is worth repeating: "O men of little faith! Have you not
yet understood that the kingdom of God is neither here nor there, that it
cannot be objectified, that all our notions of it are provisional, in constant
movement, and rather conventional?"

---

[73] Several other translations follow: "He who has faith in me will do what I am doing;
and he will do greater things still because I am going to the Father" (New English Bible);
"Whoever believes in me will perform even greater works, because I am going to the Father"
(New Jerusalem Bible); *Wer an mich glaubt, der wird die Werke, die ich tue, aber selber tun.
Ja, grössere als die wird er tun, weil ich zum Vater gehe* (Stier); *Chi crede in me, compierà le
opere che io compio e ne farà di più grandi, perche io vado al Padre* (Episcopal Conference of
Italy).

Christophany illuminates every being. Neither a manifestation of another nor a human alienation, it is rather the maximal actualization of our true identity. The phrase of the African slave who had become free may also be said of Christ: *Homo sum; humani nihil a me alienum puto*[74] ("I am a man; I consider nothing human foreign to me").[75]

This *humanum* is humanity, "the perfect Man." It is therefore not a question of reducing everything to the one sole center, which would be Jesus the Christ. Reality exhibits as many different centers as there are centers of consciousness—which means that it manifests as many centers as there are beings. This is not, therefore, any kind of panchristism because Christ has left and thereby allowed the Spirit to bestow our identity on us. In a certain sense this last *mahāvākya* sums up the quintessence of Jesus's message: no certitude, no assurance, no external rule, total faith in us, in each of us. The Spirit will come.

Not only does he go, not only does he in fact leave us, not only does he trust us and give us responsibility, but it is good that it be so. All this should remind us of Lao Tze and Chuang-zu.

There is a strong temptation to criticize organizations and emphasize the betrayal of many Christians and, above all, of the official churches for having wanted to rigidify everything, regulate life, and proclaim laws. We are, of course, justified in sustaining a critical and open spirit and in not fearing to denounce what appear to us as abuses and deformations of Christ's spirit. But let us not forget that it is good that he has gone, and good that we realize it was not necessary for him to remain, just as it was not necessary for an omnipotent God (to give one example, without pursuing the argument) to prevent us from abusing our freedom. It is good for the church to be in human hands, that humanity forge its own destiny, and that we become co-responsible for the world's dynamism (Qoheleth 3:11). "And he left the world to their disputations," we read in the Latin version of a biblical text,[76] even though it does not correspond to the original. The immutability that breaks life's dynamism is death.

This trust in the Spirit, which in reality means trust in Man, this freedom is the testament of that "prophet powerful in deeds and words" (Luke 24:19). "Where there is Spirit there is freedom" (2 Corinthians 3:17), *Ubi Spiritus, ibi libertas!*

The traditional interpretation of Jesus's "last discourse" (John 13-17) is well known. Jesus seems to be aware of both his mission and his responsibilities. This discourse alludes to the Trinity and the church and contains an undeniable example of the climate in which the first generations of

---

[74] Terentius, *Heautontimoroumenos* 77 (circa A.D. 163). The phrase became very widely known because Cicero (*De Officiis* I, 9, 30; *De legibus* I, 12, 33), Seneca (*Ad Lucilium* XCV, 53); Juvenal (*Satir.* XV, 140ff.), and Ambrose (*De officiis* III, 7, 45) quoted it.

[75] Here we have an example of the meaning of a phrase that tradition has gradually deepened over the centuries.

[76] *Et mundum tradidit disputationi eorum.*

Christians lived. Without these chapters, it would be difficult to understand them.[77]

Modern scholarship has accomplished marvels in filtering strata of texts and in analyzing the historical events that gave rise to the text being examined. Yet it is undeniable that, in one sense or another, the promise of the Spirit belongs to Jesus's *kerygma*.[78]

Perhaps the first Christian generations to believe that the Son of God decided to found his church and was conscious of a role entrusted to them by the divine Father, may have held the discourse reported in the Gospels, which can be understood as the apex of the teaching of Jesus. It is undeniable, however, that the attitude it reflects is typical of the man of Galilee. Here we can see that, instead of visualizing a triumphalistic "representation" toward the works of Christian communities in which Jesus seems to have had no doubts about his church, it is surely possible to interpret his words as narrating a realistic situation that crushes every idealistic expectation.

We could say that Jesus failed and lost the opportunity to found his church. The enthusiastic crowd wanted to make him king: he walked away. The apostles wanted him to remain on the mountain: he rebuked them and went down to the plain. Satan wanted to offer him all the kingdoms of the world: he refused. He did not even want to listen to the scriptures and convert the stones into bread for himself: he preferred that the stones remain stones. He was certainly not a diplomat capable of ingratiating himself with those in power. But in this last situation he could no longer leave. They seized him and got rid of him: he died abandoned.

We are not therefore commenting on a single statement and elaborating a specific exegesis. We are seeking to understand Jesus's experience and asking ourselves whether, ultimately, our experience corresponds to the fundamental attitude that we grasp in what he said and did. Jesus repeated that message constantly. He lived and preached it. "Do not be anxious" (μὴ μεριμνᾶτε, *mē merimnate*, Matthew 6:25-34) about the future, be serene, do not think about what you should say (Matthew 10:19).

It seems appropriate to append a teaching passage that reveals Jesus's humanity. It is not a question of an omniscient being who hopes to arouse repentance for Peter's betrayal—whoever it is who might have written the passage and whatever may be its historical level of reality. I refer, of course, to the question, "after eating": "Simon, son of John, do you love me more than they love me?" (John 21:15-16). Even though he has risen, he must nevertheless go and implore love, human love. He may leave if he is reas-

---

[77] The following is found in a classical Italian commentary by St. Catherine of Siena (1935), 845: "I shall go and return to you, for when the Holy Spirit returned to his disciples, he did not return alone but came with my power, the Son's wisdom (which is one and the same with me) and the clemency of the same Holy Spirit, who proceeds from me, the Father, and the Son."

[78] Cf. González-Faus's expression (1995) 124: *Extra Spiritum nulla salus.*

sured of being loved. He does not ask, "Simon of John, have you understood my message? Have you understood who I am?" We discern an autobiographical (and prophetic) tone even in the reported fact that Jesus was in no condition to go where he would have liked and say what he had dreamed of doing.

> I leave everything to love—and neither to my will nor to projects of any type whatsoever. I must go, simply go, and I leave you with a question: Have I aroused love in you? I entrust my message to you—to you who, like Peter, are not sure of yourselves because of your many betrayals, but you still do love me.

Jesus behaved truly as a servant, not as a *pantokratōr*. Let us also note how the roles are overturned. Jesus neither asks Peter if he repents, nor does he say that he forgives him: he asks if he loves him. It is then that he will be forgiven, for love alone cancels sin: "Her many sins are forgiven because she has loved much . . ." (Luke 7:47).[79] The text's ambivalence constitutes a vital, not a vicious circle. Love leads to forgiveness and forgiveness to love. Listen to what the risen Christ says: "Receive the Holy Spirit: those whose sins you forgive will be forgiven" (John 20:22-23). We have the power to forgive, to cancel the offense only if we love—that is, if we have the Spirit, which is Love. It is the Spirit that enables us to forgive. By ourselves, even with the greatest good will, we cannot do so. But in going away, it is the Spirit that he leaves us.

It is not by chance that we have presented this *mahāvakya* last. One of our reasons for doing so resides in the central dogma of Jesus's life—the resurrection. Unless Jesus leaves, the Spirit will not come and his resurrection will not acquire its full meaning. "Men of Galilee, why are you looking at the heavens?" (Acts 1:11). In a paradoxical sense the text at issue constitutes a discourse on the resurrection. God's children are children of the resurrection (Luke 20:36), and the resurrection reveals the trinitarian life in us. It is good that he leaves; in what other way could we find him risen? The resurrection is the real presence of the absence. "He has risen. He is not here!"—neither here nor there, just like the Kingdom (Luke 17:21).

The Apostle said, *Praedica verbum*, "Preach the word" (2 Timothy 4:2), but Jesus went further: "Become the Word," let your self "continue" the incarnation, a process that does not end with me, for it is indeed in this me that you exist. This is the ultimate meaning of the eucharist. As we have seen, loss of the mystical sense of reality has brought us to confuse the messenger with the message and reduce the latter to a doctrine if not to an outright ideology. The *kerygma* of this and many other texts consists not in

---

[79] Significantly enough, only Luke reports these words.

making speeches but in incarnating a life in the selfsame glorious proclamation of Life in its plenitude.

We have already seen how the scholastic *creatio continua* liberates us
from a fixed and conditioned universe. We must now mention still another
experience that is difficult to communicate because both words and
thoughts fail, as one Upanishad asserts.[80] This experience, which could be
expressed as an *incarnatio continua*, liberates us from living in a merely
historical and temporal universe and makes us conscious of our divine dignity. The Christian incarnation is not an accident, not something that happens by chance in human "nature."

This incarnation is in fact the trinitarian vision of creation. The divine
mystery makes itself flesh, makes itself matter, "creates" not *ex se* but certainly *a se*—since outside of God, there is nothing.[81] (To "create" *ex se*
would constitute pantheism; hence, in dialogue with Plato, we say *ex
nihilo*—without a "prime matter.") We are not inquiring now whether
Christ, the second Adam, assumes nature (in its entirety) or the nature of
man as an individual (in his singularity). We do say that the Word's incarnation in Jesus is the revelation of the mystery that has been hidden since
"the eternal eons" (Romans 16:25), and that in him we see the fullness of
the "last times" (Hebrews 1:2) realized in the head of "creation" (Colossians 1:15-20). The destiny of the head is one and the same as the destiny
of the members, and indeed of the whole universe (Romans 8:19-23).

Although this is not the place to present a "theology" of the eucharist
understood as *incarnatio continua*, we shall refer to it in the third part of
this work as an example of the harmony and coherence of Christian intuitions. Too often the eucharist has been reduced to a private devotion or a
quasi-superstitious act or a disincarnate faith. Surely the church fathers
intended to say something when they spoke to us of the eucharist as "the
medicine of immortality" (φάρμακον ἀθανασίας, *pharmakon athanasias*).[82]

In this sense it seems no exaggeration to assert that this *mahāvākya*
represents the acme of the experience of Jesus the Christ, more or less conscious of being "the splendor of God's glory and the imprint of God's
being" (Hebrews 1:3). In fact, "leaving" on the part of Jesus is a symbol of
the trinitarian *perichōrēsis*, the revelation of the divine—that is, trinitarian—life in the whole of that reality I have called theanthropocosmic or
cosmotheandric, in order to join the Christian tradition, which extends the
expression of the divine glory (Psalm 19:2) to the whole cosmos.

---

[80] "When both word and mind fail because of their inability to teach it (*brahman*), those
who in this fashion know the joy of *brahman* no longer experience any fear" (*Taittirīyaa-
upaniṣad* II, 9; II, 4, 1).

[81] See Panikkar (1966), "Creazione in metafisica indiana," 71-98, esp. 82-83.

[82] *Ad Ephesios* XX, 2 2 (PG 5:661). See my 1952 article "La Eucaristia y la Resurrec-
ción de la carne," in Panikkar (1963) 335-52.

There are not two universes, one divine and the other material.[83] Creation does not exist outside (*extra Deum*) God. Rather, it is a moment, a dimension of the radical trinity. The trinitarian life circulates through the whole universe. "The Father has created everything; everything was in him, and everything desires to know him."[84]

Let us resume our inquiry regarding the profound "reason" for Christ's words. It is necessary that he leave so that the dynamism of Life will not be reduced to an arid dualism. This is the nonduality of which St. Thomas writes explicitly: *Unum idemque actu quo Deus generat Filium creat et mundum* ("By the same act through which God generates the Son he creates the world").[85] This sentence expresses the trinitarian dynamism that is usually defined improperly in an external sense as *ad extra*.

The Christian tradition has seen in Christ the "mediator" (μεσίτης, *mesitēs*), the one who comes from the Father and goes to the Spirit without separating himself from them: the true way that leads to Life. But this mediator is undivided.[86] God's life is trinitarian. For us life comes and goes and does not stop; we exist within this dynamism and live in its passing. Expressed in grammatical terms, Being is a verb, an action, an *actus* in scholastic language, an activity, ἐνέργεια, *energeia*—not a substance. It is good that he leaves, and it is also good that we too leave. He represents the model. Life is a gift, a gift that has been given to us and that we in turn give back; in this fashion we participate in the Father's activity—otherwise we would not be One. "The one who loves *his* life will lose it" (John 12:25), because, as the Buddha would say, this life is transitory.

The Experience

The question we pose now is whether we can understand this statement without either minimizing or diluting it, as well as without transferring Jesus's words into declarations of a sovereign human consciousness. As a normal human being, I ask myself how I can understand what transpires in a human heart that pronounces these words. Do we not call him our brother and friend, as he has told us? Allow me, then, once again to speak in the first person.

---

[83] See Sherrard (1992) esp. 157ff. "The visible universe is God's living body; it is the temple of the living God" (p. 163). This idea is present in many religions which, without falling into pantheism, see God's body in the world.

[84] The *Gospel of Truth*, in Vannucci (1978) 326.

[85] *Summa theologiae* I, q. 34, a. 3.

[86] According to Aquinas, *In filio est esse Paternitatis quia in divinis non est nisi unum esse* ("The being of Father is in the Son because in divine things there is but one being"; *In IV Sententias* I, d. 33. q. 1, a. 1, ad 2).

I must go; otherwise the Spirit will not come. I must not be intent on perpetuating my life because, if I do, Life will be neither continued nor transmitted to others. Everything that I have been, I have experienced, lived and seen, yet it will remain fruitless if I carry it with me into the tomb. I am not the exclusive master of my life, of that Life which has been granted me. If I cling, Life will not flow, will not live. Life has been given us, Rabindranath Tagore has written, and it is only in giving it that we merit it. We have already mentioned John's phrase (12:25), which the other evangelists echo (Matthew 10:39; 16:25; Luke 9:24; Luke 17:33; Mark 8:35), and which, expressed in different words, tells us that we, that I, must not cling to my "life" but, rather, consecrate it to something larger than my ego. It is well that I leave, that we leave. As I go, I leave many of my projects unfinished, many of my aspirations unsatisfied. The longer I live, the more surely I discover what it is that I could have done.

I must not yearn to make myself immortal or worry whether my projects and ideals will be followed to the letter and observed according to my desires. In life we find dynamism, in reality that Spirit of truth which flows from me too, if only I do not enclose myself within myself. This Spirit will pervade others by its own initiative, without any need for me to program myself first. This is what freedom is. "Where the Spirit is there is freedom" (2 Corinthians 3:17). Freedom is the fruit of truth (John 8:32).

Jesus's experience manifests a truly liberated soul, and what this implies is clear: Jesus achieved a total transparency and transcended both the burden of the past and the fear of the future.

Have we not learned that although Lao Tze, Socrates, Śaṅkara, Kant, Gandhi, our ancestors (to give but a few disparate examples) have all gone, their spirit surely has not? To be a man is to be unique for a certain period of time—and then pass the flame to others. Although we all know that we shall leave, a certain wisdom is required to learn that it is good that it be so. Eternity is neither a long nor a definite time. Eternal life is no continuation of living in the future: it is, rather, the infinite life lived in the experience (and also hope) of the "tempiternity."[87] The individual drop that we are disappears in time although the personal water that we are (the drop's water) lives eternally—if, that is, we have succeeded in realizing the (divine) water that we are.[88]

---

[87] There is a fundamental difference (at least in the Greek text) between the words ζωή and βίος (*zōē* and *bios*). The meaning of the first is simply "life," while the second refers to one's individual life. Jesus did not promise *bios* eternal, an individual continuing life, but infinite *zōē*. Christ is the bread of life, the bread of *zōē*, not *bios*. See Kerenyi (1976) XXXI-XXXVII for this distinction in the Greek world.

[88] Panikkar (1980).

The first *mahāvākya* is in a certain sense turned toward the past: the Father exists "before" us, is more powerful than we are: he is the Source. The second statement somehow concerns the present: we are the same in nature and surely are not two. Our bond gives us life and, in fact, constitutes our very existence. The third expression is directed toward the future and toward overcoming its grip on us.

> I must go, I shall surely go, yet I am not sad. I do not burn with a desire for "immortality" as if it were a prolongation of my sheer existence; I do not even yearn for a continuation of my ideals, thoughts, plans, and projects. Those who love "to the utmost" (John 13:1) believe in those whom they love. I do not wish to freeze the flow of Life that springs from the Father and will continue to flow. I share this life, I participate in this adventure, I do not need any heavy baggage. *Consummatum est!* The Spirit will come even though it is not I who will send it, even though I have no power over him and indeed I feel it is not I who sends him. He will come, "The Spirit and the Bride say, 'Come'" (Revelation 22:17).[89] And we who listen repeat, "Come!"
>
> This surely does not mean that I should retire before my time, escape my destiny, refuse to follow my dharma, not accept my karma. I am ready to leave when my time arrives, but not because I am tired of life. We always face the risk of being misinterpreted. The fact that the exact time for us to leave is uncertain seems to me a great lesson of Life, and above all for our contemporary generations, tormented as they are by a desire for certainty and the obsession with security.
>
> This uncertainty, this *not* knowing whether there will be a tomorrow for me, allows me to live the today in all its intensity, as if it were the last and definitive moment. I can then redeem the time (see Ephesians 5:16; Colossians 4:5) and discover the tempiternity in every moment. Every act is unique and unrepeatable. Every day contains life in its entirety. (Matthew 6:34). In this way I live, *not* in the repetition of mechanical acts but in a continuous creation. Nor can I forget that I will take my last step only after the next to the last. It is surely appropriate that every step be unique—and that at a certain moment I will be leaving.
>
> It may well be, of course, that I am not capable of always living at the height of this intuition, although I cannot deny that I do *know* it (in an experiential sense) when I live a truly authentic life,

---

[89] It is both significant and moving to read the text in Revelation as the motto for Sergei Bulgakov's 1933 *Lamb of God*, "a book about Christ's and our theanthropy." It begins with the statement, "The salvation that Christ worked within man's soul, which is more precious than the world" (Bulgakov [Boulgakov] 1982, IX).

free of every ego. I then find a force in myself that is free of the ego, a power (*exousia*) that sends the Spirit into the world: it is the Spirit with which I succeed in identifying myself when my heart is pure.

And there is more. Unless I leave, the Paraclete will not come.

Let us not examine now what is described as the "one called to our side," the "consoler," "intercessor," the "invoked," the "implored." Everything may be summed up in the traditional word "Spirit."

If I cling to life, to my ego, to my mission, to my task, to my ideal, or, even worse, to my goods, to my family, to people, to the world; if I do not let everything go, if I do not renounce every desire to prolong my life (even though I call it immortality) and insist rather on constructing monuments to my creation and aspire to control all that has cost me so much toil to produce so that it might not all get lost, Life will be suffocated. It is not for the future but for the present that I must order my life. I am but transient or, better, a participant in the *perichōrēsis*, the dance of the entire universe, the constant rhythm of everything, of the trinitarian or cosmotheandric unfolding of reality.

I understand the extraordinary experience of Jesus: to be free of thoughts, to overcome the anxiety for the future, learn from the flowers that blossom today and tomorrow will have withered, renounce every fantasizing about the future by living a life always projected toward the future, thereby allowing the tempiternal moments of our human existence to escape us.

It is only then, with neither fear of death nor attachment to existence that we achieve the full freedom to pursue justice at all levels, from "justification" [by faith] to political justice. We then experience the fact that the search for "the kingdom of God" is inseparable from "his justice" (Matthew 6:33). This Kingdom is within *us*—among us; it is not the kingdom of an individualistic me. This is the reason why I do not feel the tragedy of failure, even if the large chariot of "external history" does not seem to travel the right road. It is true that you, Jesus, have suffered abandonment but not despair.

I can well understand that the man of Nazareth experienced sadness but not anxiety, sorrow but not despair. I understand, too, that he experienced a profound serenity not devoid of joy as he felt that it was good for him to leave: he had lived—and lived life in its plenitude. Others might well produce works even greater than his—if they entrust themselves to the Spirit, which lives in each one of us.

Jeshua [Jehoshua] ha nōzeri, Jesus of Nazareth, is about to leave us, all of us are about to leave. He neither lays foundations for anything nor does he initiate any religion. He does not play the role of a teacher, a title that he does not like. His time has arrived and he leaves after accomplishing his mission, which was not, it seems—and this we must acknowledge—a great success. His sole testament is his Spirit, which means that his followers have a perfect right to establish a church, create rites, and continue his work creatively—even at the risk of making mistakes. Theology is not archaeology. Faith does not deal with the past nor hope with the future: they both deal with the invisible (to the senses and mind, but not the intellect).

> To assume my human condition, to become conscious that my time has ended and I must leave, to be convinced that the Spirit must be neither suffocated nor controlled nor directed, constitutes the supreme human experience. The Son of man does not want for himself either exceptions or privileges.
>
> This is the last test I will undergo. I must go. The ego will die and thus make room for the Spirit: this is Life and Resurrection.

The experience of the three *mahāvākyāni* is only one. They do not constitute three experiences, inasmuch as one is interwoven with the other. If they did live separately, they would be false and would then lead to dualism, monism, pantheism, or nothingness.

Even though we feel that "the Father is greater" as we live the experience of the *Abba Patēr!*, we also feel "I and the Father are one." The *Abba* is not outside us. If for one moment the Father should cease to give us life, to "generate" us, it would not only be we who would perish, but he himself, for he would no longer be the Father, that is to say, he who gives life. The source is within us. We are the One, we are the thou that the "I" originates. Expressed in somewhat paradoxical form, the Father gives himself life by giving that same life to us. It is because of us that he is Father, that he is Life.

In addition, the discovery of the One, which comes after seeing the Father, leads to the discovery of the Whole. The Father is not the property of any one person alone. He is the Father because he gives Life to everything, and inasmuch as I am one with him, "I" too am everything. In other words, when the Christian discovers Christ in himself, when he lives the immanence to which he has been invited, he does not discover Jesus (Jesus is the mediator) but he does see the Father ("Philip, he who has seen me has seen the Father"), and becoming God, becomes everything. This kind of knowledge may be described as assimilation without loss of personal differentiation. What we are witnessing here is the mystery of the Spirit.[90]

Within the innermost depths of experience the I is grasped as micro-

---

[90] See the reflections of St. Thomas in *Summa theologiae I, q. 37, a. 2, ad 3: Pater non solum Filium, sed etiam se et nos diligit Spiritu Santo . . . Unde sicut Pater dicit se et omnem creaturam Verbo quod genuit, inquantum Verbum genitum sufficienter repraesentat Patrem et*

cosm. Each of us is not a world in itself, as if a variety of little worlds existed. Each one of us is the unique world in our totality, although miniaturized. And so the Christian tradition has completed the Greek intuition by saying that man is also a *mikrotheos*, a micro-God, not a small God alongside the great God but God, the very Godself. Again, substantializing thought renders the phrase inaccessible, interpreting it atomistically. We are not small Gods.

The Spirit comes when I leave; and as I leave, I leave space for the dynamism of reality. The Father "leaves" into the Son, gives God's whole self and disappears as Father—or rather, disappears as Father if, by virtue of the trinitarian *perichōrēsis* through the work of the Spirit, he did not become resurrected into fatherhood. In the same manner, the Son "leaves," and it is the Spirit that "renews" all things, or rather, brings it about that reality is an "absolute novelty" and not simply a "circular" renewal (Revelation 21:5; 2 Corinthians 5:17). But here all metaphors collapse.

Even the virtually universal experience of love that moved Ibn 'Arabī to exclaim, "The lover, the beloved, the love," reveals one and the same experience. And it is precisely the experience of love that constitutes the key that allows us to enter into this mystery, into the *guhā*, the greatest secret, which is not, however, according to Abhinavagupta, a secret at all, nor is it hidden in any distant, arduous, esoteric place.[91] Light in itself is darkness, cannot be seen, is invisible: in order to become luminous, it needs me, an opaque body. Without me, light would indeed be darkness, and without light I would be nothing.

Among the three *māhvākyāni* there is a gradation. Only when all this is complete and an echo of divine transcendence in its immanence and when I dwell in this presence and that presence is the final cause of my being—and in some way conscious—only after the *Abba, Patēr*, can I say, "I and the Father are one." Only when the light flows like molten metal enveloping the chalk of my skeleton by penetrating all the cavities can I say, I have reached the original, the Christ. Only when my image is completed and my icon painted and consecrated can I reflect the Father. Then those who see me see God in the Spirit that envelops us. Likewise, it is only when this plenitude has been reached that I can say *consummatum est* and discover that it is good that I leave because the Spirit is coming—and continues to come.

---

omnem creaturam; ita diligit se et omnem creaturam Spiritu Sancto, inquantum Spiritus Sanctus procedit ut amor bonitatis primae, secundum quam Pater amat se et omnem creaturam ("The Father loves not only the Son but he also loves himself and us in the Holy Spirit . . . Just as the Father 'speaks' himself and every creature in the Word he has generated inasmuch as that Word represents the Father and every creature, so does he love himself and every creature in the Holy Spirit inasmuch as the Holy Spirit proceeds as the love of the primal goodness whereby the Father loves himself and every creature").

[91] See Bäumer (1988) 53ff. (Sanskrit text, p. 18).

3

The Mystical Experience of Jesus Christ

Jesus says to the disciples: "Compare me, and tell me whom or what I am like." Simon Peter answered him: "You are like a great angel." Matthew answered him: "Master, you are like a great philosopher." Thomas said to him, "Master, my tongue is absolutely incapable of saying whom you are like." Jesus said to him: "I am not your master because you have drunk and you have been inebriated at the bubbling spring that I have measured." Then he took him aside and spoke three words. And when Thomas returned to his companions, they asked him: "What has Jesus told you?" Thomas answered, "If I tell you just one word that he has spoken to me, you would take up stones and throw them at me, fire would come out of the stones and would burn you."

—*Coptic Gospel of Thomas* 13

Eva Me Suttaṃ

"This I have heard," as many Buddhist scriptures say, or also ἤκουσα (*ēkousa*), as Socrates said (*Phaedrus*, 274c).

Once there was a man who came to the world and asserted that he was one with the Origin of the universe, although in fact he was not the Origin; he had come from the Source and he had to return to the Source. He spent the time granted him doing good deeds without any programmatic calculation and did nothing out of the ordinary, though what he did was intense, finished, authentic. He was simply a man who went about without joining any extremist groups, a man wholly disposed to forgive everything but hypocrisy. Moreover, even though he did not discriminate against any group, he always seemed to take the side of the oppressed and the disinherited, and thus he ended his life. Although he saw the Origin that originates everything and suffered the impact of the forces of evil, he had an unlimited faith in the blowing of that wind which he called Spirit and which pervades everything. It was, in fact, the only thing that he left us as our inheritance.

135

He saw himself as Man: Son of Man, *barnasha* (eighty-two times in the Gospels). He loved the name and discovered, for himself and others, that his humanity was nothing other than the face of divinity, inseparable even though distinct, so distinct, in fact, that he, in the form of that humanity, was painfully conscious of the existence of sin. Yet in himself as well as in every other human being, he did not see evil but rather the kingdom of the heavens. This is what he preached and lived.

The man's birth was obscure. He spent a great deal of his life in the shadow, and his death was even more obscure. Yet he never experienced any frustration whatsoever; the moment power tempted him, he despised it; and when he failed he dared to promise his friends that he would really be present, not only through the Spirit but likewise through simple food and drink which they would consume in common. He neither employed violence nor allowed himself to be impressed by power; he preached forgiveness and love and uttered words that, he insisted, did not originate from him. He did not elaborate any doctrinal system: he spoke the language of his time.

"I have also heard" something else. I have heard twenty centuries of reflection on Jesus and dozens of doctrinal systems of every kind. I can neither ignore nor study them all. Great minds have offered us stupendous syntheses. I have learned from many of them. I have also heard of other extraordinary human figures of the past as well as the present. Holiness (if I may use the word), wisdom, and fulfillment may well be a rare plant yet it is a plant that grows in all climates and at all times.

I have also heard of painful controversies and prejudiced confrontations among and between followers and disciples; I have even been compelled to take sides. A phrase I heard came to my help: "He who is not against you is with you"—although the opposite assertion, "He who is not with me is against me," has saved me from literal readings and unchallengeable assertions out of context. The "you" of the community is not the "me" of the Resurrected One who is always present and hidden in every man of good will.

I have heard, furthermore, that we must necessarily practice discernment. This realization has led me to discover the priority of personal experience, thus achieving what a different tradition knows as *nitya-anitya-vastu-viveka* (discernment between the temporal and the eternal—reflected in a famous work by a virtually forgotten Jesuit, Juan Eusebio Nieremberg). Since it is on myself that I must rely, it is on purifying my entire self that I must work. Although the task never ends, it has liberated me from absolutizing my convictions.

I have, moreover, heard so many things that I have been

obliged to listen ever more attentively to the Spirit. And then, if I may return to the theme in part 3, I have simplified everything in a "trinity" of words. It is neither the fear of being stoned nor declared a heretic—I am always ready to make corrections—that restrains me, much less the fear of saying what others prefer not to hear; it is, rather, the impossibility of embodying in words what I have heard. I can only hope that the words will resonate whenever true listening occurs in the depth of the heart where Life vivifies us, while rocks ("the living stones") become fire, purifying everything, and God becomes all in all.

"Itipaśyāmi"

"This I see." The inner life of Jesus reveals a universal experience. History proves it. But it is I too—intensity and purity aside—who am in a position to understand and live that experience. In fact, every human being is able to do so, even though the language and therefore the doctrines may be different, even reciprocally incompatible.

I am not assuming a dialectical position when I assert that I have no hesitation in saying "I am God"—because God has said "I am Man." That would be wrong. What I am doing, rather, is describing my own experience in an intimate, personal way. I simply feel that the divine is in me and, moreover, that I experience the unity that makes my life truly real. Yet I am fully aware how far I still am from that achievement. Paradoxically, the closer I think I am to that ideal, the farther away do I feel. And when I look around me and analyze human history, I understand the anguished question: "How many have achieved salvation, plenitude, fulfillment?" (See Matthew 19:25; Mark 10:26; Luke 18:26). Perhaps the door opens at the last minute—I do not know.

The *kenōsis* of the Son of Man is neither his singular privilege, nor did it occur because he was humble: it occurred because he was Man. Moreover, it is perhaps one of the most pregnant manifestations of the human condition. We are all kenotic, emptied of the divinity that is lodged hidden in each one of us; we are all naked, so to speak, without our most authentic clothing. Even though we all have a divine origin and are temples of divinity, we appear, all of us, not only to others but even to ourselves, as mere individual members of a species subject to suffering and death. Jesus did not hide this situation from us—in fact, it is only a divine person who can reveal so much humanity, a humanity brimming with divinity.

Even though I find it difficult to express, I can surely observe that not only Jesus's life but mine too bears an infinite value precisely because it is limited in form and manifestation. My life is unique and thus beyond comparison; it cannot be compared to or placed on the same plane as anything else. It is precisely in my being finite, being concrete, being contingent that I touch the infinite, the divine.

"I see" that the man of Galilee shared my human condition. It is this sense of uniqueness that constitutes my dignity. Nothing and nobody can take my place precisely because there *is* no substitute for my place in the universe: this is the mystery of man. The Son of Man shows me that I too must fulfill myself as son of man—precisely as man.

Many persons tend to identify themselves with the role they play in society: citizen, politician, worker, physician, farmer, parent, spouse. Religious identifications are even more subtle: Christian, Buddhist, monk, priest, or spiritual roles such as saint, *iguru, saṃnyāsin*. Yet these ways of living neither exhaust our being nor touch the heart of what we essentially are: a microcosm of the whole of reality, the lineage of the *sat-puruṣa*, an icon of divinity. I know the All, the Father, *brahman*, God, and (at the same time) I am a spark, the Son, *ātman,* a creature: the you of the I by virtue of the Spirit. The man Jesus actualized this union, *henōsis*, as Origen defined it (or *anakrasis*, which he distinguished from the hypostatic communion of the incarnation that he called *koinōnia* in *Contra Celsum* III, 41). The early councils defined the union as both completely human and completely divine; and this kind of union constitutes the divine aspect of the human condition that is common to all of us, and which included, naturally, Jesus Christ.

"Sat-puruṣa"

The mysticism of Jesus Christ is simply human mysticism. What else could it be? It is the ultimate experience of man as Man. *Sat-puruṣa* signifies not only an individual or exemplar of the human species but also the plenitude of what we all are. Although we speak of divinization, we must observe that the moment we cease being men, that divinization may turn into alienation. In addition, although we may believe in annihilation, the moment we abandon what we truly are, that annihilation may become evasion. We may indeed accept our humanity, although this too may be synonymous with a passive acceptance of our defeat if we renounce what we truly are or fall into a plain "homocentrism" closed to any form of self-transcendence.

I would dare say Jesus's experience was that pure human experience which, without denying any of them, transcends all kinds of peculiarities. It is only by being concrete that we can become universal. Jesus's experience did not consist in his being a male or a Jew, much less a Christian, a member of a class, a caste, a party, or a religion: it was solely the experience of being man, Son of man. This, his *kenōsis*, made it possible for him to speak to all of us from the depths of our true humanity, from the authentic center of what we truly are. Paradoxically enough, the more we free ourselves from every attribute or role, the more we are ourselves and discover ourselves to be completely human and even more divine.

Insofar as we are human beings, we must leave as individuals. Everyone has left, including Jesus. Insofar as we are divine, after we have left, the Spirit will remain. We do not leave reality deprived of our experience. We have been—forever.

All this may be incompatible with a rigid monotheism. We are not God; God alone is God. But Christ is God's Son, one with the Father inasmuch as the divine mystery is pure gift, donation. In traditional words, the Son is generated and the Spirit proceeds from the Source. The whole universe is engaged in the process. In Christian language, the whole of reality is Father, Christ, and Holy Spirit. It is not only all the divine mysteries but likewise the whole mystery of creation that is held within this Christ—in a process of growth and maturation.

Seen from this level of experience, let us also say that if any follower of Shiva or anyone else should claim that he needs neither Jesus nor even the name of Jesus, the answer is unequivocal: let him indeed go, let him not cling to Jesus, to that name, to that symbol. Otherwise the Spirit will not come "to teach us the whole truth," a truth that in fact reveals to us that nobody possesses a monopoly on personal realization. It is fitting, both for Christians and for others, that Jesus leave. "Why do you call me good?" "The Father is greater than me," or as Marius Victorinus said after his conversion from Neoplatonism to Christianity in 360, "The Father is related to the Son as Nothingness (ὁ μὴ ὤν, *ho mē ōn*) to Being (ὁ ὤν)." It is in the *kenōsis* of our ego that what we really are arises. Meister Eckhart, too, in his treatise *Abgescheidenheit* (*Deutsche Werke* 5:431) cites our third *mahāvākya* to tell us that if we do not detach ourselves even from Jesus's humanity, we will not be given the perfect joy (*volkomene Lust*) of the Holy Spirit.

Every word we employ is loaded with specific connotations, yet if we attempt to describe the mysticism of Jesus the Christ, we could not express it without recourse to words. "The *puruṣa* is everything." A vedic verse recites (*Ṛg-veda* X, 90, 2). Everything depends on how it is interpreted: cosmic man, divine man, perfect humanity. *Ecce homo!* Pilate said. *Puruṣottama*, "the highest man" (see *Bhagavad-gītā* VIII, 1; X, 15; XV, 18-19) is the supreme divine form, *paramaṃ rūpam aiśvaram*, the *Gītā* says (XI, 3, 9).

If I should assert that Jesus Christ is he who has fully realized his human condition, I would only be uttering an empty phrase unless I were to explicate it by adding that this also constitutes our destiny. Were it to be explained outside its proper context, it would constitute, moreover, a limiting assertion—the *paramaṃ puruṣaṃ divyam*, "the supreme divine man," again the *Gītā* says (VIII, 8, 10). We are touching lightly the ineffable.

We cannot understand mysticism in the third person, nor even in the second. But the first person, in order to break the silence, must have someone to talk to. This someone, however, cannot be an imaginary reader: he must be a Thou, an *iṣṭadevatā* who, in turning everything upside down, converts me into a thou. Silence is therefore the final experience inasmuch as it reveals the fact that the Word emerges out of Silence by virtue of Love. The Word, as we have already said, is nothing other than the ecstasy of Silence.

To sum up, the mystery of Christ is the mystery of the whole of reality—divine, human, cosmic, without confusion yet without separation. Christ would not be Christ were he not divine, were he indeed not God. The divine cannot be splintered into parts. Were he not human, were he not the whole of humanity, Christ woud not be Christ. Yet this humanity, distended in time, is not yet nor ever will be finished as long as time is time, and time has no end because the end is itself already temporal. And Life is precisely this novelty or constant creation. Were not Christ corporeal, were he indeed not the whole of coporeality, Christ would not be Christ. Yet this bodiliness or materiality extended in space is not yet nor ever will be finished as long as space is space, since the limit of space is already spatial. Matter is part of reality, together with the other "two" dimensions, in infinite interpenetration. In Jesus Christ Christians see this symbol as a radiant point that, in blinding us, makes us glimpse—and therefore not "see" but rather "feel," "live," enjoy—the experience of Light on Mount Tabor in its totality.

The human tongue must remain silent; every *logos* is insufficient by itself. "It is good that I leave."

Perhaps the most theological expression that corresponds to the philosophical formulation according to which transcendence can be discovered only in immanence is to say—reflecting the patristic tradition—that God can be seen only in the Spirit.

Psalm 36:9 raises a hymn to this truth with extreme simplicity and beauty:

> For with you is the fountain of life
> in your light we see the light.

In the Latin Vulgate:

> *Quoniam apud te est fons vitae*
> *et in lumine tuo videmus lumen*

I now invite the reader to a contemplative pause. In order to grasp the living reality of symbols, we need the third eye.

Part 3

Christophany
The Christic Experience

καὶ αὐτός ἐστιν πρὸ πάντων
καὶ τὰ πάντα ἐν αὐτῷ συνέστηκεν

ipse est ante omnia
et omnia in ipso constant

He is first of all things
and all things subsist in him.
(Colossians 1:17)

Nine *Sūtra*[1]

The problem of Christ has unleashed some of the most profound reflections of the Western mind, not only of professional theologians but also of philosophers, irrespective of the differences in creeds or ecclesiastical communities.[2] Classical theology maintains that in Christ's revelation there is a *novum*, both for the history of humanity and human nature itself. Philosophical thought, on the other hand, tends to say that what theologians are discussing is inherent in human nature, although under different forms. In any case, philosophy seems to have enjoyed the better part and to have virtually swallowed up the *novum* of Christ.[3] We have already spoken of theology as the handmaid of philosophy (*theologia ancilla philosophiae*), despite positions that hold the contrary.

These *sūtra* intend to constitute a middle way between classical theology, which inserts the figure of Christ in a monotheistic frame, more or less qualified, and a theoclastic current that wishes to "free" Christ (and Christianity) from every bond with "God."

I use the word *sūtra* rather than thesis because the deductive method is not valid for the *sūtra*, which speaks to us from within a level of consciousness that must already have been attained before we can grasp its meaning. Human thought cannot be limited—I would say degraded—to the formula induction/deduction, as the predominance of modern scientific "thought" frightens us into believing. No one can deduce an oak from a seed; some of the oak's properties may be derived from its physico-chemical composition but not the oak itself.

These nine *sūtra* are not theses to be defended. They are, rather, condensations of experiences lived (and often suffered) within the framework of tradition. They are "threads" that, along with others, form the texture of reality. It is up to the reader to make a carpet out of them, perhaps even a tapestry. After all, not even the seed is born of itself: it needs the humus in which to ground itself.

These threads should link us to the past and open us to the future.

---

[1] The third part of the book deepens, amplifies, and corrects a hastily published small work entitled *Cristofania* (Bologna: EDB, 1984) and a too radically abbreviated article prepared for a conference and published as "A Christophany for Our Times," *Theology Digest* 39 (1992) 3-21, as well as in Panikkar (1993b) 64-73.

[2] See, among many others, Weischedel (1975), who shows to what extent we find an implicit christology in Western philosophers when they take up the problem of God.

[3] See Duquoc (1977), who, along with many others, confirms our "virtually" by demonstrating Jesus's distance from a certain judaic and hellenistic monotheism, from which, however, he has not liberated himself. There is a brief summary of this theme in Fraijó (1996).

1

Christ Is the Christian Symbol
for the Whole of Reality

Any assertion that says less than this first and crucial *sūtra* cannot do justice to either Christian faith or the experience of virtually all human traditions—though under other names and in different contexts. More or less explicitly, the various cultures of the world claim to possess a coherent cosmovision. Coherence does not necessarily mean the rationality of a logical system as much as the exigency of an ultimate experience, a central symbol. I use the word "symbol" to express an experience of reality in which subject and object, the interpretation and the interpreted, the phenomenon (φαινόμενον, *phainomenon*) and its *noumenon*, are inextricably linked. Symbolic knowledge is irreducible to rational evidence and any kind of dialectic. God, being, matter, energy, world, mystery, light, man, spirit, and idea are examples of such symbols. The symbol symbolizes the symbolized in the symbol itself and is to be found nowhere else. It is different from a simple sign.[1] Those who, faithful to the Enlightenment mentality, confuse the sign, epistemic in nature, with the symbol, ontological in character, could misunderstand this *sūtra* as if it defended a gnostic interpretation of Christ. Nothing could be further from the spirit of this *sūtra*, which employs the word "symbol" in the same sense in which Christian tradition refers to the sacraments.[2]

As the Christian tradition emerged from judaic monotheism and confronted a certain Greek polytheism, on one hand, and philosophical monism, on the other, it has reconquered the most ancient trinitarian tradition concerning reality as Heaven–Earth–Man, or as God–World–Humanity, or even as Spirit–Matter–Consciousness. Christ is that central symbol that incorporates the whole of reality. By this I don't mean to say that the notion of the Christian Trinity (without which the symbol "Christ" loses its full meaning) is the same as that of other religious traditions, since every culture constitutes a symbolic world. I do insist, however, that the

---

[1] Panikkar (1981a).
[2] See Dupuis (1989) 187; and Wong (1984) 624.

experience of reality as trinitarian, though very differently understood, seems to be virtually universal.

Christ is "that light which illuminates all those who come into this world" (John 1:9);[3] "everything has been made through him" (John 1:3), and "in him all things subsist" (Colossians 1:17); "he is the only born" (John 1:18) and "the first-born" (Colossians 1:15); "the alpha and omega" (Revelation 1:8), the beginning and end of all, the "Son of God" equal to God, the *icon* of all reality, the "head of a body" (Colossians 1:18) still "in becoming in the pain of childbirth" (Romans 8:22). The adventure of reality is a spatial and temporal *egressus* ("going out") from God and a *regressus* ("return") to the source, constantly proceeding beyond, to the infinite—by the "work" of the Spirit, which "prevents" reality from becoming duality. The "return" does not carry us back to the point of departure inasmuch as God is not a geometrical point but an *actus purus* (pure actuality, dynamism). This extension (spatial) and distension (temporal) are united in the (human) tension of man as he "grows to the full awareness of Christ" (Ephesians 4:13). "God becomes man so that man may become God," as I have said before, in the light of patristic tradition. This "becoming" is a way that does not lead anywhere else inasmuch as God is everywhere. Jesus's phrase, "I am the way, the truth, and the life" (John 14:6) is not to be understood necessarily in an objective nor even conceptual sense. The *way* is precisely the *truth* of our *life*. Although the meaning of the way does reside in the goal, it is on the road of life itself that the goal is found—and found in every step that is authentic—without the need of quoting Meister Eckhart (*Deutsche Werke* 5:35). We are talking about the symbol "Christ," which Christian culture has often identified as goodness, truth, and beauty.

Here I should comment on the song of Christ of Philippians or the cosmic texts of Colossians, Ephesians, Corinthians, and Romans, or the Book of Revelation, or John's Gospel and even the Synoptics. Christ was "before Abraham" (John 8:58) and will be "the last" (1 Corinthians 15:28). Whatever is done to the smallest and most insignificant is done to him (Matthew 25:40). "In him are hidden all the treasures of wisdom and knowledge" (Colossians 2:3). We are simply remembering—that is, bringing into our minds and hearts, the central point of the Christian understanding of reality, which is precisely "the man Jesus Christ"—"mediator" (1 Timothy 2:5) and not intermediary—that is, "fully divine and fully human," "inseparable yet distinct" from divinity, as later tradition will express.

The cosmovision that prevailed throughout the patristic period, in which the church's chistological consciousness was formed, made the cosmic interpretations of Christ's function plausible. The world of the angels

---

[3] See *Bṛhadāraṇyaka-upaniṣad* IV, 3, 2; 3, 7-8; *Chāndogya-upaniṣad* III, 13, 7-17, for a homeomorphic equivalent of this interior and divine light.

was particularly important. One tenth of the angels were lost (the fallen angels), just as the woman in the Gospel lost one of her silver coins (Luke 15:8-10). This loss was made up by mankind—thereby completing the ten orders of angels. One hundredth of creation—that is, humankind—is lost, as the lost sheep, and Christ, the good shepherd, abandons everything in order to recover man lost in sin. Origen goes so far as to say that "Christ, the whole of mankind—indeed, the whole creation as body, and each one of us—is a member according to the part he plays in creation."[4] Tradition reechoes the scriptures in a free interpretation (Matthew 5:48; Colossians 4:12; James 1:4; 3:2; Philippians 3:12; 2 Corinthians 13:11; Ephesians 4:13; Colossians 1:28), as it speaks to us of the perfect man, τέλειος ἄνθρωπος (*teleios anthrōpos,* "the whole man"), who unites and represents the whole of human nature.[5] And this Christ *is* from the very beginning. St. Jerome fights the heresy of the Ebionites, who assert that "Christ did not exist before Mary" (*Christum ante Mariam non fuisse*), and argues that this is the reason John the Evangelist strongly accentuates Christ's divinity (*De scriptoribus ecclesiasticis,* 9).

Although it is not necessary to accept this vision of the world, we certainly cannot be satisfied with scientific cosmology—which in any case does not wish to entangle itself in "theological" questions. The Christian vision today, however, has lost its foundation inasmuch as it lacks an adequate cosmovision, while theology runs the risk of either engaging in empty talk or being misunderstood. The modern cosmovision has lost a sense of the third dimension.

A nonreductive Christian vision should be able to assert that every being is a christophany, a manifestation of the christic adventure of the whole of reality on its way to the infinite mystery. I repeat, the whole of reality could be called, in Christian language, Father, Christ, Holy Spirit— the *Font* of all reality, *reality* in its act of being (that is, its becoming, the existing reality which is "the whole Christ" (*Christus totus*), not yet fully realized, and the *Spirit* (the wind, the divine energy that maintains the *perichōrēsis* in movement).

It should thus be clear that the homeomorphic equivalent of Christ, in a comparative study, is not that of an *avatāra,* a descent of the divine for the purpose of sustaining the dharma and saving a particular *kalpa* ("eon"; see *Bhagavad-gītā* IV, 7-8). An *avatāra* is not a real being in the world of the *saṃsāra* but a true manifestation of the divine in docetic form. Krishna is not a man; he is a God, a manifestation of God in human form. Christ, in the eyes of the Christian church, is neither a member of the pantheon nor a realized, divinized individual; his divinization is not an accident. Christ is

---

[4] PG 12:1330A; see von Balthasar (1938) 399.

[5] See Haas (1971) 52-63, who summarizes the patristic conception and gives us a pertinent bibliography.

the very incarnation of God, his first-born, to cite anew a different tradition: *pūrvo hi jataḥ (Śvetāśvatara-upaniṣad* II, 16).

Let us note again that, within a monotheistic theology, the incarnation is nothing but an accident in God and represents, to say the least, a great difficulty. The Absolute cannot become man—nor can anything else. Within a trinitarian vision, however, the centrality of Christ with respect to the whole of reality is a direct consequence of the incarnation. It is not christocentrism precisely because the Trinity has no center and nothing human and created stands outside that Word through which all things were made—intuitions that have been expressed in many traditions. Meister Eckhart is not the only one to assert that the dignity of man originates in the incarnation.

The assertion that "there is no salvation outside of Christ" is almost a tautology. Salvation means full realization or, in traditional terms, divinization, and divinization occurs only in union with the divine—whose symbol in Christian language is Christ. If this *theōsis* is not an illusory aspect but a real "participation in the divine nature" (2 Peter 1:4), it is realized only if we become one with Christ—that is, if we become part of the *Christus totus* so as to be *ipse Christus* (Christ himself). This is what St. Paul suggests when he attempts to interpret the Gospel's invitation to be perfect like the Father who is in heaven. That "mystery that has been kept secret for long ages" (χρόνοις αἰωνίοις, Romans 16:25) is what Christians understand as Christ. Christ is human and divine without confusion of the two natures and nevertheless, without rupture of any kind.

When we say that "Christ is the symbol of the whole of reality," we intend to say that not only are "all the treasures of divinity" included in Christ, but that "all the mysteries of man" as well as the thickness of the universe are also hidden in him. He is not only the "first-born" but the "only begotten," the symbol of reality itself, the cosmotheandric symbol par excellence.

As the symbol of the whole divinization of the universe, Christ is the *theōsis* of the Greek fathers.[6] The Roman liturgy for centuries has chanted, *Per ipsum, cum ipso, in ipso* ("Through him, with him, in him") all the dimensions of reality meet and "all things hold together in him" (Colossians 1:17). The whole universe is called to share the trinitarian *perichōrēsis*, in and through Christ. Some speak of the cosmic Christ, others of the *Christus totus*. I would prefer to call him the *cosmotheandric Christ*, or simply the Christ.

I close this first *sūtra* with a text of St. Bonaventure that sums up the tradition of the past and contains an intuition that is also valid for the future:

---

[6] See Gregory Nazianzen, *Oratio* XXV, 16 (PG 35:1221); ibid., XXXIX, 16 (PG 36:353); John Damascene, *De fide orthodoxa* III, 17 (PG 94:1069); ibid. IV, 18 (PG 94:1184); Cyril of Alexandria, *De trinitate* XIV (PG 77:1152).

Respice ad propitiatorem et mira,
quod in ipso principium primum iunctum est cum postremo,
Deus cum homine sexto die formatum (Genesis 1:26),
aeternum iunctum est cum homine temporali,
in plenitudine temporum de Virgine nato,
simplicissimum cum summe composito
actualissimum cum summe passo et mortuo,
perfectissimum et immensum cum modico,
summe unum et omnimodum cum individuo composito
et a ceteris distincto,
homine scilicet Jesu Christo.

Look at the propitiator and admire, because in him
the first principle is joined to the last,
God with man formed the sixth (last) day (of creation),
The eternal is joined to the temporal man
born of the Virgin in the fullness of time(s),
the simplest with the most composite,
the most real with him who suffered and died,
the most perfect and immense with the small,
the absolutely one and multiform with an individual composite
and distinct from others:
that is the man Jesus Christ.
            —St. Bonaventure, *Itinerarium mentis in Deum* VI, 5

2

The Christian Recognizes Christ *In* and *Through* Jesus

It is known that "Christ" is a Greek name that translates the Hebrew word *mashiah*, which simply means "anointed." The generic meaning of this word has acquired a specific connotation within Judaism: the Messiah awaited by the people of Israel. Later the specific Hebrew meaning was again transformed and individualized in the Christian tradition, as it came to mean Jesus, Mary's son. This Jesus, "a prophet powerful in works and words before God and the whole people" (Luke 24:19), became for Christians the revelation of Christ that was mentioned in the first *sūtra*. Christians gradually stopped competing with the Jews and abandoned the pretension that Jesus was Israel's Messiah. The name of Christ assumed a new meaning, although it was still capable of arousing tensions and perplexities.

The Christian revolution manifested itself in the First Council of Jerusalem, which abolished circumcision (Acts 15:1ff.), the primordial pact of God with the Jewish people. This revolution consisted not in supplanting the Jewish Messiah with a condemned Jew but in recognizing in Jesus the man in whom "the whole fullness of divinity lives corporeally" (Colossians 2:9), and the revelation of the "heir of all things . . . who sustains the whole universe with his word of power" (Hebrews 1:3).

In the Christian vision Jesus does not compete with the Hebraic Messiah. The Christian transformation does not consist in affirming that Jesus is the Hebrew Messiah—the reticence of Jesus himself should indicate this with utmost clarity. It consists, rather, in proclaiming that in Jesus "the mystery that has been kept secret" since the beginning has now revealed itself (Romans 16:25), and that "through him all things have been created" (Colossians 1:16).

In other words, it is in Christian revelation that the Christian discovers the living Christ through whom the universe was made (John 1:3; Colossians 1:16). He who believes that "Jesus is the Christ" is a Christian. The existential confession manifests the salvation of whoever professes it. It is a confession, an existential affirmation, not an objective or objectifiable phrase. Nobody is saved by uttering a simple theoretical phrase (for example, the Pythagorean theorem), or a statement of fact (King Aśoka existed), or even a prayer ("Lord, Lord"). The confession of his name is the same as the personal testimony of having encountered the reality which the name reveals. This is the reason why his name is "a name that saves," and "there is no other name under the sky through which we can attain salvation" (Acts 4:12; cf. Philippians 2:9-10).

Nobody can say "Jesus is Lord" (*Kyrios Iēsous*) except through the Holy Spirit (1 Corinthians 12:3). *Jesus is the Christ*: this is the Christian *mahāvākya* (great assertion). In fact, Christian tradition has joined the two in one sole name. Jesus Christ as undivided experience constitutes the central Christian dogma. The copula "is" collapses: otherwise, it would introduce an epistemic split of the unity of that experience.

It is interesting to observe that the expression employed in the sacred texts is not only "Jesus Christ" but also "Christ Jesus,"[1] although we do find a homology and must not push this argument beyond its limits. In any event, this inversion bears a profound meaning: it confirms distinction on the one side and equivalence on the other. Christ is certainly not Jesus's surname.

Jesus is the one whom "the Spirit of the Lord" has consecrated with unction (anointed, Messiah, Christ, ἔχρισεν, *echrisen*; see Luke 4:18). This is what he sought to make the inhabitants of Nazareth understand during his first period of preaching, citing the prophet Isaiah (61:1). The relation between Jesus and the Christ was elaborated later by means of the Council of Chalcedon's four adverbs: ἀσυγχύτως, ἀτρέπως, ἀδιαιρέτως, ἀχωρίστως (*asynchytōs, atrepōs, adiairetōs, achōristōs*; Denzinger, 302), which Latin tradition renders as *inconfuse, immutabiliter, indivise, inseparabiliter* ("not confused," "immutable," "undivided," and "inseparable").

The trinitarian background within which this way of understanding the central reality of Christ makes sense: Jesus Christ cannot be God without qualification. He must be God of God, Light of Light, God's Son, the Father's first-born, only-begotten (*prōtotokos, monogenēs*). And this Christ is acknowledged as one sole person in which the two natures subsist "in an unconfused, immutable, undivided, inseparable way." We need these four adverbs (not adjectives) in order to have an enlightened faith, to accomplish that requirement of "spiritual worship" (τὴν λογικὴν λατρείαν, *tēn logikēn latreian, rationabile obsequium* of Romans 12:1), as tradition has interpreted it.

I underscore the *in and through* of this *sūtra* in order to avoid possible misunderstanding: Jesus is Christ, but Christ cannot be identified completely with Jesus of Nazareth.

---

[1] For "Jesus Christ," see, e.g., Matthew 1:1; John 17:3; Acts 2:38; 3:6; 8:37; 9:34; Romans 1:6, 7; 13:14; 1 Corinthians 1:1-3, 9-10; 8:6; 16:22; Colossians 3:17. For "Christ Jesus, see, e.g., Acts 5:42; Romans 1:1; 15:16; 8:1; 1 Corinthians 1:2, 30; 9:1; Galatians 3:14; 4:14; Ephesians 1:1; 2:20; 3:21; Philippians 2:5; 3:3; 3:12; 4:7; Colossians 1:2; 1 Timothy 1:2; 3:13; 4:6; 2 Timothy 1:2; 4:9; 2:3; 3:15; Titus 1:4; Philemon 6; 2 John 1:3.

The misunderstanding derives from the unwarranted extrapolation of the modern scientific method applied to a reality that cannot be reduced to an algebraic formula that can be written on the blackboard. If A is B, B is A. But neither is Jesus A nor Christ B. The result, *pars pro toto* ("the part for the whole"), which in this context refers to symbolic knowledge, in our *sūtra* is applied to the *iconophanic* consciousness: the icon A is not the original of B, much less is it a simple image. Seen in the light of Mount Tabor, the icon is revelation, the unveiling of the original, the symbol that represents it, that makes it present to those who discover it as icon and not as copy. Jesus is the symbol of Christ—for Christians, obviously.

As for what concerns us, the eucharistic example would suffice. The eucharist is the real presence of Christ, of the resurrected Christ (but does not contain the protein of Jesus of Nazareth).

The confession "Jesus is the Christ" presupposes a very concrete conception of history and matter and a particular anthropology, because Jesus is indubitably a corporeal reality and a true man. To assert that "the Jesus of history," Mary's son, is "the Christ of faith," the Christ of our first *sūtra*, is precisely what constitutes the scandal of Christian concreteness.

However, the Christian scandal remains a scandal not only for others but for Christians themselves. This is the reason why to speculate about "Christian folly" and criticize non-Christians because they cannot understand and accept the greatness of Christianity—as if Christians were capable of understanding it!—signifies not only a deplorable pride but an apostasy as well. The cross cannot constitute a weapon against others. As Paul exclaims, "In that case the scandal of the cross has been removed" (Galatians 5:11).

This is the reason why the confession "Jesus is the Christ" is constitutively open. The predicate of the proposition is a mystery, even though the subject is a concrete historical figure, Mary's son, the Jeshua who, faithful to his name *Jeho-shua* ("God is salvation") "has done all things well" καλῶς, *kalōs*, Mark 7:37). Using a bold metaphor, it has been said, "whoever enters into contact with the *logos* touches Jesus of Nazareth," because "in Christ God's being enters into unity with man's being."[2] Or, as more than one council has said, Christ assumes human nature, "as there is not, nor was, nor will be any man whose nature has not been assumed in him [Christ], so there is not nor was not, nor will be any man for whom he has not suffered" (*Sicut nullus homo est, fuit vel erit, cuius natura in illo assumpta non fuerit, ita nullus est, fuit vel erit homo, pro quo passus non fuerit;* Synod of Quiercy in 835; see Denzinger, 624). This statement echoes the entire patristic and medieval tradition.[3]

This second *sūtra* asserts that the Christian encounters Christ in and through Jesus. It is a personal meeting, an "existential touch." At the same

---

[2] Ratzinger (1993) 707.
[3] See the discussion of Eckhart's similar thesis in Haas (1971) 26ff.

time it is necessary to return to the *gnōsis* of Christian tradition, in which "experiential knowledge" often recurs in the writings of Paul and John. This is in conformity with both Hebrew and Greek traditions, as well as all those human cultures in which knowledge is an ontological activity and not a simple epistemological operation. "This is eternal life, that they know you, Jesus Christ" (John 17:3). This salvific knowing is something more than a conviction of the mind or a doctrinal affirmation. Neither Christian nor the *vedic gnōsis* is gnosticism—which occurs when *gnōsis* becomes purely epistemic.

3

The Identity of Christ Is Not
the Same as His Identification

Modern nominalistic and scientific methods of approaching reality have so infiltrated theological thought that the question about *what* an individual is becomes confused with *who* that person is. Despite such nominalism, having understood a concept leads many to believe that they have grasped the thing. It is significant that the very "individuality" of an elementary particle should become problematic even in theoretical physics. According to Werner Heisenberg's widely known theories, we can now record the discovery that the observer always modifies what is being observed. It is surprising that this fact has been forgotten by modern philosophers, who conceive thought as only an epistemological reflection (the thing's image) and not an ontological activity (the action of being itself). This is the price that has been paid when the third eye or the mystical vision has been eliminated from philosophy. Thought about reality is not, in fact, a simple mirroring of reality but an action on it—nor are we referring only to parapsychological facts, much less magic, but to the spiritual life as well, to prayer and our entire psychic life. In brief, the Cartesian coordinates help us to identify a phenomenon but not to know the identity of the event. Perhaps it will be useful for me to repeat briefly what I have said above in part 2 of this book.

Although identity and identification cannot be separated, they are not the same thing. A boy, for example, may be identified by the police as intent upon taking drugs. Although his identity is that of the boy his parents know and *love*, his identity cannot be separated from the police's identification. In an analogous way, we can know the objective identification of Jesus. He was born and died at a specific time and place and left sufficient signs to make it possible to identify him. We are certain that we are referring to a precise individual. We can know all this, but his true identity may still escape us. As in the example of the boy, in order to know the identity of a person, love is required.

As I have said, Peter discovered the thou of Christ in his famous answer to the question about Jesus's identity (Matthew 16:13-20; Mark 8:27-30; Luke 9:18-21). The apostle answered with the titles at his disposal. Jesus is identified as "the Messiah, the Son of the living God" (words that his teacher told him not to make public). Nevertheless, Peter was called blessed, not because he had given an exact answer but rather because he had discovered the thou, the profounder identity of Christ, which required revelation on God's part. I abstain from giving an *upanishadic* understanding of Peter's answer, but its essence was "Thou art" (*tvam asi*). In this context it is enough to underscore the discovery of the personal "you" in the meeting with Christ. This discovery is the work of "neither flesh nor blood," nor calculation nor feeling.

The difference between identity and identification can explain Jesus's reticence in revealing his own identity. Whoever has experienced the unbridgeable abyss of the "I" will feel the necessity of keeping his own identity veiled, revealing it only to those for whom the subject–object division is overcome—that is, to those one loves, to the innocent (see Matthew 11:25-27; Luke 10:21). Jesus answered neither Herod nor Pilate.

Too often christologies have concentrated on the identification of Jesus. They have forgotten that identity is not an objectifiable category and have proceeded to project into different contexts the identity of Jesus Christ, which was discovered in a particular cultural situation. The predicate will never lead us to know the subject fully. "S is P" is not identical with "S is"; and this last formulation is not identical with "S," as Buddhist thought emphasizes. For example, the assertion that Jesus is Messiah is destined to be both misunderstood and alienating in India. India does not belong to the lineage of Abraham. Nor is the identity of a person the sum of his attributes: on the contrary, attributes serve to identify a person.

The corollary of this point is the specific ontological and epistemological status of theology and philosophy, inasmuch as Christian theology is only a particular field of philosophic activity. Except in certain periods like the "Enlightenment," philosophy has never pretended to be an exclusive work of reason (*opus rationis*). If philosophy is the name that signifies man's intention to discover the meaning of life and reality through every means *we believe* we can utilize, then it is the intellectual (and not only rational) companion of the wisdom of life directed toward salvation, whether one calls it realization, liberation, or something else. Philosophic meditation is the conscious companion of man's pilgrimage on earth, and this pilgrimage is religion.

If a contemporary reflection on Christ is to be faithful to the real—and not only conceptual content—it must reflect Christ and not limit itself to the exegesis of texts; it must seek the identity of Christ and not be content with his identification. Now the fact of approaching a knowledge of Christ's identity implies an attempt to know both his self-consciousness to the extent that it is possible and our experience of faith to the extent to which experience permits an intelligible reflection. "Who do the people say that I am?" (Mark 8:27). This is what I have sought to answer in part 2.

In terms of religious phenomenology, the neologism *pisteuma* (from the Greek word *pistis*, "belief") complements the *noēma* (from the Greek word *nous*, "mind") of Edmund Husserl's phenomenology. While the latter is a content of human consciousness purified of any extrinsic connotation through the *eidetic* intuition, the former is an enlightened and critical consciousness in which the believer's faith is not bracketed in the phenomenological *epochē*. What the believer believes (the *pisteuma*), and not what the observer thinks (the *noēma*), is the aim of religious phenomenology.

The relation between identity and identification presents a particular tension in Christian history. If the *who* of Christ is "his divine person," Christian spirituality will tend to be in tune with Neoplatonism and will rise to the mystical heights of a Dionysius the Areopagite, of Christian *gnōsis*, or the ideas of Pierre Teilhard de Chardin, to offer some examples. If the *who* of Christ is "his human nature," Christian spirituality will tend to be in tune with the living and loving Jesus and will develop the nuptial mysticism of Bernard, Catherine, or Teresa, to cite some examples. We speak of tension, not a split, because the great Christian figures have maintained the creative polarity between the human and divine dimensions. Appropriately, it was Origen who first wrote a Christian commentary on the Song of Songs; John of the Cross, the disciple of Teresa, the great lover of the humanity of Jesus, penetrated the depths of his divinity, where nothing more exists; in his *Summa theologiae* Thomas Aquinas cites Dionysius more than anyone else; William Law was converted by reading Jakob Böhme. In recalling the last verse of the *Divine Comedy*, "the love that moves the sun [of the intellect] and the other stars [of the heart]," we are reminded that *bhakti* ("devotion") and *jñāna* ("knowledge") cannot be separated, as the medieval mystic Jñāneśvar has shown so magnificently.

The identity that is discovered in a personal encounter must accept the criteria of identification and thus must seek to discover the identity, which in turn confirms that the identification is correct. The devil, after all, can quote scripture to his advantage (Matthew 4:6). Even the angel of light that pretends to be Christian (and believes he has achieved identity) can conceal the same demon. And let us remember that the personal meeting we have mentioned is not to be understood in the sense of a two-dimensional anthropomorphism.

4

Christians Do Not Have a Monopoly on the Knowledge of Christ

If faith in the mystery of Christ transcends but in no way denies or contradicts the manifestation that takes place in Jesus, reflection on the acts of Jesus, including the Christian experience of Christ, does not exhaust the richness of the reality Christians cannot but call Christ.

"The name above all names" (Philippians 2:9, τὸ ὄνομα τὸ ὑπὲρ πᾶν ὄνομα, *to onoma to hyper pan onoma*) also stands above the name of Jesus. It is a "supername," a name present in every authentic invocation. It is surprising that the hymn in which it appears (Philippians 2:5-11, which does not recognize any distinctive property right to the point of praising the *kenōsis* as the self-emptying of Christ Jesus), should have been understood as a justification for Christians to appropriate to themselves the one who so "emptied himself" as to "accept obedience and death on the cross"— v. 8. It is a paradox that Christians should fight to make exclusive that "no other name" precisely of the one who renounced all names and emptied himself even of human dignity by assuming the form of a slave—which at the time meant someone deprived of every right.

My book *The Unknown Christ of Hinduism* (1964) was dedicated to the unknown Christ as a parallel to the "unknown God" of whom St. Paul speaks (Acts 17:23). However, the book has at times been misunderstood as if it were speaking of the Christ known to Christians and unknown to Hindus.

The "unknown Christ of Hinduism" is unknown a fortiori to Christians. And Hindus have no need to call him by the Greek name. Similarly, calling the Christ "Messiah" in the Judaic sense would be going astray, attributing to the same name of Christ homeomorphic equivalences of other religions. Just as a unique relation exists between the Hebrew *mashiah* and the *Christos*, so too there are relations that have not yet been brought to light between Christ and homeomorphic equivalents in other religious traditions. But the relation must occur from both sides. Thus, for example, although from a Judaic-Christian-Islamic point of view we can speak of a cosmic testament that refers to other religions, it is not enough to use this concept without listening to how the Christ is seen in other cultures.[1]

No religion that is lived in depth will be content with representing a part of the whole. It will rather yearn for the whole, even if in a limited and imperfect way. Every religion wishes to show a path to "realize" reality, and reality is whole. But every person and every religion participates in, enjoys, arrives at, lives in that whole in a limited way. Nobody has a monopoly on the whole, and no one can completely satisfy the human thirst for the infinite and content herself with a part of the whole. Once again, we apply an inadequate method if we limit ourselves to quantifying and calculating when we treat such vital problems. The whole exists in every *iconophany*, but it does so "as in a mirror and in a dark manner" (1 Corinthians 13:12).

The fact that Christians do not have full knowledge of the symbol they call Christ shows that they are not masters of Christ and confirms that Christ transcends all understanding. If, in Christian language, Christ is the savior of humanity and the redeemer and glorifier of the cosmos, we must again ask who this Christ is. We need to explain how the mystery Christians call Christ is manifested in other religions. Although the latter do not speak of Christ, they possess different symbols to which they attribute a salvific function, which, in a homeomorphic sense, is equivalent to the function of Christ. Christians assert that, even though unnamed and unknown, it is Christ who exercises this salvific function. Is it a question, then, of the same unique Christ?

The question requires a threefold answer. First, *from a philosophic point of view*, a given answer depends on the question itself: there is no answer that is universally and "objectively" valid. Every answer depends on the precomprehension of the question itself, which delineates the context in which the answer takes place. Moreover, when the question regards the ultimate problem, we cannot apply the more or less crypto-Kantian idea of a "thing in itself," named "the self-same Christ." The self of "Jesus Christ, yesterday, today, and throughout the centuries" (Hebrews 13:8), is an ever-new present, a constant new creation (see 2 Corinthians 5:17). The mystery of Christ is not, in terms made familiar by Kant, a *Ding an sich* (a thing in itself).

I have already mentioned different parameters of intelligibility; I must add that the philosophical problem is inescapable. When there is reference to Jesus of Nazareth, what are we talking about? About a man, the son of a Jewish woman who lived centuries ago and was followed by a small group of disciples who left written testimonies about him, and who then spread throughout the whole earth—and also left behind a jungle of interpretations of his very personality. Jesus was certainly a historical person who lived in a specific period in history. But who was this man? Is history

---

[1] In this sense we should complement Dupuis (1997).

the decisive factor of reality? What is man? Certainly more than a body, and even more, perhaps, than a soul. Again, what does body, what does soul mean? To limit the human person to being an exemplar of the race of anthropoids in time and space is to remain within a reductionistic anthropology. Are we certain that a historical biography and a reading of his writings are sufficient to reveal who Rajagopalachari really was—which includes, perhaps, that he was more than a statesman of India's independence? If we think that a person's reality is one and the same as his historical existence, we are eliminating a priori any answer that does not include the person's historical dimension and context. If, moreover, we believe that what a person thinks of herself does not touch her being, we are already presupposing an answer conditioned by a contemporary understanding of objectivity. These problems indicate that the very subject of christophany depends on the conception we have formed of the subject in question. While this study does not intend to negate Jesus's historicity, neither does it accept a priori the presupposition that a person's historicity exhausts his whole being.

To speak of a historical (that is, real) being and to believe that this is the way man can be understood presupposes that historical existence is the formal constitutive of the person and that the person is an individual.

Second, *from the point of view of other religions*, the answer to the question whether the matter being treated is "the self-same Christ" under different names, is decidedly no. These religions possess a self-understanding and validity that they can sustain with arguments based on their experience; they have no need of employing any Christian parameters but will use their own categories of understanding and will interpret the other religions of the world, including Christianity, on their own terms. Christ neither is nor has any reason for being their point of reference. Of course, Buddhists may be called "anonymous Christians" on condition that Christians are seen as "anonymous Buddhists." Nevertheless, there is a difference: while for Christian self-understanding the discourse of the anonymous Christian can have a certain meaning, for a large part of the Buddhist world an anonymous Buddhist is an unnecessary hypothesis since no comparable problem exists.

This requires a change of perspectives for Christians, because a true understanding among the various religions can never be a one-way street. The whole effort to understand what Christians call Christ within the sphere of other religions must be related to the problems that concern the nature of the *Buddha*, the *Qur'an*, the *Torah*, the *Chi*, the *Kami*, the *Dharma*, and the *Tao*, as well as *Truth, Justice, Peace*, and many other symbols. What Christ represents in other religions is to be confronted with the complementary question of what the other symbols might represent within Christianity. It would then be possible to find a common ground in which dialogue may become fruitful.

I do not intend to assert that every name that is evoked might represent "the self-same Christ." Such names may be, at best, homeomorphic equivalents—although it is not necessary that such equivalents exist. We should respect pluralism in the sense that, within this perspective, incompatibility and incommensurability become possible—something that excludes neither dialogue nor the defense of each person's own beliefs.

Third, *from the perspective of Christian reflection*, the answer is affirmative, though qualified. It is affirmative in the sense that Christ—symbol of reality's ultimate mystery—implies a certain aspiration for the universal, which is common to virtually all religions. Everything that has been said that is true, both Buddhists and Christians say, is respectively Buddhist and Christian.[2] In the view of Islam, before society confines one within a particular religion, every person is born a Muslim. Here is the same human syndrome that cannot easily accept the fact that its own truth is not objective and universal.[3] Reservations, on the other hand, regard the fact that every culture can understand only in the light of its own parameters of intelligibility which, moreover, cannot be uncritically extrapolated. In addition, we cannot answer the question of whether or not we are dealing with the same Christ, because the "unknown Christ" of other religions is truly unknown to Christians who, in any event, possess no other name to designate him. In order not to make Christ a sectarian figure Christians speak of an unknown Christ. When they refer to the ultimate mystery, other religions legitimately use other languages and thus prevent Christian language from becoming a universal language.

There are two difficulties in accepting this *sūtra*'s intelligibility. The first, which I have already sought to clarify, arises when we identify Christ and Jesus; the second, when we turn Christ into a substance. This is the same difficulty we encountered when the Trinity is thought of as a substance.

This *sūtra*, which is clear enough if we listen to the sacred texts about Christ, is likewise the fruit of the human experience that faith makes possible. Nevertheless, it has often been received with a certain reticence, on one hand, because the mystical dimension in Christian life and theology has been forgotten, and on the other, because of the thought patterns (the *forma mentis*) of the Mediteranean people. This mentality is, above all, sensitive to differences and considers "the specific difference" to be the essence of a thing. In contrast, let us consider the form of thought of the *Chāndogya-upaniṣad* and, more specifically, the introduction to the greatest *mahāvākyāni* ("maxims") in the vedic tradition so as to see a different form through which one reaches the intelligibility of a thing or an event. The prevalent form for reaching intelligibility in modern Western culture is based on classification and differences. In the Hindu mentality, as I have tried to explain elsewhere, intelligibility rests on identity.

---

[2] See the inscriptions of Aśoka; Lamotte (1958); Justin, *Apologia* II, 13 (PG 6:465).
[3] See Panikkar (1990).

In this brief philosophical digression, I have tried to explain why, because of the *forma mentis* of the primacy of differentiation for so many centuries, Christian thought believed that Christ's identity would be lost if it abandoned the specificity that differentiates it. A further deepening of this hypothesis could be of great importance for the Christian thought of the next millennium.

5

Christophany Transcends Tribal and Historical Christology

The fifth *sūtra* constitutes another corollary to the discovery that Christ is not absolutely identical with Jesus. For Christians, Jesus is the means through which we gain access to salvation. He is the way that leads to the Father (God, salvation, fullness, realization), a way that is authentic life itself (John 14:6). Christians in general believe that Jesus is also the life for others. They must, however, acknowledge that they do not know how this is, because this Jesus does not appear in this way in the eyes of others. The latter often have a very vague idea of who he might be and no interest in being saved by him, for they admit that salvation is a notion sufficient for expressing the different homeomorphic equivalents concerned the meaning and end of human life. Should Christ save them, he would do so only in an anonymous way. This is the first consequence, on which I have already commented, of the fact that Christians do not possess an exhaustive knowledge of Christ.

Another consequence is that the figure of Christ has been forged almost exclusively in dialogue with Mediterranean cultures. This is why I sometimes use provocative language and speak of the tribal christology that has prevailed for the past two thousand years of Christian history, and that has been almost exclusively centered on its own interests, accompanied by a sad indifference to other human experiences. What has been practiced has been a christology for private use (*ad usum nostrorum tantum*)—that is, for the internal use of Christians, perhaps even for aiding to conquer the world. "Who do men say is the son of man?" Jesus asked (Matthew 16:1-3). The first Christian generations opened themselves to a dialogue with Syrians, Persians, Ethiopians, Greeks, Romans, and even "barbarians."[1] But once they developed an answer, they ceased referring to the other civilizations with which they came into contact. Instead, they created the *Congregatio de propaganda fide* in 1622 and diffused only their own answer.

---

[1] The Goths, Visigoths, Ostrogoths, and other European "immigrants" were all called "barbarians" by the Romans. What these people called a "migration," Romans called an "invasion."

They did not imitate their Teacher by asking once again, "Who do the people"—the Buddhists, the Hindus, the Africans—"say the son of man is?"

The majority of scholars today agree that for about two thousand years Yahweh, the God of the Hebrews, was a tribal God, one among many others, often more powerful or in any event equally cruel. A long and painful evolution was necessary, above all with the help of the great prophets of Israel, to convert the Hebrews' tribal God into the God for all and of all. The task of Christians—perhaps our *kairos*—may be the conversion—yes, conversion—of a tribal christology into a christophany less bound to a single cultural current.

I would like to pay homage to the idea of tribe. Westerners have attributed to it, and to so many words that refer to different civilizations and religions, a certain contemptuous meaning. To begin with, tribe is more primordial than the idea of a people. The idea behind tribe is not just ethnic. Christian ethnocentrism is on the way to becoming transcended, at least in theory. But the tribal vision has more profound roots. It is neither a strictly biological entity like the family nor purely political like the state; it is eminently historical and telluric—even chthonic, and related to the underworld. Here we encounter a very important and delicate problem. Although a tribal christology is not necessarily completely illegitimate, christophany cannot be reduced to it.

When I say that history is the modern myth of the West, I am not asserting that history is a "myth" in the all-too-common meaning of the word, but that historical events are seen as the horizon in which the real is manifested in such a way that the historical Jesus is identified with the real Jesus. If Jesus of Nazareth were not a historical personage, he would lose all his reality.

Christophany does not contest the historicity of Jesus. It merely affirms that history is not the only dimension of the real and that Christ's reality is thus not exhausted with Jesus's historicity.

Christophany's transcendence of historical christology belongs to the cultural moment in which we live.

Before our so-called modernity—centered in an anthropocentric ontology and concentrated on epistemological problems—emerged, traditional christology did not ignore the role of Spirit even though, inevitably, it expressed itself within a Ptolemaic cosmovision. Once the Copernican cosmography, in which there was no place for angels and spirits—and not even for God, who at most may be a transcendent engineer on sabbatical leave—prevailed, Christ's cosmic and universal function was reduced to the human world, and this became identified with the history of humankind. This is evident even in Vatican II, which did not wish to be either antimodern or anti-Semitic (problems that the church urgently needed to confront). But that council did not know how to overcome the parameters of the Enlightenment [rationality]. The council, therefore, presented the church as "the people of God" in imitation of the "chosen people of Yahweh," Israel. The cosmovision of the council thereby effectively forgot the angelic and cosmic dimension of reality and ignored the perspectives of other cultures. We should remember that, according to the most ancient tradition, accepted without question until Peter Lombard's *In IV Sententias* (II, d. 9, c. 6), Christ redeems even the fallen angels. Similarly, the "restoration of everything in Christ" (the *apokatastasis pantōn* of Acts 3:21), the "recapitulation" (*anakephalaiōsis*) of everything in Christ (Ephesians 1:10), and other great affirmations of scripture speak to us of a cosmic Christ, the alpha and omega of the whole divine adventure of reality. Nor should we forget that Jesus's life was a constant battle with devils, that he remained in the desert with animals and angels (see, e.g., Mark 1:13), and that the first thing he did after the resurrection was to "descend into hell" (Denzinger, 16; 27-30 and *passim* in the Creeds).[2]

The legitimate preoccupation with not breaking totally with Jesus's Hebrew roots and not abandoning monotheism—because the alternative of a "pagan polytheism" was considered even worse—led to the reduction of Christ to a universal Messiah and a special son of God. Although the concept of the Trinity was a necessary premise for understanding the incarnation, the trinitarian experience did not enter into common Christian experience—with some laudable exceptions in every period.

The shift in our cosmovision has brought it about that several traditional christological assertions, such as *extra ecclesiam nulla salus* ("outside the church there is no salvation") came to be considered sectarian and narrow. Platonic and Neoplatonic influence on Christian thought lent themselves to commentaries, in a monotheistic (John 1:1) and non-christic-trinitarian framework, on John's revelatory phrase that "everything has come to be through him (the Logos)" (John 1:3). In this way, inspired by St. Augustine, Aquinas could write in *Contra gentes* IV, 13: *Verbum Dei est ratio omnium rerum* ("God's word is the principle of all things"), although for him this "principle" (*ratio*) refers not to the existing things of this world but to the *rationes aeternae* ("the eternal ideas") in God's mind—because the idea (*ratio*) was considered more real than the thing itself. Christ is thus split in two, as an intratrinitarian Logos and the descent of this Logos into time and space—with consequent metaphysical difficulties for a God understood to be "Absolute Being" (or as "being itself" *ipsum esse*). All these ideas were advanced despite the clear assertions of many councils (see Denzinger, 301-2, 317ff.). St. Thomas finds himself compelled to say that in the incarnation it is not so much that God becomes man as that this man (Jesus) becomes God.

It is significant that the concept of the mystical body of Christ has been forgotten.[3] The reason is obvious. Monotheism fears that the incarnation might lead to pantheism. If a human body is capable of being divine, it

---

[2] See Doré (1990) 558-62. See commentaries on 1 Peter 3:19 and Ephesians 4:9.
[3] See the valuable studies of Mersch (1933 and 1949).

must be treated in a particularly exceptional way. While the field of the *logos* unfolds itself chiefly in history, spirit also transcends the temporal sphere. For human beings, the *logos* as both word and *ratio* requires temporal succession—*componendo et dividendo*, "[time for] bringing together and dividing") Thomas would say—before talk of induction and deduction with respect to the method of reason. *Pneuma*, on the other hand, the functioning of spirit, does not seem as bound to the flux of history.

Although Mary's *fiat* was a historical event, the conception by the Spirit had no need of time, even though it took place in time. Instead it belongs to another level of reality. Similarly, the "today you will be with me in Paradise" (Luke 23:43), which the "good thief" heard from the lips of the Crucified One, annulled and transcended in an instant the thief's entire historical past, and his entire negative *karma* vanished. The incarnation and the resurrection were historical events, but their actual reality (*Wirklichkeit*) is irreducible to either history or a memory of these facts. In short, for christophany, speaking of the so-called preexistent Christ is not a happy formulation, for the "Only Begotten" is also the "First Begotten." Once we understand that, from the very beginning, christophany constitutes a Christian vision. In the following *sūtra* we shall treat some fundamental points that have their origin in tradition, while deepening it.

6

The Protological, Historical, and Eschatological Christ Is a Unique and Selfsame Reality, Distended in Time, Extended in Space, and Intentional in Us

The doctrine of Christ's unity constitutes the fulcrum of the Christian tradition. There are not three Christs—one the *creator* who has made all things (Genesis 1:3); the second the *redeemer*, or a Second Adam, who redeems some elect persons, or the whole human race, or the entire universe (according to different theologies) from slavery, sin, *avidyā*, *saṃsāra*; nor third, the *glorifier*, who brings all things to their total divinization (1 Corinthians 15:28).

For this reason the Christian tradition does not separate the understanding of Christ from that of creation, on the one hand, nor that of the Trinity, on the other. Christ is not just the savior; he is also the creator. Christ is not a divine meteorite; he is one of the Trinity. Christophany makes sense only within a trinitarian vision, since it is in Christ that we find the full manifestation of the Trinity. *Per ipsum, cum ipso, et in ipso!* ("Through him, with him, and in him!").

From outside such a vision we have only a "microdoxic" conception of Christ's mystery. In it he is reduced to a more or less divinized personage or an abstract gnostic principle. Starting from their respective points of view, we may say that Judaism is right in considering the incarnation of Yahweh an absurdity; Islam, in seeing the incarnation of Allah as blasphemous; and many other religions in considering the doctrine of Christ as meaningless or imperialist.

From a modern secularized point of view, prevalent today among the dominant classes of society in both East and West, the figure of Christ is interpreted as a more or less "scientific" phenomenon—that is to say, as something more or less observable in its historical singularity and its repercussions in communities of so-called believers, especially in the past but likewise also in the present. Some believe in the phenomenon; others do not. Polite people respect the private beliefs of each other person so long as "real" life—the world of work, economics, and politics—is developed independently of the ideas that both believers and nonbelievers entertain about this Christ. In a word, at most the prevalent cosmology may accept an abstract philosophy and theology completely torn from daily life. Collective "religious" phenomena are seen as sociological manifestations of the remnants of superstition and undeveloped, primitive beliefs, or perhaps even a challenge that science will have to resolve in the future. Modernity can believe only in a *Deus otiosus* (a remote, uninvolved God), as Mircea Eliade has so ably pointed out.

What I am saying is that the vision we have of Christ necessarily depends on a determinate cosmovision. Much of modern christology has accepted, in a generally uncritical way, the reigning cosmology and endeavors to present a "believable Christ" to what it calls "modern man." One of the shocks provoked by liberation theology occurred when it convinced many that the poor are a privileged *locus theologicus* (source for theological reflection). It would be opportune to recall not only that the poor have less money but also that they often exhibit a different mind-set and live in a different cosmovision, closer to that of an earlier time.

As a challenge to this modern world, it would be appropriate to remember a certain traditional cosmovision by recalling our first *sūtra*: "Christ is the Christian symbol for the whole of reality." We should, however, first reflect on the vocabulary employed, since every word is pregnant with meaning within a specific cultural context.

For example, in this sixth *sūtra* I have, though with some reluctance, called Christ creator, redeemer, and glorifier. The three words are in fact ambiguous and bear a potential for connotation that today may obscure the primordial intuitions that inspired them. We must know the context in which they were used and change them appropriately when the context is changed. Christ as creator constitutes an abuse of language within a rigid monotheism, where God alone is creator. The word "redemption," as the Victorines and Scotists noted, suggests an almost sadistic theory of Christ's salvific action. Perhaps we should find another word. Glorification reflects an imperial theocratic vision, and divinization is equally unacceptable within a strict monotheism. To introduce new words might lead some to think that we wish to break with tradition. To continue to use the same terms requires complex qualifications and could generate confusion. To find a middle way is the task of wisdom. For the moment, a simple mentioning of the problem must suffice.

In any event, let us return to our *sūtra*. While always mediated by our personal interpretation, human experience discloses a threefold tension in our consciousness of reality. First, we feel ourselves *distended in time*. Our human consciousness is temporal, our life is not lived wholly in an instant but rather runs along a temporal path, howsoever that may be interpreted—straight, linear, circular, spiral, and so on. Our experience of the world shows that everything of which we are conscious is temporal: the world is a *saeculum*, an interval of time, an eon. The distension of time pervades everything, every being. Yet we also note that everything is connected, that there is also something that is not distended—without time or full of time, immanent or transcendent as it might be. Eternity is neither a simple concept nor anything posttemporal. The infinite is not only a mathematical entity nor reducible to a limit concept.

Second, we are conscious that everything that exists—that is to say, everything—is *extended in space*, corporeal, and has parts. The universe, including ourselves, is a material place. Reality is spatial and material. If we abstract matter from reality, reality collapses. Yet we also experience a fugitive intuition—at times, only a suspicion—that there is something "more" than matter. Spirit is not a pure concept. Distance itself is something that is not corporeal—it exists *between* bodies.

Third, we are also conscious of our *intentional* nature—striving and purposeful. Everything in us tends toward something more or something else. We are in *epektasis*, as the Cappadocian Fathers say, projected ahead, with an intentionality that is not only epistemic but likewise ontic. There is "a" transcendence, although we do not know *where*; we cannot know it; we only know that it is outside us. There is in us a "tending," a tension toward the whole that makes us intentionally a microcosm and in the last analysis a *mikrotheos*. Aristotle wrote that "the human soul is in a certain sense all things" (*De Anima*, III, 8; 431 b21).

Where do we come from? Where we are we going? What are we? These are the fundamental questions men and women have raised from time immemorial. They arise from the constitutive intentionality that drives us to investigate precisely that which is unknown.[1]

To sum up, although we are temporal, we know we are also "more"—eternal. Although we are spatial, we know we are "more"—spiritual. Although we are conscious, we know we are capable of always knowing "more"—infinite. We are suspended between being and nothingness.[2]

Unless the figure of Christ is to be reduced to the level of a private devotion, christophany must deal with these fundamental human questions. The classical Christian answer consists in elaborating Christ's triple function as creator, savior, and glorifier. And although the triple action has been attributed, respectively, to the Father, the Son, and the Spirit, it has likewise been underscored that we cannot compartmentalize any divine action. Unless Christ is a dead symbol, all three actions refer to him.

There is no need to interpret these ideas within an obsolete cosmovision. Our intention is not to defend or criticize any cosmology or christol-

---

[1] This has been discussed since Socrates. See the Buddhist criticism of these ultimate questions as well as the Upanishads *Praśna* and *Kena*.

[2] See Panikkar (1972a) 109-13; Nishitani (1982) 77-118 and *passim*.

ogy whatsoever, but simply to note that a christopany for our age must raise these questions and that the past already offers us enough connecting ideas so that we need not break with tradition. Nevertheless, let us repeat that christophany is neither pure exegesis nor archaeology.

If the eschatological Christ, for example, tells us nothing about the physical future of the earth, if it tells us nothing about what I have called "ecosophy," he fails to enlighten us on a vital problem. Athens may have nothing to do with Jerusalem—recalling Tertullian's famous phrase—but Christ has to deal with both, as well as with mother earth. In a word, ecology (science of the earth) is a problem that also belongs to christophany and in its light becomes "eco-sophy" (wisdom of the earth, not just *our* wisdom of the earth).

Although history must not be neglected, neither may Christ's historical role be ignored, Christ's reality is not limited to saving souls, making them, so to speak, ascend to heaven. Christ's full reality cannot be split into three nor reduced to one function. Christ is the Only Begotten and First Begotten, Mary's son and son of Man, the beginning and the end, the alpha and the omega, this is why his reality transcends the categories of substance and individuality, as well as other concepts that need to be reexamined, like those of creation and redemption.

A spiritual comment may help us understand what such a christophany accentuates. Our fidelity to and love of Christ do not alienate us from our kindred—which includes angels, animals, plants, the earth, and, of course, men and women. Christ is a symbol of union, friendship, and love, not a wall that separates. Jesus is certainly a sign of contradiction, not because he separates us from others but rather because he heals our hypocrisies, fears, and egoism, while leaving us as vulnerable as himself. Instead of rejecting others because they are pagan, nonbelievers, sinners—whereas we are righteous and justified—Jesus impels us toward others and makes us see the negative which is in us too. Insofar as we share love, sympathy, suffering, and joy with all our neighbors, we discover the true face of Christ that is in all of us. "You have done it to me" (Matthew 25:40) is no simple moral exhortation to do good; it is rather an ontological assertion of Christ's presence in the other, in every other, in the smallest of the small— not for the purpose of discovering an "other" hidden in the neighbor but in order to discover the neighbor as part of ourselves. In fact, neither those on the right nor the left are conscious of the presence of Christ (Matthew 25:37) because what matters is the human face of the neighbor.

This explains my refusal—as a Christian—to belong to a simple religious sect that has existed on its own for only two thousand years. On this point, too, the Christian tradition sustains us. As St. Augustine said, the Christian religion is traceable to the dawn of humanity (*Retractationes*. 1, 12). *Ecclesia ab Abel* ("The church since Abel") is an ancient Christian belief.

Precisely because religion, in the best sense of the word, is the most profound human dimension that "binds" (*religa*) us to the rest of reality through its most intimate constitutive bonds, it is not reducible to an exclusive belonging to any particular human group. On the contrary, it is precisely the conscious belonging to reality that makes us Christians and happens precisely through a very concrete bond by means of which we are not only fully human but also fully real, although in a contingent and limited way. It is within and through this concreteness that we are able to realize, to the extent of our limitations, the fullness of our being—as microcosm and *mikrotheos*. This *sūtra* opens the way to further considerations, which we have already developed in the previous sections.

We should also remember that creation is continuous (*creatio continua*, as the scholastics say), not something that happened "at the beginning of time"—a phrase that makes no sense, since "beginning" is already temporal. It is not a simple cosmological assertion as to where to place the big bang. *Creatio* is at the basis of all temporal existence, the foundation on which time—the concrete time of every instant—rests. Time is not an absolute "before" of things but a constitutive element of every single thing.

The protological Christ, at times improperly called preexistent, is one with and the same as the historical Christ, and the historical Christ is inseparable from the eucharistic and resurrected Christ. The eucharist, we have said, is the continuation of the incarnation and so makes it possible for us to speak of an *incarnatio continua*.

In an analogous sense, the eschatological Christ, in his last coming or *parousia*, is inseparable from the eucharistic and risen Christ. Hence the "second coming" is neither another incarnation nor a second appearance of Christ. We have been warned not to believe in any appearance of the Messiah that might be reported here or there. The Kingdom does not arrive at a specific moment, nor can we say when it comes (Luke 17:20-24). All this does not deny the reality of time; on the contrary, it places time on two powerful pillars—the beginning and the end. Since neither the one nor the other is temporal, they are neither pre- nor posttemporal but tempiternal. These columns sustain every temporal moment. The particular judgment and the universal judgment, to use the language of the catechism, coincide. There is no waiting when we leave time.

It is in this sense that christophany helps us to live consciously our tempiternal life, the fullness of a life that has integrated past, present, and future (the *trikāla* of certain Indic traditions) so that we may live in fullness (John 10:10).

7

The Incarnation as Historical
Event Is Also Inculturation

Some theologians have expressed fear that this christophany would make the Christ of history disappear in the clouds of a non-Christian gnosticism. Nothing could be further from the intention of this work, even though I have often criticized the implicit "historiolatry" of a certain kind of theology. History in the concrete is so important as to justify this seventh *sūtra*, whose truth is often neglected when one thinks about the geographical expansion of Christianity. As a historical act in time and space, the incarnation is also a cultural event, intelligible only within a particular religiocultural context, that of a specific history. The divine incarnation as such is not, however, a historical event but a divine trinitarian act. The Only Begotten is also the First Begotten, as we have stressed repeatedly. The incarnation is the total reality of the *Logos*. That "mystery hidden for centuries in God" (Ephesians 3:9; Colossians 1:26) has "manifested itself [φανερωθέντος, *phanerōthentos*] at the end of the ages" (1 Peter 1:20), "in the fullness of time" (Ephesians 1:10), in the historical christophany of Jesus, Mary's son.

History must not be absolutized. It is significant to note that, when the heliocentric system (known since Aristarchus of Samos in the third century B.C.) was accepted, not only was the earth no longer considered the center of the universe, but the angels, demons, and spirits, which constituted parts of that cosmovision began to vanish, and Christ began to lose his cosmic function—which had been obvious in the canonical scriptures—as center of the entire universe (Ephesians 1:21; Colossians 2:10). After this, humankind found itself at the margin of physical reality and consoled itself that it possessed those mental powers that had created the world of history. Although our salvation does occur in history, it is not a historical fact. "Salvation history" (*Heilsgeschichte*) is neither the salvation of history nor the historical salvation of humanity but the historical sequence of events in which salvation occurs—not salvation itself, which is not a historical event.

A "sociology of knowledge" would explain the tension internal to the history of Christianity that became conscious of itself only with the fall of colonialism. To which must be added the fact that the colonialist ideology has taken refuge in the presumption that modern science is universal and culturally neutral. The essence of colonialism, in fact, consists in the conviction that one single culture is sufficient to embrace and understand the whole spectrum of human experience. Christianity had allied itself with this mentality or perhaps simply contributed to its consolidation. The moment we do not believe, at least in theory, that one single culture is humanity's ideal destiny, we cannot defend Christianity's claim to universality without emancipating ourselves from the culture with which it has lived in a symbiotic relationship for more than fifteen centuries.

We can speak, then, of Christianity's inculturation—that is, of its right to graft itself onto the different cultures of the world inasmuch as it is considered a "supercultural" fact. But it is precisely here that the internal tension arises. If Christianity is in essence historical and bound to a historical current of humanity, it cannot claim that Jacob's sons or Shem's grandchildren represent the whole of human history. Alongside Abraham's children there are other human brothers and sisters. Hence a contradiction arises: we cannot say that Christianity is historical and not historical at the same time. We cannot pretend that Christianity is a gift for everyone if at the same time it is essentially bound to a determinate history. Such a history can be made universal only by eliminating the children of Cain, Ishmael, and Esau—to remain within the biblical world.

The "evolutionistic" mentality of modern cosmology makes plausible the belief that the whole of humanity is journeying toward one single point in history, which has been called the "omega" point. In this framework other cultures find themselves "on the way to developing"—and of course Christianity and scientists are already on the right road. This is the soteriology that we do not accept.

Judaism considers itself a historical religion and the people of God, although it has never pretended to be universal. Christianity, on the other hand, has claimed in recent centuries to be historical and universal at the same time.

While not historical, the incarnation is also an event that has in fact occurred in history and, as such, radically changed the sense of how Christians perceive history. But to proceed from this fact in order to assert that Christians are the new people of Israel—apart from the well-grounded criticism expressed by Judaism—is to leap across an abyss. The crisis in the Jewish religious consciousness after the atrocities of Nazism is well known. How could "the people of God" be exterminated? The belated acknowledgment that Christians have their share of responsibility for the horrors of the Holocaust is surely praiseworthy, but it is surprising that the Christian consciousness did not suffer the same crisis after forty-five million African slaves were sacrificed for the economic benefit of Christian peoples. The Hebrew Bible's God is the God of history, while the Christians' Christ has been, rather, a victim of history.

Insofar as it has happened in history, the incarnation is certainly an event irretrievable in time—in linear time. We can only remember it, commemorate it. Christophany is not only a christology that seeks to interpret the historical facts of Jesus of Nazareth. It seeks above all to accept critically "the mystery that has appeared, been manifested, and now revealed" (φανερωθέντος δὲ νῦν, *phanerōthentos de nun*, Romans 16:26) with every cognitive means at human disposal. From the very beginning, this mystery was "in the Father's bosom" (John 1:18) and thus, like Jesus's statement that he was "before Abraham" (John 8:58), it is neither historical nor temporal.

Here we see clearly delineated a twofold dimension of Christianity that a dualistic vision of reality has difficulty keeping in harmony, despite the fact that nonduality is the quintessence of Christ's mystery—*totus Deus et totus homo* ("the whole God and the whole man") according to the classical expression. An inevitable consequence of this "panhistorical" vision of Christianity would be that the eucharist cannot be Christ's real and true presence, but only an *anamnēsis* ("memory") of a past fact. In other words, without a mystical vision, the eucharistic reality disappears.

The incarnation as historical event cannot be considered a universal human fact unless we reduce men and women to simple historical beings and history to an exclusive human group whose mission would be to swallow up all other groups—with the pretension of saving them. Such an attitude is in keeping with a certain doctrine which defends the thesis that outside this particular group there is no salvation. All of this is certainly coherent, although it does undermine the very meaning of the incarnation, which consists in the divinization of the entire flesh, both as a return to the original state and the final completion of creation. The exclusively historical conception of the incarnation has certainly been enfleshed in the monarchical and imperialistic idea that has been the dominant ideology of Europeans throughout at least the last six millennia.

The intelligibility of the incarnation as historical event depends on a particular series of cultural premises proper to the vision of the abrahamic world. Precisely for this reason we must reconsider the presumed right to inculturation that a certain contemporary theology of mission advances, as if the incarnation were a fact that, being above culture, had the right to inculturate itself in every civilization. The very idea of incarnation represents a cultural revolution. The reaction of Hindu fundamentalism, for example, with respect to the adoption of Indian costumes on the part of Christian missionaries—however incorrect it may seem to some—is in fact justified: we cannot wear clothing and practice forms of ritual that do not belong to us. Jesus was not a Hindu *saṃnyāsin*, nor the angel Gabriel a *deva*. If those historical events that have given rise to Christianity claim relevance for other cultures, they need to demonstrate their transhistorical validity. Otherwise, they will be interpreted as another, perhaps more peaceful, colonial invasion. A certain type of christology finds it difficult to refute this objection.

We are not defending either a cultural or an intellectual solipsism or a vision of a compartmentalized humanity. Osmosis and symbiosis are not only physical or biological but also human and cultural events. We are simply calling attention to problems that a contemporary christophany cannot avoid. Perhaps it would be better to speak here of reciprocal interculturation and fecundation.[1]

Here is an example of the incarnation's historical-sociological implications among those who feel themselves furthest from Christianity. In certain North American academic circles one can see a return—with repercussions elsewhere—to the most bigoted Christian colonialism, along with the good intention of overcoming it. It has been suggested that the terminology of the Western calendar, Christian in origin, be replaced by one that presumably would be neutral and universal. It is understandable that some would protest the use of A.D. (*anno Domini*), but by eliminating B.C. (before Christ) and substituting B.C.E. (Before the Common Era) scholars betray the depths of the cultural impact of the historico-Christian event. After all, Jesus was not born in the year 1. We select a single event but without any value judgment. To call our age "the Common Era," even though for the Jews, the Chinese, the Tamil, the Muslims, and many others it is not a common era, constitutes the acme of colonialism.

Christianity too is a cultural construct, inextricably bound to Western history and culture. No christology is universal, and one aspect of christophany consists in its being conscious of that fact in confronting the problem of Christ's identity.

We face two options. Either this culture, for which the historical Christian incarnation is meaningful, must become a universal culture—with the many other cultures reduced, so to speak, to folklore. Or we must realize that christophany itself is pluralistic, which means there can be no univocal christophanic concept. Hence christophany does not belong to the order of *logos*, though we must not ignore the Logos's exigencies. In other words, "logomonism" is a philosophical reductionism—and, let us add, a heresy. Once again, the Trinity provides the key. Although inseparable from the Logos, the Spirit is not the Logos. In the Trinity, equality and difference mean that there is nothing superior and external that allows us to say in what it is that the "persons" are equal or different. The Trinity is pure relationality.

Let me try to clarify this. Christianity is a historical religion. If we abolish history, we destroy Christianity. But Christ, the Christ in whom historical Christianity claims to believe, is more (not less) than a historical reality, in the sense in which Semitic culture has understood history. The fact that in Hindu India the experience of the Christian Christ is perceived more in the sacrifice of the eucharist than in the story of Bethlehem is a sign of this problem.

---

[1] Panikkar (1991).

A pluralistic christophany does not mean that a plurality of possible christologies exists. This is, rather, a fact. But pluralism is not synonymous with plurality. A pluralistic christophany challenges the *reductio ad unum* ("reduction to uniformity"), considering it an exigency of the intellectual *logos*—while christophany properly so-called is not reducible to *logos*. Christophany includes *pneuma*, spirit. The two are inseparable and irreducible. In other words, christophany does not limit itself to the identification of Christ but aims at reaching some understanding of his identity. And this, as we have already seen, requires the mystical vision, the third eye.

At this point we discover an extremely important corollary. A realistic christophany cannot avoid political problems. From the time of Pontius Pilate, such problems are inherent in an understanding of Christ, since he is not a politically neutral figure. He challenges us to make decisions—to choose a side. But he reminds us that a side is only a side, After twenty centuries of history in which we have seen Christ's assertions used to defend the most opposed ideas—from the Crusades to just war theory to total pacifism—our christophany should be more cautious and mature. To begin with, it should understand that cultural factors, with all their limits and ambivalences, are inherent in every christophany insofar as they are bound up with the very fact of the incarnation. Tertullian, Basil, Augustine, Luther, Comenius, Münzer—to cite only a few names—were all Christians who invoked Jesus's words to justify their diverse and sometimes incompatible positions. Despite the indubitably acute intelligence and good will of the great theological geniuses of the past, the figure of Jesus Christ seems to induce them to make contradictory statements insofar as they underwent different experiences. Christophany is pluralistic: Christ, it appears, *has* appeared as king, soldier, knight, pacifist, friend of the poor, rebel, and madman.

The first lesson to draw is the insufficiency of simple exegesis. We know that the devil can quote the scriptures to his own advantage. More than a question of hermeneutical caution, we recognize the correctness of the adage, "the letter kills." Like the vedic religion, Christianity is not a religion of scripture but of the word. "From hearing [*śruti* in Sanskrit] comes faith" (Romans 10:17), despite the fact that a narrow exegesis tells us that the original meaning was different.

Our *sūtra* takes a step forward: it does not simply state that Christ's epiphanies exhibit many aspects and that they are psychologically and historically conditioned. It also tells us that the incarnation itself, as a historical event, has taken place within a specific cultural milieu. The effect is twofold: the incarnation is already an inculturation and can therefore be received only within a certain culture. At the same time, it profoundly transforms the culture that receives it. The Bethlehem event that is grafted onto Semitic culture changes it radically.

The consequence is obvious: no such thing exists as an absolute christophany, since christophany is not a logical corollary of a purely deductive theology. A "chemically pure" christology from which we can deduce Christian ideas and a Christian praxis does not exist. No Christian life, no Christian theology and, in our case, no christophany is the conclusion of a syllogism. Jesus Christ himself warned us that he would become a "sign of contradiction" (*sēmeion antilegomenon*, Luke 2:34).

This does not mean, however, that we cannot invoke Christ in our support, or that we must renounce a christophany that would be convincing for our time—for example, one that favors the oppressed. It means only that we cannot absolutize our interpretations and enthrone a particular christology with universalist pretensions. This would entail reducing the mystery of Christ to our categories. The Son of man bears many names because no name exhausts the one named. We should distinguish *experiential Christianness* from *cultural Christianity* and *doctrinal Christendom*.[2] The problems remain open.

We encounter an example of this inculturation in the history of the so-called theology of liberation. It represents proof of the vitality of theology, such that it resists the caution of the so-called official churches. The picture of Christ most convincing in the concrete consciousness is that which represents him as the Jesus of the oppressed making us aware of the institutionalized violence of this our new world.

Some theologians cry, "Jesus Christ is not God," in contrast to a Christianity spiritually detached from the world. Jesus Christ is certainly not Yahweh. Jesus Christ is the son of God, but we are also that—and all of creation is a trinitarian adventure.

Such an opening is not a simple concession to theoretical pluralism. It also implies not closing ourselves deterministically to the human adventure. Understood in the deepest and most traditional interpretation, under the inspiration of the Spirit (*sit venia verborum*), the Christian church may decide to remain the "little flock" (Luke 12:32) different from the rest or the "salt of the earth" (Matthew 5:13) that flavors everything. The adventure of creation is also in our hands (Qoheleth 3:11 in the Latin Vulgate interpretation). Human beings are not marionettes in the hands of God, Destiny, or Providence. Divine freedom is constrained by neither physics nor metaphysics, and we are co-creators of our own destiny, which is inseparable from that of the universe. It is in this that our dignity consists. The future depends on us too (1 Corinthians 3:9). Jesus confessed that he did not know all the secrets of the "Kingdom" (Mark 13:32).

---

[2] Panikkar (1994b) 201-18.

8

The Church Is Considered a Site of the Incarnation

The fact that the Reformation and Counter-Reformation have clashed almost exclusively in areas of socioecclesiological polemics has created an image of the church as something similar to a civil institution. In the first fifteen centuries, in contrast, Christians were virtually unanimous in believing in what today is called "the cosmic church" (the μυστήριον κοσμικὸν τῆς ἐκκλησίας, *mystērion kosmikon tēs ekklēsias*)[1]—although immersed in secular affairs that it considered sacred.

Vatican II (*Lumen gentium*, 1) underscores again this ampler understanding of the church, returning to the traditional notion of the church as μυστήριον τοῦ κοσμοῦ (*mystērion tou kosmou*) or the *sacramentum mundi*—that is, the mystery of the universe. With this affirmation, the church shows its consciousness of being the place where the Holy Spirit is active and thus an integrating element of the unique trinitarian act of Christian faith: "I believe." This should suffice. But inasmuch as a person is self-conscious, one searches for a symbol adequate to this faith. This symbol is God—who is not an objective concept. In fact, this philosophy distinguishes between *credere in Deum* (that is, "believing in God," *credere Deum* (i.e., "believing God exists") and *credere Deo se revelanti* (i.e., "believing in God revealing himself"). The expression *in Deum* opens us to the trinitarian life—in God, Father, Son, Spirit. . . . And "holy church" here is in apposition to the Holy Spirit. One of the first creeds, after the active εἰς (*eis*, "in" [God]), which expresses the dynamism of the act of trinitarian faith, ends by saying that this assertion is made (ἐν τῇ ἁγίᾳ καθολικῇ ἐκκλησίᾳ, *en tē hagia katholikē ekklēsia*), "in the the holy catholic [universal] church" (Denzinger, 2). Already Lorenzo Valla, one of the first to turn from the Latin to the Greek text in order to overcome the split of the Middle Ages, proved that the *mystērion* of the New Testament was infinitely more profound and ample than the Latin *sacramentum*, understood as the global nature of the church's sacraments. That the church had

---

[1] De Lubac (1953); Holböck and Sartory (1962); and H. Rahner (1964).

existed "since Abel" (*ecclesia ab Abel*), the first human being born of woman, was virtually accepted as a foregone conclusion. The idea that God had created the world out of love for the church was considered virtually synonymous with the idea of the mystical body. This meant that God created the world for the purpose of divinizing his creation by making it become his own body, with Jesus as head and we the members. The church is understood as Christ's spouse, called to be "one single flesh" in the eschatological *hieros gamos* ("sacred matrimony") at the end of time.[2] Aquinas summarizes the traditional understanding of the church, saying: *Corpus Ecclesiae constituitur ex hominibus qui fuerunt a principio mundi usque ad finem ipsius* ("The body of the church is constituted by the people who existed from the beginning of the world until its end"; *Summa theologiae* III, q. 8, a. 3).

For now it is sufficient to quote the fathers of the church and their insistence—as Clement of Alexandria says—on "the church of the first-born," (ἐκκλησία πρωτοτόκων, *ekklēsia prōtotokōn*, see Hebrews 12:23). In Tertullian's bold formulation, the church is "the body of the Trinity's three persons," and "wherever the three are, that is to say, the Father, the Son, and the Holy Spirit, there is the church which is the body of the three" (*Ubi tres, id est Pater et Filius et Spiritus Sanctus, ibi ecclesia quae trium corpus est*).[3]

When Origen (PG 12:841) and St. Cyprian (PL 4:503), toward the middle of the third century, formulated the celebrated statement *extra ecclesiam nulla salus* ("Outside the church there is no salvation")—which found virtually universal acceptance until a short time ago—*ecclesia* was understood as *locus salutis* ("the place of salvation"), so that wherever salvation occurred, there was the church. "Where Jesus Christ is, there is the catholic church," maintained Ignatius of Antioch (*Ad Smyrnaeos*, VIII, 2; PG 5:713).

This cosmic and soteriological understanding is the primary meaning of the Greek word *katholikē*—the church that coexists with the universe. It would be misleading to identify this church directly with an institution, as Pius XII made clear. Subsequent discussions concern the bond between this *ecclesia*, this universal community, within which salvation occurs, and the juridical Roman church, between the visible church and its invisible boundaries. Contemporary ecclesiological disputes belong to a different order altogether.

To reduce the church to a visible or official church or to a simple historical phenomenon would constitute a "microdoxic" interpretation. The church is the "spouse of Christ" or, as Irenaeus said, the place of the Spirit: "Where the Spirit is, there is the church." Here we face a question of terminology. Some theologians criticize the conception according to

---

[2] H. Rahner (1964).

[3] Tertullian, *De Baptismo* VI, cited in de Lubac (1953) 30. See Colossians 1:18.

which the church would be the continuation of the incarnation.[4] If by church is understood an institution or even the living visible organism (and not just the organization), then these theologians are fully justified in criticizing a neo-Romantic mysticism. The distinction between "church" and "kingdom" is also well known. It is clear that we cannot escape the "politics" of terminology. However, while I agree with the criticism of pseudo-mysticism, I still believe that the concept of *ecclesia* also includes the universal ἐκκλησία.[5] My formulation of the problem does not eliminate an ecclesiology that is more sociological than theological, but it does not accept any "fundamentalist" conception of church. What it does seek to do is reach a level at which communication with other cultures and religions becomes possible.

To sum up: salvation consists in reaching our plenitude—that is, in sharing the divine nature, since nothing finite can ever satisfy the being that is *capax Dei*. Humanity and all of creation are capable of reaching that fullness because, at the very root of "creation," we find the mediator, the bond, Christ. Generated by the "source and origin of the whole of divinity," not only does Christ create everything but he divinizes everything by the grace of the divine Spirit, so that, after the spatiotemporal adventure of creation, the divine life of the Trinity will pervade everything and God will be all in all (1 Corinthians 15:28). What we are describing is a God that is as transcendent as immanent, therefore irreduced to a Trinity *ab intra* ("from within").

In the meantime, as long as we are pilgrims, as long as the whole of creation groans in the pains of childbirth, we remain immersed in the process until the full revelation of the children of God will be manifested (Romans 8:19-23). The place in which this process occurs is the church; it is also realized in the "visible church" despite all her human shadows and sins. The church is the very place in which the whole universe pulsates until its final destiny. Man is the priest, the mediator in that cosmic-divine battle—the *daivāsuram* of India's "myths." Christophany shows us our role in the universe in the *anakephalaiōsis* ("recapitulation") of all things in Christ (Ephesians 1:10), to which man is called, a creature who, though ontologically inferior to the angels, has a higher task to fulfill precisely because of the divine paradox that chooses those things that are not in order to confound those that are (see 1 Corinthians 1:26-31). To see in the word "church" only an institution is a residue of clericalism or an unhealed trauma.

With a fresh critical consciousness, christophany returns to these fundamental truths: the place of the incarnation is Man, indeed "the flesh." The place of man is the earth, indeed the church in its journey. The goal of this pilgrimage is plenitude, not nothingness (not to be confused with

---

[4] Mühlen (1968) 173-216.
[5] See Mühlen's important contribution of 1966.

emptiness). It is this which constitutes Christian hope. The human adventure is ecclesial, cosmic, and divine.

In order to grasp the profound meaning of this *sūtra*, we must recapture the scholastic intuition of *creatio continua*, and extend it to *incarnatio continua*. We find timid hints of the latter in the writings of a few mystics, such as Maximus the Confessor and Meister Eckhart.[6] Just as God's creative activity in every moment takes nothing away but makes creation from the "beginning" stand out more profoundly, so the continuous incarnation of the Son in every creature does not diminish the central place of the incarnation of Jesus (John 1:14). Rather it allows us to become conscious of what was from the beginning (Romans 16:25-26; 1 John 1:1-3). It is here that the title of Son of man which the Son of God gave himself reveals its innermost depth.

---

[6] On Maximus, see von Balthasar (1961a) 274ff.; on Eckhart, see Wilke (1995) 237-48.

9

Christophany Is the Symbol of the *Mysterium Coniunctionis* of Divine, Human, and Cosmic Reality

The cosmic and trinitarian aspect of the mystery of Christ does not obscure his historical reality, since the mystery of Christ resides precisely in this harmonious *coniunctio*. As St. Leo the pope says in his *Seventh Homily on the Nativity*, Christ's equality with the Father does not come at the expense of his equality with us. His cosmic function does not eliminate his historical role. If the *lex orandi* ("the law of praying") is the *lex credendi* ("law of believing"), we may then discover how the Christian tradition has seen in Jesus Christ something more, not less, than a savior of souls. In fact, a great many liturgical texts constantly describe this polarity. Let us look at the eighth antiphon of the office of matins for the liturgy of January 1. There we sing:

> *Ante luciferum genitus et ante saecula Dominus Salvator noster hodie nasci dignatus est.*

> Our Lord the Savior, generated before the light and before the centuries, deemed worthy of being born today.

And in the seventh antiphon, is found:

> *In principio, et ante saecula Deus erat Verbum, et ipse natus est hodie Salvator mundi.*

> At the beginning and before the centuries was the Word, and he was born today, the Savior of the world.

The meaning is clear: Jesus was born a man among us. Both texts emphasize the word *hodie* ("today"), a transhistorical today. The texts do not say that he was born *olim* ("then," "once upon a time") but today. It is therefore not a simple commemoration but the celebration of something contemporary, today's new birth. The historical reality of Mary's son transcends time not only in a vertical divine direction (Only-begotten Son of the Father) but likewise in a horizontal one. *Hodie* is neither *ante saecula* ("before the ages," and by extension, "before time began") nor *in principio* ("in the beginning"), outside of time, but as a temporal reality that is not limited to the historical fact that occurred twenty centuries ago. To repeat: if we forget either the mystical or the faith dimension, we deform the figure of Mary's son. This figure is as much human as it is divine and cosmic, belonging to the past, the present, and the future.

For centuries the liturgy has sung the praises of this figure in the Advent hymn at matins:

> *Verbum supernum prodiens*
> *e Patris aeterni sinu*
> *qui natus orbi subvenis*
> *latente cursu temporis.*

> Supreme Word proceeding
> from God's eternal bosom;
> by being born you save the world
> when the passage of time falls away.

The entire cosmotheandric experience is implicit here—the divine, the human, and the world. Christ's function is not limited to "redeeming" humanity but embraces the restoration of the world; the cosmic *mandala* (both *orbis* and *mandala* mean circle).

"Whoever sees me sees the Father" (John 14:9). Jesus Christ is pure transparence, the Way. At the same time, whoever sees Jesus Christ sees the prototype of the complete man, the *totus homo*. Whoever discovers Jesus Christ experiences eternal life—that is, the resurrection of the flesh and therefore the reality of matter, of the cosmos (material universe). Jesus Christ is the living symbol of divinity, humanity, and the cosmos. Whatever experience does not entail these three dimensions can hardly be called a living encounter with the young rabbi who one night told Nicodemus that man's new birth must spring out of water (matter) and the Spirit (John 3:5-6).

In Jesus Christ the finite and the infinite meet, the human and the divine are joined. In him the material and the spiritual are one, and also the male and the female, high and low, heaven and earth, the historical and the transhistorical, time and eternity. From the historic-religious point of view the figure of Christ could be described as that of a person who reduces to zero the distance between heaven and earth, God and man, transcendent and immanent, without sacrificing either pole—which is precisely the principle of *advaita*. Jesus prayed, "That they be one" (John 17:21). The Coptic *Gospel of Thomas* says, "When you make one out of two and make the internal the external . . . then you will enter (into the Kingdom)" (22). *Qui facis utraque unum* ("You who you make one of two") the great "O" antiphon of Christmas (sung on December 22) amplifies the scriptural meaning (Ephesians 2:14), and Peter spoke of the *apokatastaseōs pantōn* ("the restoration of all things") in Acts 3:21.

If, as we have said, we separate the figure of Christ from the trinitarian mystery, we fail to grasp the meaning of christophany. In this respect one may speak of the "radical Trinity" as a complement to the intuition of the unity between the immanent and the "economic" unity. The immanent Trinity would be God's mystery "within" (*ab intra*) the divine interiority, while the economic Trinity would be the action directed "externally" (*ad extra*), the "work of creation" (*opus creationis*), especially as it refers to humanity. After Tertullian this distinction became classical and was consecrated by the Christian consciousness, often because of the fear of falling into pantheism, as a famous thirteenth-century text asserts: *Inter creatorem et creaturam non potest similitudo notari, quin inter eos major sit dissimilitudo notanda* ("Between the creator and the creature no similarity can be noted without calling attention to the dissimilarity, which is greater" (Denzinger 806).

To keep us from forgetting the Trinity, Karl Rahner formulated the thesis that "the economic Trinity is the immanent Trinity"—and immediately added, "and vice versa." Some theologians criticize this "vice versa" because they hold that it contradicts the Lateran Council's affirmation cited above.[1] Without entering into the heart of that discussion now, I would like to underscore again the difficulty that Western thought has experienced in admitting that an a-dualism could exist between monism and dualism. "The Father is equal to the Son," the trinitarian doctrine asserts, because everything that the Father is he gives to the Son without holding anything back, yet the Son is not the Father; otherwise he would not be the Son, and the immanent Trinity would vanish. According to the Council of Toledo, *Quod enim Pater est, non ad se, sed ad Filium est; et quod Filius est, non ad se, sed ad Patrem est; similiter et Spiritus Sanctus non ad se, sed ad Patrem et Filium relative refertur: in eo quod Spiritus Patris et Filii predicatur* ("What the Father is, he is not for himself but for the Son, and what the Son is, he is not for himself, but for the Father; in the same way the Holy Spirit does not refer to himself but to the Father and the Son: therefore he is called the Spirit of the Father and the Son" (Denzinger 528).

It is worth saying that the nondual *advaita* to which I refer is neither a dialectical negation of duality nor a secondary act of the intellect—or perhaps better, the human spirit. Rather, it is a direct vision that transcends rationality (without denying it). I do not intend to say that duality comes "first" and is subsequently denied but that we see relationality immediately "before" any duality. In this sense we may also call it "non-unity." The constitutive relational nature of reality—or, better, its correlationality—cannot be characterized as either unity or duality. In fact, both the latter are

---

[1] See B. Forte (1985) 18-24.

no more than what human thought requires when it breaks out of the primordial silence from which it originates.

The way in which the radical Trinity manifests itself in Christ presents us with the nondualist unity between the divine and the human (the *theandric* mystery of Eastern theology). But the human being, too, constitutes a nondualist unity between spirit and body. Each of us is a nondualist unity between spirit and body, and each of us exists in the corporeality proper to material things. The "three" (the "divine," the "human, and the "material") go together with neither confusion nor separation.

I have called this experience the *cosmotheandric* or the *theanthropocosmic* intuition. At times this intuition has been misunderstood, as if it were a question of three substances. Again, Christ remains the central symbol. Christ is one, and not a union of "three" elements, even though we can and must acknowledge this tridimensionality in him, as well as in the whole of reality. It is enough to remember that the traditional vision of Jesus Christ has always recognized in him the harmonious conjunction of these three dimensions of the real, even though every period and every person accentuates now one, now the other element of the triad.

Maximus the Confessor writes that in Christ the five great "conjunctions" are realized: the masculine with the feminine (Galatians 3:28), the world of the damned with paradise (Luke 23:43); the terrestrial world with heaven (Acts 1:9-11), the sensible with intelligible things (Ephesians 4:10), created with uncreated nature.[2]

Rather than a *coincidentia oppositorum*, Jesus Christ has been described as the reconciliation between the divine and the universe, the one who has called upon those who believe in him to act in "the service of reconciliation" (διακονία τῆς καταλλαγῆς, *diakonia tēs katallagēs*, in 2 Corinthians 5:18). Thus, overcoming "otherness" could be experienced as the *mysterium coniunctionis* (the sacrament of conjunction), as the center of the cross as *quaternitas perfecta* ("fourfold perfection"). In fact, Christ is more the "conjunction" than "coincidence." For in him all Christian teachings are conjoined.[3] As we have said, creation cannot be separated from the incarnation, nor the incarnation from the Trinity.[4]

St. John Damascene emphasizes that we "do not have to say that man has become God but rather that God made himself man" (*De fide orthodoxa* III, 2). This has been a great difficulty for monotheism. How can Being, absolutely one and simple, become anyone whatsoever? Let us repeat it again: the incarnation makes no sense except in the Trinity.

If we separate Jesus Christ from the Trinity, his figure loses all credibility. He would then be a new Socrates or any other great prophet. If we separate Jesus Christ from humanity, he becomes a Platonic ideal of per-

---

[2] See von Balthasar (1961a) 271-72 for quotations.
[3] Scheeben (1941) developed this understanding in a profound way.
[4] See Sherrard (1992) 163.

fection—and frequently an instrument for dominating and exploiting others by becoming a God. If we separate his humanity from his actual historical journey on this earth and his historical roots, we turn him into a mere gnostic figure who does not share our concrete and limited human condition.

The conjunction of these three elements constitutes the task of christophany for our age.

Epilogue

It is no surprise that a new period in world history should reflect a fresh understanding of Jesus the Christ. If Christ is to have any meaning for Hindus, Andines, Ibos, Vietnamese, and others who do not belong to the Abrahamic lineage, this meaning can no longer be offered in the garb of Western philosophies. Such an understanding can be achieved neither by a simple repetition not by a mere adaptation of traditional doctrines, but by a "new life in Christ," by the *fides oculta* ("hidden faith") that never stops "looking at the heaven," as the men of Galilee did, but relives the *incarnatio continua*, with which the ancients were also familiar. The salutary reaction of a "christology from below," such as liberation theology represents, must be complemented by a "christology from within," which might at the same time serve as a bridge to a "christology from above." All three forms are necessary, but this does not require us to wed an adoptionist christology (God adopts Jesus as his son) or a pneumatic christology (a divine spiritual being took on flesh at a particular point in history). At the beginning (of time) Jesus did not exist, but at the beginning (ἐν ἀρχῇ, *en archē*), at the origin (tempiternal) was the alpha and omega that Christians call Christ.

Were I to label everything, I would speak of a *christophany from the center*—not to be confused, however, with so-called christocentrism. And let us remember that the "rule for praying is the rule for believing" (*lex orandi, lex credendi*) and that the liturgical hymns that express it were not only an exercise in poetic license but also represented theocosmological intuitions. Let us recall the ancient Christmas Vespers Hymn, first in Latin and then in English:

Jesu, Redemptor omnium,
Quem lucis ante originem
Parem Paternae gloriae
Pater supremus edidit.
Tu lumen et splendor Patris
Tu spes perennis omnium.

Jesus, Redeemer of all things,
who before light's origin
equal to the fatherly glory,
the supreme Father generated

Thou, light and splendor of the Father,
Thou, eternal hope of all things.

Although the same hymn praises the day as *currens per anni circulum*
("coursing through the cycle of the year"), and the hymns of praise still call
Christ *beatus auctor saeculi* ("blessed creator of this world/age"), in the
modern Western world the general tendency has been to read such texts
within a linear conception of time. In greater agreement with the great
christological texts of scripture, we should read this hymn within a different temporal framework—from the beginning, at the origin (*en archē, in
principio*), reality was (is) Father, Christ, Spirit (to use Christian names).
When "the fullness of times" arrived, there occurred in space (and also in
time) what we call the incarnation, so that the manifestation (φανέρωσις,
phanerōsis) of Jesus constitutes a revelation of reality—of what we are. We
should remember that, unless we wish to make God an anthropomorphic
and composite being, the revelation of God can be only God himself (not
a simple production of his mind). God's *logos*, the trinitarian intuition
asserts, is God. The mystery of time is the unfolding—the distension,
Augustine would say—of the Trinity *ad extra*. But "outside of" God nothing exists. The whole of reality is not an exclusively transcendent God: it is
the Trinity.

Let us end with another hymn, this one from the monastic breviary for
matins during the Easter season, remembering that Augustine said, *Cantare
amantis est*, which can be roughly but correctly translated as "singing is
what lovers do."

Ut hominem redimeres,
Quem ante iam plasmaveras
Et nos Deo coniungeres
Per carnis cantubernium.

So that you may free man,
whom you had already formed
and unite us to God
through your union with the flesh.

The greatness of the Christian vision, let us recall, does not take anything away from other intuitions of the ultimate mystery of reality. The
Christian faith is confirmed when we find homeomorphic equivalences in
other traditions. I call attention to a little-known hymn which comes from
one of the most ancient documents—probably seventh century—of the
Tibetan people:

From a divine son
Will rise a human race . . .

and a hero will dominate the world,
and his fame will spread over the earth. . . .[1]

We have repeated several times in these pages that the experience we have called christophanic is a concrete form of living the human experience in its fullness. Many people today hesitate to accept this language either because it has been banalized or abused. We have tried to demonstrate that two millennia of human experience partake of our common patrimony and that we should neither relegate it to a museum nor accept it uncritically. My intention has been not so much to present the past from a new angle of vision as to live the present "in communion with the others," like all those pilgrims to whom we have dedicated this study.

The language of this book may disturb the experts in psychoanalysis and analogous disciplines. We should make clear that we admire those who have contributed to the investigation of the human soul in the last century; their contribution to the exploration of the human psyche is precious. It would be a mistake, however, to believe that their theories reflect the human spirit at the level at which we have treated it.

The reader is surely aware of our critical attitude toward contemporary culture, but this does not mean that I do not admit a secularized "original sin" that makes us speak of an "unhappy consciousness" (*unglückliches Bewusstsein*, in Hegel's phrase), or even an excessively complex or wrong conscience.

It is true that evil exists in the world and in man; the divinization of which we have spoken does not mean a return to paradise. Indeed, such a "dream" seems like a monotheistic conception of divinization or an Apollonian idea of perfection. Human perfection does not have the character of a machine, nor human health that of an elephant. Man is not the same as the Platonic idea of man. We should be grateful that psychology has dismantled the mirage of *second innocence*. But that does not require us to deny that our ultimate destiny is a leap from an instinctive animality to participation in the infinite adventure of reality. Even the Gospel is full of Jesus's battles against demons of all kinds.

In other words, christophany is not an idyllic vision of either reality or the human condition but a *phania*, a light that appears as light insofar as we are wrapped in darkness. Perhaps those who are most sensitive to the human condition may be able to see christophany as "good tidings." We began by describing the *Sitz im Leben* that gave birth to these reflections. We end by referring to another, broader *Sitz*—the social-political-economic-spiritual field of our overall human situation. What does a christophany have to say to three quarters of those whom we call our neighbors and yet fail to achieve even a minimal level of humanity because

---

[1] Olschak (1987) 36.

of unjust human systems? The cry *Venceremos,* "we shall overcome," expresses a powerful psychological explosion, although for the millions of victims who perish along the way to an ever more problematic "promised land" it is either a pious wish or an alienating drug. We must go deeper and furnish an answer to the ʿ*am haʾaretz,* the *dalit,* the Amerindians, and all the oppressed—not only economically and politically, but also in a spiritual and human direction. We should constantly keep in mind all those who will not "succeed," who will not "survive."

Let us again employ poetic language, this time in the mouth of a Latin American Catholic bishop, Pedro Casaldáliga, who, in summing up the sorrows of the Amerindian, provides a compendium of what I have been trying to say. It is perhaps in today's crèches that christophany is best manifested.

> From the Amerindia to Holy Mary,
> both in the state of Nativity.
>
> Who says it was good news?
> And the child not yet fully born . . . . !
> The caravels of greed are panting
> and Herod shields himself in his power.
>
> They opened me in the middle seeking money
> and they have broken the fire of my voice.
> Can it be the God of life who is killing me?
> This God, Guadalupe, can it be God?
>
> Will the wind not know to come by my road?
> Will my blood not be good for His wine?
> Does the Kingdom not ferment in me as well?
>
> In the slum of the empire and inconsolable,
> I offer you the poverty of the beaten one,
> which may be, finally, our Bethlehem.

The sociopolitical implications of this vision should be clear. Jesus Christ destroys all our dualisms. He is the one *Qui fecit utraque unum* ("who makes one from both") chants the liturgy as it echoes scripture. Yet this *unum* is neither a philosophical monism nor a theological monotheism. We repeat: the δικαιοσύνη (*diakaiosynē*) of the Gospels does not mean "justification" (by heaven) on one side, and "justice" (on earth) on the other. "On earth as it is in heaven," the best-known Christian prayer says. The Son of Man is the Son of God. It is not the case that God is here, Man is there, and the Earth somewhere underneath. The spiritual and the celestial are not on one side, and the material and the political on the other; time is not now and eternity later; the isolated individual is not in opposition to the undifferentiated collectivity. Jesus was neither a political liberator nor an ascetic who denied the world, much less a member of the clergy, but simply a being (we do not have any other word) who lived the fullness of the human. What Jesus did was to participate in the affairs of the earth and the vicissitudes of men and women, while knowing that it is the obligation of each of us to assume our responsibilities so that the common effort will achieve a greater justice. But this human fullness also includes participation in the divine—thereby recalling what we are called to become.

Once again: Christ as pure God, even though the only Son of God, does not convince. He neither descended from the cross nor is he the God of history. Nor does it help if we consider him simply as a "man for others," a historical hero or marvelous model. Although once in a while David is lucky, there are innumerable occasions when it is Goliath who wins. Where do all revolutions lead us? The struggle for justice is not "justified" by an eventual victory (judged again in terms of linear time) but by the fact—I dare say while leaping to another tradition—that it is our human vocation—the *lokasaṃgraha* ("the cohesion of the universe"), as imaged in the *Bhagavad-gītā* (III, 20 and 25).

In other words, if the mystery of Christ is not our very own, if christophany means no more than the archaeology of the past or the eschatology of the future, it might as well be considered a museum piece. The cry for a new spirituality is a cry of the Spirit which, according to tradition, is the very Spirit of Christ himself. The christophany of the third millennium must be neither sectarian nor a mere consolation for "believers." The Son of man died outside the holy city.

The christophany *from within* which we are timidly suggesting constitutes the deepest interiority of all of us, the abyss in which, in each one of us, there is a meeting between the finite and the infinite, the material and spiritual, the cosmic and the divine. The christophany of the third millennium is a summons to us to live this experience.

A Final Word

ἐκ τοῦ πληρώματος αὐτοῦ ἡμεῖς πάντες ἐλάβομεν.

Et de plenitudine ejus nos omnes accipimus.

From his fullness we have all received.
John 1:16

"In order that we may fill up
the fullness of God
in all."[1]

---

[1] . . . *ut impleamini in omnem plenitudinem Dei,* says St. Bonaventure in the prologue of his *Soliloquies,* citing Ephesians 3:19 (ἵνα πληρωθῆτε εἰς πᾶν τὸ πλήρωμα τοῦ θεοῦ, *hina plērōthēte pan to plērōma tou theou*), as Paul speaks of receiving the love of God so that "you may be filled with the fullness of God."

Glossary

Abgescheidenheit (German). "Detachment," an expression Eckhart coined in his treatise *On Detachment*. It constitutes one of the central points of his mystical conception and implies, at one and the same time, both a passive and an active attitude.

Abgrund (German). Abyss.

Abhinavagupta (Abhinavaguptacārya) (Sanskrit). Shivaitic mystic-philosopher of the tenth century.

adhyāsa (Sanskrit). "Superimposition," false attribution of divine attributes to reality.

ādhyātmic (Sanskrit). Qualification applied to the spiritual life that transports us to a knowledge of Self (*ātman*), to the inner experience that corresponds to the deepest dimension of our being.

ādi-puruṣa (Sanskrit). The primordial *puruṣa*.

advaita (Sanskrit). Nonduality. Metaphysical expression for the irreducibility of reality to pure unity (monism) or mere duality, which many religions, especially Eastern, elaborate philosophically.

advaitin (Sanskrit). A follower of *advaita*, one who professes the nonduality *ātman-brahman*.

agora (Greek). Public square in Greek cities where citizens met and celebrated assemblies.

ahambrahmāsmi (Sanskrit). "I am *brahman*," a *mahāvākya* that expresses the idea *ātman-brahman*.

aliud (Latin). The other ("thing"), neuter.

alius (Latin). The other ("person" or "I").

ʿam haʾaretz (Hebrew). "People of the earth," commoners, the poor and ignorant; disadvantaged and untouchables, those who do not know the Torah.

antistrophē (Greek). Inversion, new meaning achieved by inverting the components of a word or phrase.

anuttaram (Sanskrit). That which cannot be transcended, the *non plus ultra*.

apauruṣeya (apauruṣeyatva) (Sanskrit). Of nonhuman origin, without *puruṣa*.

ʿaql (Arabic). Intellect, intelligence.

asat (Sanskrit). Non-being; negation of being.

āśrama (Sanskrit). Spiritual community, generally under the direction of a guru or spiritual master. It also means a stage in human life, usually written unitalicized in English as "ashram."

astiti nāstiti (Sanskrit). "It is this it is not this"; being-non-being.

ātman (Sanskrit). The "self" of a being or reality. The ontological nucleus in Hinduism, the purely impermanent in Buddism.

Aufhebung (German). "Transcending"; in Hegel's philosophy it signifies at one and the same time "transcending" and "conserving"—that is, one of opposite meanings. It consists, moreover, in the process of negating a reality in order to make room for a different aspect in which, however, it does not lose the whole of its starting point.

Aum (Sanskrit). The sacred symbol, the highest and most comprehensive symbol of Hindu spirituality; Buddhism also employs it as a mantra. A manifestation of spiritual energy, it indicates the presence of the Absolute within the world of appearance.

191

avatāra (Sanskrit). "Descent" of the divine, physical manifestation of Vishnu. Traditionally, Hinduism speaks of ten of Vishnu's *avātara*. Often written without italics in English as "Avatar(s)."

barnasha (Aramaic). Man's son.

bedhābheda (Sanskrit). Philosophy of difference and nondifference (between God and the world).

Bhagavad-gītā (Sanskrit). *The Song of the Glorious Lord*, the most widely known sacred book in India.

bhakti (Sanskrit). The mystic way of devotion, of loving the Lord. One of the ways to salvation through union with the divinity.

bodhisattva (Sanskrit). Buddhist who has achieved liberation on earth and then commits himself to help all other sentient beings to achieve liberation in their turn.

Brāhmaṇa (Sanskrit). Designation of absolute reality (according to some schools), identical with the *ātman*, foundation of everything.

Bṛhadāraṇyaka-upaniṣad (Sanskrit). One of the most ancient and important Upanishads.

buddhi (Sanskrit). Intellect, discriminative faculty. Intellect as higher faculty; intuitive intelligence; knowledge, mind; at times thought, meditation.

capax Dei (Latin). The soul's capacity for perceiving and receiving God.

Chāndogya-upaniṣad (Sanskrit). One of the most ancient Upanishads. It treats of the mystical value of sound and song, and of the identity of *ātman-brahman*.

Christāloka (Sanskrit). From *āloka*, light, splendor; Christ's light.

circumincessio (Latin). Compenetration of the three persons of the Trinity. Its Greek equivalent is *perichōrēsis*.

cit (Sanskrit). Consciousness, intelligence, spirit, intellect.

coesse (Latin). To exist jointly, to be united; to co-exist.

cogito (ergo) sum (Latin). "I think (therefore) I am."

cogitamus (ergo) sumus (Latin). "We think (therefore) we exist."

colloquium salutis (Latin). Dialogue about salvation.

compunctio cordis (Latin). Repentance, heartache; essential disposition of monastic spirituality.

daivāsurām (Sanskrit). Struggle between *deva* (good divinities) and *asura* (bad divinities).

dalit (Sanskrit). Oppressed, crushed. Name that the marginalized groups in India give themselves.

dharma (Sanskrit). Cosmic and ritual norm; natural law and ethical order; religion. It is extended also to the very manifestations of the norm that governs different levels of existence, such as obedience to duty, fulfillment of precepts, etc.

dharma-kāya (Sanskrit). In Mahāyāna Buddhism, the mystical body of dharma.

disciplina arcanis (Latin). Body of secret doctrines and their teaching, reserved for the initiates of the ancient mystery religions and early Christianity; the obligation to keep silent on such matters.

Durgā (Sanskrit). "Of difficult access, the inaccessible." One of the most ancient names for the divine Mother, Shiva's consort.

Erfahrungverschmelzung (German). Fusion of experiences.

extra ecclesiam nulla salus (Latin). Outside (of) the church, there is no salvation.

fania (phania). Direct manifestation, derived from *phanos*, lamp, light.

fides quaerens intellectum (Latin). "Faith seeking understanding."

fontanalis plenitudo (Latin). Name that St. Bonaventure gives God the Father as the font whence everything emanates.

guhā (Sanskrit). Cave, grotto, secret place.

guru (Sanskrit). Teacher, guide.

Heilsgeschichte (German). History as "salvation history."

hypostasis (Greek). Substance, underlying reality (literally, "what lies beneath"). Key word that became controversial in the early trinitarian disputes, above all because of the ambiguity of its Latin translation as either person or substance.

identité-idem (French). According to Ricoeur, the identity of temporal permanence (with an ontic identity), which does not entail an immutable nucleus of the person(ality).

identité-ipse (French). According to Ricoeur, the self-awareness that entails otherness so that no self-identity exists without the other.

intellectus agens (Latin). "Agent intellect," which some authors consider to be one of the emanations of the divine intelligence which thus defines its unique and universal character.

Īśā-upaniṣad (Sanskrit). One of the shortest Upanishads. It deals with the divine presence in everything.

iṣṭadevatā (Sanskrit). Icon of the divine which best corresponds to every person's culture, idiosyncrasies, and circumstances; the concrete symbol through which we experience the ultimate mystery that many call "God."

Īśvara (Sanskrit). Lord of the universe, personal God, as distinct from the impersonal Brahman.

jagat-guru (Sanskrit). Universal teacher.

jīvanmukta (Sanskrit). Liberated, living person who has fulfilled her ontological identity, *ātman-brahman*; she who has fulfilled her very being inasmuch as she has become totally integrated.

jñāna (Sanskrit). Conscious experience of reality, one of the paths to liberation.

kairos (Greek). Decisive moment, crucial point at which destiny changes its phase; epoch.

karma or *karman* (Sanskrit). Work, deed, action, originally the sacred action of sacrifice, and also a moral act. The result of all the actions and works according to the law of *karman*, which governs actions and their results in the universe. As a consequence, linked to rebirth.

kenōsis (Greek). Emptying of oneself, annihilation.

kērygma (Greek). Message, proclamation (of the word of God); corresponds to the primary level of evangelical teaching.

koinōnia (Greek). Community. communion.

Kṛṣṇa (Sanskrit). Commonly spelled "Krishna" in English. Manifestation of Viṣṇu (commonly spelled "Vishnu" in English) the Savior. The *Bhagavad-gītā* contains his revelation to Arjuna.

kṣetra (Sanskrit). Field. Consciousness begins with the distinction between the field and the knower of the field, which means, between the world (as an object of knowledge) and the conscious subject.

light, taboric. The light that illuminated Jesus in the transfiguration; can be considered the visible character of the divinity, of the energies of grace through which God makes himself known; man is capable of receiving this light.

locus theologicus (Latin). A legitimate source or location for theological activity.

mādhyamika (Sanskrit). The school of the "middle way" in Mahāyāna Buddhism.

Mādhyamika-kārikā (Sanskrit). Nagarjuna's philosophical treatise.

mahāvākya (Sanskrit). "Great saying." Indicates important expressions in the Upanishads that articulate in a very concise way the content of the experience of the Absolute.

Mahāvīra (Sanskrit). "Great hero." Founder of Jain religion (sixth-fifth century B.C.).

metanoia (Greek). Transformation, conversion, to go beyond (*meta*) the mental or rational (*nous*).

mīmāṃsā (*mīmāṃsāka*) (Sanskrit). Vedic philosophical school that concentrates on the exegesis of texts.

mokṣa (Sanskrit). Final liberation from *saṃsāra*, from the cycle of birth and death; from ignorance, limitation, with the extended meaning of "salvation." Homeomorphic of *sōtēria*; commonly spelled *moksha* in English.

mysterium coniunctionis (Latin). The mystery of conjunction, reintegration into unity of the broken parts; the reunification of opposites, of the sexes in the original unity.

Nāgārjuna (Sanskrit). One of the most important philosophers of Mahāyāna Buddhism, founder of the *Mādhyamika* school.

nirvāṇa (Sanskrit). Extinction, liberation from every limit; the ultimate goal for Buddhism. Commonly spelled "nirvana" in English.

noēma (Greek). In Husserl's phenomenology, the unity of intellectual perception.

noēsis noēseos (Greek). The thought of thought, characteristic of the pure act or the Aristotelian first mover.

noumenon (Greek). That which is hidden behind the appearance *(phainomenon)*; beyond sensible experience; "that which is thought"; the thing in itself.

opus operantis Christi (Latin). By means of the work done by Christ (and transmitted to man as grace).

opus operatum (Latin). The work done, used mostly in the phrase *ex opere operato,* referring to the fact that the grace which the sacraments transmit is not produced *ex opere operantis* (by the action and virtue of the one who acts, the celebrant) but by virtue of the sacrament being performed and conferring the grace promised by Christ *(ex opere operato Christi).*

pati divina (Latin). Man's passive attitude in facing the "touches" of (encounters with), the divine (often in mystical experience).

perichōrēsis (Greek). Concept of early church's trinitarian doctrine describing interpenetration of the divine persons, equivalent to the Latin *circumincessio.*

phaneros (Greek). Shining, derived from *phanos*, light.

pisteuma (Greek). From *pisteuō*; what the believer believes, the "intentional" meaning of religious phenomena, in contrast to *noēma.*

plērōma (Greek). Fullness, the full, the complete.

Prajāpati (Sanskrit). "Lord of the creatures."

pratītyasamutpāda (Sanskrit). The Buddhist doctrine about the conditioned of "dependent origination," which asserts that nothing exists for itself, nothing bears within itself the conditions for its existence; instead everything is relational.

preambula fidei (Latin). Presuppositions or preambles of the faith (God's existence and unity, the soul's immortality, etc.).

primum analogatum (Latin). The point of reference for every analogy in a train of linked analogies.

puruṣa (Sanskrit). The original, archetypical man, the person, is both the primordial man marked by cosmic dimensions and the spiritual being or inner man. Commonly spelled *purusha* in English.

puruṣasūkta (Sanskrit). One of the last hymns in the *Ṛg-veda*, in which the primordial man is described *(puruṣa).*

Puruṣottama (Sanskrit). The supreme person, the supreme Spirit or supreme Soul; designation of the Self insofar as it is transcendent.

res cogitans/res extensa (Latin). Thinking thing/extended thing—division of reality according to Descartes.

Ṛg-veda (Sanskrit). The most ancient and important Veda; commonly spelled *Rig-veda* in English.

ṛta (Sanskrit). Cosmic and sacred order, sacrifice as universal law, and also truth; the ultimate dynamic and harmonious structure of reality.

sadguru or *satguru* (Sanskrit). Eternal teacher, archtypal teacher, universal guru.

sahṛdaya (Sanskrit). "Man-of-heart."

śakti (Sanskrit). Energy, force, power. The active, dynamic—feminine—aspect of reality or a God (generally Shiva); is personified as Shiva's goddess consort who discharges the creative function.

saṃnyāsin (Sanskrit). One who renounced, an ascetic; belongs to the fourth *āśrama*, or period of life, which some consider the highest stage.

saṃsāra (Sanskrit). The phenomenal world, temporal existence; the cycle of birth and death; state of dependency and slavery.

sanātana dharma (Sanskrit). Eternal law, imperishable law, name that Hinduism attributes to itself inasmuch as it does not trace itself either to a founder or to any temporal origin.

Śaṅkara (Sanskrit). Hindu philosopher and teacher of the eighth century; one of the greatest exponents of nondualistic vedanta.

sarvam-sarvātmakam (Sanskrit). Everything is related to everything else.

Śatapatha-brāhmaṇa (Sanskrit). The *brāhmaṇa* of the hundred ways; the most complete and systematic of the *Brāhmaṇa*.

sat-puruṣa (Sanskrit). Universal man.

satyāgraha (Sanskrit). Active nonviolence of those who live for the truth.

Selbstgehörigkeit (German). Self-belonging, a characteristic of the person.

shōbōgenzō (Japanese). Custodian of the vision of authentic reality—chief work of the Japanese master, Eihei Dōgen, who introduced Zen.

śiṣya (Sanskrit). Disciple.

Sitz im Leben (German). Literally, the situation in life, context.

Śiva (Sanskrit). One of the most important Gods in Hinduism; commonly spelled "Shiva" in English.

śivaism, śivaite (Sanskrit). One of the two great families of the Hindu religion whose God is Shiva.

sola fides (Latin). By faith alone, scholasticism's adage concerning theological questions that unaided reason and philosophy can never resolve—the fundamental Pauline idea about salvation, retrieved by Martin Luther in its existential dimension of *fides fiducialis* ("trusting faith").

speculatio (Latin). Speculation, from *speculum* ("mirror"), a type of thought that in Neoplatonism denoted the act of seeing God by starting from his reflection in created things; different from *contemplatio*, which is to consider God as God is in Godself.

śraddhā (Sanskrit). Faith, trust (in the Veda's doctrines).

śravaṇa (Sanskrit). Heard, listened to, to know how to listen or receive the teaching from the master's lips. Hearing the Vedas is the first of the three stages that vedanta considers necessary in order to achieve spiritual knowledge.

śūnyatā (Sanskrit). Empty, emptiness, nothingness; represents Buddhism's ultimate reality.

Śvetaketu (Sanskrit). The character in the *Chāndogya-upaniṣad* who receives from the father the teaching about *ātman* and *brahman* that ends with *tat tvam asi* (this you are).

Śvetāśvatara-upaniṣad (Sanskrit). The chief among the last Upanishads, frequently cited in the Vedanta, which tends to personify the supreme principle (Brahma), which it identified with the gods Shiva or Rudra.

Targum (Aramaic). "Interpretation"; different collections in Aramaic of translations and commentaries on the canonical texts of the Hebrew Bible.

tat tvam asi (Sanskrit). "This thou art," a upanishadic expression which signifies that, to the eye of the enlightened person, *ātman* is *brahman* ("ordinary" being is "absolute" being).

theologoumenon (Greek). A theological assertion; the result and expression of the effort to understand the faith.

unglückliches Bewusstein (German). Unhappy consciousness. Hegel's expression for a lacerated self-consciousness.

Ungrund (German). Without bottom, without foundation, abyss.

Upadeśasāhasrī (Sanskrit). "The (book) of the thousand instructions," one of Śankara's principal works.

Upaniṣad (Sanskrit). Fundamental sacred teaching in the form of texts that constitute the end of the Veda; part of revelation (*śruti*) and foundation of later Hindu thought.

vāc (Sanskrit). Word, speech, language; the primordial word, sacred and creative.

Veda (Sanskrit). The totality of the Hindu sacred scriptures.

vedānta (Sanskrit). Regarding the end of the Vedas, or one of the last philosophical schools of Hindu thought; among its most eminent representatives are Śankara, Rāmānuja, and Madva.

visio beatifica (Latin.). Beatific vision, direct and immediate vision of God that is achieved, on the whole, after the death of those who have been saved; it entails the full and definitive experience of communion with God.

Viṣṇu (Sanskrit). He who fulfills, one of the principal Gods of Hinduism, often written "Vishnu" in English.

viṣṇuita (Sanskrit). Followers of *vishnuism*, one of Hinduism's three great orientations.

Vivekacūḍamaṇi (Sanskrit). Joy-diadem of discernment, Śankara's important work of the *advaita-vedānta*, which treats of the distinction between true reality and the phenomenal world (the world "as it appears").

Bibliography

Abhiṣiktānanda (Swami). 1986. *La montée au fond du coeur.* Paris: OEIL.

Akhilānanda (Swami). 1949. *Hindu View of Christ.* Boston: Branden.

Alegre, Xavier, et al., eds. 1995. *Universalidad de Cristo: Universalidad del pobre.* Santander: Sal Terrae.

Amaladoss, Michael, et al., eds. 1981. *Theologizing in India* (Collection of papers presented at a Seminar in Pune in 1978). Bangalore: TPI.

Amalorpavadass, D. S., ed. 1974. *Research Seminar on Non-Biblical Scriptures.* Bangalore: NBCLC.

Atanasio, Jevtić. 1996. *L'infinito cammino: Umanizzazione di Dio e deificazione dell'uomo.* Sotto il Monte (Bergamo): Servitium-Interlogos.

Augstein, Rudolf. 1972. *Jesus Menschensohn.* Munich: Bertelsmann.

Baird, William. 1977. *The Quest of the Christ of Faith: Reflections on the Bultmann Era.* Waco: Word Books.

Baldini, Massimo, and Silvano Zucal, eds. 1989. *Il silenzio e la parola da Eckhart a Jabès.* Brescia: Morcelliana.

Balthasar, Hans Urs von. 1938. *Origenes: Geist und Feuer.* Salzburg: Müller.

———. 1961a. *Kosmische Liturgie: Das Weltbild Maximus des Bekenners.* Einsiedeln: Johannes Verlag. 2nd ed. translated into Italian as *Liturgia cosmica* (Rome: AVE, 1976).

———. 1961b. *Herrlichkeit: Eine theologische Ästhetik.* Volume 1, *Schau der Gestalt.* Einsiedeln: Johannes Verlag.

———. 1980. *Kennt uns Jesus—Kennen wir Ihn?* Freiburg: Herder.

Barbaglio, Giuseppe, and Severino Dianich. 1991. *Nuovo Dizionario di Teologia.* 6th ed. Milan: Paoline.

Barr, James. 1970. "The Symbolism of Names in the Old Testament." *Bulletin of the John Rylands Library* 52:11-29.

———. 1976. "Story and History in Biblical Theology." *Journal of Religion* 56, no. 1:1-17.

Bastian, Hans-Dieter. 1969. *Theologie der Frage.* Munich: Kaiser.

Bäumer, Bettina, ed. 1988. *Abhinavagupta: Parātrīśikā-vivaraṇa.* Eng. trans. with notes by Jaideva Sing. New Delhi: Motilal Banarisdass.

———. ed. 1997. *Mysticism in Shaivism and Christianity.* New Delhi: DK Printworld.

Bayart, Julian. 1966. "Cosmic Christ and our Evaluation of other Religions." *Clergy Monthly Supplement.*

Bellet, Maurice. 1990. *Christ.* Paris: Desclee.

Ben-Chorin, Schalom. 1967. *Der Nazarener in jüdischer Sicht.* Munich: List.

Benedikt, B., and A. Sobel. 1992. *Der Streit um Drewermann.* Wiesbaden: Sobel.

Benjamin, Roger. 1971. *Notion de personne et personnalisme chrétien.* Paris: Mouton.

Berdyaev, Nikolai. 1933. *Esprit et liberté: Essai de philosophie chretienne.* Paris: Cerf.

Boff, Leonardo. 1983. *Jesucristo el Liberador: Ensayo de cristología crítica para nuestro tiempo.* Santander: Sal Terrae. Eng. trans. *Jesus Christ Liberator* (Maryknoll, N.Y.: Orbis Books, 1978).

Bordoni, Marcello. 1991. "Cristologia" and "Gesu Cristo." In Barbaglio and Dianich 1991, 234-71, 530-68.

Borne, Étienne. 1987. "Ideologie antipersonaliste." In Pavan and Milano 1987, 393-414.

Botterweck, G. Johannes, and Helmer Ringgren, eds. 1973–. *Theologisches Wörterbuch zum Alten Testament.* Stuttgart: Kohlhammer.

Boulgakov, Serge [Bulgakov, Sergei]. 1982. *Du Verbe Incarné. L'Agneau de Dieu, L'Age d'homme.* Lausanne.

Bouyer, Louis. 1960. *La spiritualité du Nouveau Testament et des Pères.* Paris: Aubier.

Breton, Stanislas. 1981. *Unicité et monothéisme.* Paris: Cerf.

Buber, Martin, ed. 1984. *Mystische Zeugnisse aller Zeiten und Völker.* New edition edited by P. Sloterdijk. Munich: Diederichs.

Büchner, Frederick, et al., eds. 1974. *The Faces af Jesus.* New York: Simon & Schuster.

Bultmann, Rudolf. 1958a. *Jesus and the Word.* New York: Scribner's.

———. 1958b. *Jesus Christ Mythology.* New York: Scribner's.

Buri, Frits. 1969. *Der Pantokrator.* Hamburg: Herbert Reich.

Caba, José. 1977. *El Jesús de los Evangelios.* Madrid: BAC.

Cabada-Castro, Manuel. 1975. "La vivencia previa del absoluto como presupuesto del acceso teorético a Dios." In Vargas-Machuca, 1975.

Catherine of Siena. 1935. *Libro della divina dottrina.* Edited by A. Levasti. Milan: Rizzoli.

Chatterjee, Margaret. 1963. *Our Knowledge of Other Selves.* Bombay: Asia Publishing House.

Cobb, John B., Jr. 1975. *Christ in a Pluralistic Age.* Philadelphia: Westminster.

Congar, Yves. 1958. *Le mystère du temple.* Paris: Cerf.

———. 1981. "Le monothéisme politique et le Dieu-Trinité." *Nouvelle Revue Theologique* 103:3-17.

Corbin, Henry. 1981. *Le paradoxe du monothéisme.* Paris: L'Herne.

Crossan, John Dominic. 1991. *The Historical Jesus: The Life of a Mediterranean Jewish Peasant.* San Francisco: HarperCollins.

Cullmann, Oscar. 1957. *Christ et le temps.* Neuchâtel: Delachaux & Niéstle.

Danese, Attilio. 1984. *Unità e pluralità: Mounier e il ritorno alla persona.* Rome: Città Nuova.

———, ed. 1986. *La questione personalista: Mounier e Maritain nel dibatito per un nuovo umanesimo.* Rome: Città Nuova.

Daniélou, Jean. 1961. *Message évangélique et culture hellénistique.* Tournai: Desclee.

———. 1968. *La Trinité et le mystère de l'existence.* Paris: Desclee.

Denzinger, Henricus. 1967. *Enchiridion symbolorum definitionum et decla rationum de rebus fidei et morum.* Barcelona: Herder.

Deschner, Karlheinz. 1990ff. *Kriminalgeschichte des Christentums.* Reinbeck bei Hamburg: Rowohlt.

Des Rochers, John. 1977. *Christ the Liberator.* Bangalore: Centre for Social Action.

Dictionnaire de spiritualité. 1937 -1995. 17 volumes. Paris: Beauchesne.

Di Nicola, Giulia Paola. 1991. *Reciprocidad hombre/mujer.* Madrid: Narcea.

Dodd, Charles H. 1970. *The Founder of Christianity.* New York: Macmillan.

Dōgen, Eihei. 1997. *Divenire l'Essere.* Shoboghenzo Ghenjokan, ed., la Comunità Vangelo e Zen. Bologna: EDB.

Doré, Joseph. 1984. "Jésus-Christ." In Poupard 1984, 847-58.

———. 1990. "Discesa agli inferi." In Poupard 1990, 558-62.

Drewermann, Eugen. 1984-85. *Tiefenpsychologie und Exegese.* 2 volumes. Olten-Freiburg: Walter.

———. 1995. *Dieu immédiat.* Paris: Desclée.

———. 1987-88. *Das Markusevangelium.* 2 volumes. Olten-Freiburg: Walter.

Dupré, Louis. 1987. "Mysticism." In Eliade 1987, 10:245-61.

Dupuis, Jacques. 1966. "The Cosmic Christ in the Early Fathers." *Indian Journal of Theology*, 106-20.

———. 1977. *Jesus Christ and His Spirit: Theological Approaches*. Bangalore: TPI.

———. 1989. *Jesus-Christ à la rencontre des religions*. Paris: Desclée. Eng. trans. *Jesus Christ at the Encounter of World Religions* (Maryknoll, N.Y.: Orbis Books, 1991).

———. 1994. *Who Do You Say I Am? Introduction to Christology*. Maryknoll, N.Y.: Orbis Books.

———. 1997. *Towards a Christian Theology of Religious Pluralism*. Maryknoll, N.Y.: Orbis Books.

———. 2002. *Christianity and the Religions: From Confrontation to Dialogue*. Maryknoll, N.Y.: Orbis Books.

Duquoc, Christian. 1972. *Christologie II: Le Messie*. Paris: Cerf.

———. 1977. *Dieu différent: Essai sur la symbologie trinitaire*. Paris: Cerf.

Eagan, Harvey D. 1984. *Christian Mysticism: The Future of a Tradition*. New York: Pueblo.

Edwards, Denis. 1955. *Jesus the Wisdom of God*. Maryknoll, N.Y.: Orbis Books.

Eliade, Mircea, ed. 1987. *The Encyclopedia of Religion*. 16 volumes. New York: Macmillan.

Evers, Georg. 1993. "Asian, African and Latin American Contributions towards Christology." *Jahrbuch für kontextuelle Theologie*. Aachen: Missio, 174-96.

Fanon, Frantz. 1963. *Les damnés de la terre*. Paris: Maspéro.

Feiner, Johannes, and Magnus Loehrer, eds. 1970. *Mysterium Salutis: Grundriss heilsgeschichtlicher Dogmatik*. 3 volumes. Cologne: Benziger.

Felder, Hilarius. 1953. *Jesus of Nazareth*. Milwaukee: Bruce.

Festugière, André Jean. 1936. *Contemplation et vie contemplative selon Platon*. Paris: Vrin.

Flusser, David. 1968. *Jesus in Selbstzeugnissen und Bilddokumenten*. Reinbeck bei Hamburg: Rowohlt.

Forrester, Viviane. 1996. *L'horreur économique*. Paris: Fayard.

Forte, Bruno. 1985. *Trinità come storia*. Milan: Paoline.

Fraijó, Manuel. 1996. *El futuro del cristianismo*. Madrid: SM.

Frei, Hans W. 1975. *The Identity of Jesus Christ: The Hermeneutical Bases of Dogmatic Theology*. Philadelphia: Fortress.

Friedli, Richard. 1989. *Le Christ dans les cultures*. Paris: Cerf.

Fries, Heinrich, ed. 1962. *Handbuch theologischer Grundbegriffe*. 2 volumes. Munich: Kösel.

———, ed. 1981. *Jesus in den Weltreligionen*. St. Otilien. Eos.

Frye, Northrop. 1982. *The Great Code: The Bible and Literature*. New York: H. C. Jovanovich.

Gadamer, Hans Georg. 1972. *Wahrheit und Methode*. 3rd ed. Tübingen: Mohr.

———, and Paul Vogler, eds. 1975. *Neue Anthropologie*. 7 volumes. Stuttgart: Thieme.

Galtier, Paul. 1939. *L'unité du Christ: Être, personne, conscience*. Paris: Beauchesne.

———. 1947. *Les deux Adam*. Paris: Beauchesne.

———. 1954. *La conscience humaine du Christ*. Rome: Gregorian University Press.

Garrigou-Lagrange, Reginald. 1953. "La possibilité de L'Incarnation sans aucune déviation panthéiste." *Angelicum* 30, no. 4:337-46.

Geiselmann, Joseph Rupert. 1962. "Jesus Christus." In Fries 1962, 1:739-70.

Gispert-Sauch, George. 1974. "Biblical Inspiration as 'parama-vyanjana'?" (*sic*). In Amalorpavadass 1974, 136-52.

González de Cardedal, Olegario. 1975a. "Un problema teológico fundamental: la preexistencia de Cristo: Historia y hermeneutica." In Vargas-Machuca 1975, 179-211.

————. 1975b. *Jesús de Nazaret: Aproximación a la Cristología.* Madrid: BAC.

González-Faus, José Ignacio. 1984. *La Humanidad Nueva: Ensayo de Cristologia.* Santander: Sal Terrae. Eng. trans. *Where the Spirit Breathes: Prophetic Dissent in the Church* (Maryknoll, N.Y.: Orbis Books, 1989).

————. 1995. "Religiones de la tierra y universalidad de Cristo: Del dialogo a la diapraxis." In Alegre 1995, 103-43.

————. 1996. "La cristología después del Vaticano II." In *Memoria académica, 1995-1996,* 105-16. Madrid: Instituto Fe y Secularidad.

Gort, Jerald D., et al., eds. 1992. *On Sharing Religious Experience: Possibilities of Interfaith Mutuality.* Grand Rapids: Eerdmans.

Graham, Aelread. 1947. *The Christ of Catholicism.* London: Longmans, Green.

Grant, Robert M. 1961. *The Earliest Lives of Jesus.* New York: Harper & Brothers.

Griffin, David Ray. 1973. *A Process Christology.* Philadelphia: Westminster.

Grillmeier, Alois. 1975. *Mit ihm und in ihm: Christologische Forschungen und Perspektiven.* Freiburg: Herder.

————, and Michael Schmaus, eds. 1965. *Handbuch der Dogmengeschichte.* Volume 3. Freiburg: Herder.

Guardini, Romano. 1939. *Welt und Person: Versuche zur christlichen Lehre vom Menschen.* Würzburg: Werkbund.

————.1953. *Vom Wesen katholischer Weltanschauung.* Basel: Hess.

————. 1958. *Die menschliche Wirklichkeit des Herrn.* Würzburg: Werkbund.

————. 1963. *Unterscheidung des Christlichen.* Mainz: Grünewald.

Haas, Alois M. 1971. *Nim din selbes war: Studien zur Lehre von der Selbsterkenntnis bei Meister Ekhart, Johannes Tauler und Heinrich Seuse.* Freiburg, Switzerland: Universitätsverlag.

————. 1979. *Sermo mysticus: Studien zu Theologie und Sprache der deutschen Mystik.* Freiburg: Switzerland: Universitätsverlag.

————. 1996. *Mystik als Aussage: Erfahrungs-, Denk- und Redeformen christlicher Mystik.* Frankfurt: Suhrkamp.

Hamerton-Kelly, R G. 1973. *Pre-existence, Wisdom and the Son of Man: A Study of the Idea of Pre-existence in the New Testament.* Cambridge: Cambridge University Press.

Hartmann, Franz. 1890. *The Life and Doctrines of Jacob Boehme.* Boston: Occult Publications.

Hausherr, Irénéé. 1955. *Direction spirituelle en Orient autrefois.* Rome: Pontificium Institutum Orientalium Studiorum.

Haven-Smith, Lance de. 1997. "How Jesus Planned to Overthrow the Roman Empire." *Religious Studies and Theology* 16, no. 1:48-59.

Healy, Kathleen. 1990. *Christ as Common Ground: A Study of Christianity and Hinduism.* Pittsburgh: Duquesne University Press.

Hegermann, Harald. 1961. *Die Vorstellung vom Schöpfungsmittler im hellenistischen Judentum und Urchristentum.* Berlin: Akademie.

Heidegger, Martin. 1966. *Einführung in die Metaphysik.* 3rd ed. Tübingen: Niemeyer.

Heiler, Friedrich. 1961. *Erscheinungsformen und Wesen der Religion.* Stuttgart.

Hérmes—Recherches sur l'expérience spirituelle. 1981. Les voies de la mystique ou l'accès au sans-accès, n.s. 1. Paris: Deux Océans.

Hockel, Alfred. 1965. *Christus der Erstgeborene.* Düsseldorf: Patmos.

Hodgson, Peter C. 1971. *Jesus—Word and Presence: An Essay in Christology.* Philadelphia: Fortress.

Hoffman, Bengt R. 1976. *Luther and the Mystics.* Minneapolis: Augsburg.

Holböck, Ferdinand, and Thomas Sartory, eds. 1962. *Mysterium Kirche.* 2 volumes. Salzburg: Müller.

Isaac, Augustine. 1974. *Jesus the Rebel.* Mangalore: Sallak Publications.

Jaspers, Karl. 1963. *Der philosophische Glaube angesichts der Offenbarung.* Munich: Piper.

Jiménez Duque, Baldomero, and Luis Sala Balust, eds. 1969. *Historia de la espirtitualidad.* 4 volumes. Barcelona: Flors.

Jung, Karl-Gustav. 1963. *Erinnerungen, Träume, Gedanken.* Edited by A. Jaffé. Zurich: Rascher.

Kahlefeld, Heinrich. 1981. *Die Gestalt Jesu in den synoptischen Evangelien.* Frankfurt: Knecht.

Kasper, Walter. 1974. *Jesus der Christus.* Mainz: Grünewald.

Keenan, John P. 1989. *The Meaning of Christ.* Maryknoll, N.Y.: Orbis Books.

Kendall, Daniel, and Gerald O'Collins. 1992. "The Faith of Jesus." *Theological Studies* 53:403-23.

Kerényi, Károly. 1976. *Dionysios: Archetypal Image of Indestructible Life.* Princeton, N.J.: Princeton University Press.

Kittel, Gerhard, and Gerhard Friedrich, eds. 1964-74. *Theological Dictionary of the New Testament.* Translated and edited by G. W. Bromiley. 16 volumes. Grand Rapids: Eerdmans.

Kittel, Gisela. 1989-90. *Der Name über alle Namen.* 2 volumes. Göttingen: Vandenhoeck & Ruprecht.

Klostermaier, Klaus K. 1997. "The Hermeneutic Center." *Journal of Ecumenical Studies* 34, no. 2 (Spring):159-70.

Knitter, Paul F. 1985. *No Other Name?* Maryknoll, N.Y.: Orbis Books.

———. 2002. *Introducing Theologies of Religion.* Maryknoll, N.Y.: Orbis Books.

Koyama, Kosuke. 1984. *Mount Fuji and Mount Sinai.* Maryknoll, N.Y.: Orbis Books.

Krempel, A. 1952. *La doctrine de la relation chez saint Thomas.* Paris: Vrin.

Kröger, Athanasius. 1967. *Mensch und Person: Moderne Personbegriffe in der katholischen Theologie.* Recklinghausen: Paulus.

Kuschel, Karl Josef. 1978. *Jesus in der deutschsprachigen Gegenwartsliteratur.* Zurich and Cologne: Benziger. Gütersloh: Gerd Mohn.

———. 1990. *Geboren vor aller Zeit? Der Streit um Christi Ursprung.* Munich: Piper. Eng. trans. *Born Before All Time: The Dispute over Christ's Origin* (New York: Crossroad, 1992).

Lamarche, P. 1965. "Einführung in die biblische Christologie." In Schmaus and Grillmeier 1965, 3/la:1-16.

Lamotte, Étienne. 1958. *Histoire du Bouddhisme indien.* Louvain: Publications Universitaires.

Lattanzi, Ugo. 1937. *Il primato universale di Cristo secondo le S. Scritture.* Rome: Lateran University Press.

Leaney, A. R. C. 1967. *The Letters of Peter and Jude.* The Cambridge Bible Commentary. Cambridge: Cambridge University Press.

Lee, Bernard J. 1993. *Jesus and the Metaphors of God: The Christs of the New Testament.* Mahwah, N.J.: Paulist Press.

Leeuw, Gerardus van der. 1956. *Phänomenologie der Religion.* Tübingen: Paul Siebeck.

Lefebure, Leo D. 1993. *The Buddha and the Christ: Explorations in Buddhist and Christian Dialogue.* Maryknoll, N.Y.: Orbis Books.

Liébaert, Jacques. 1965. "Christologie: Von der apostolischen Zeit bis zum Konzil von Chalcedon." In Schmaus and Grillmeier 1965, 3:19-127.

Limone, Giuseppe. 1988. "Tempo della persona e sapienza del possibile: Valori, politica, diritto." In *Emmanuel Mounier.* 2 volumes. Naples and Rome: Edizione Scientifiche Italiane.

Loehrer, Magnus. and Johannes Feiner, eds. 1970. *Mysterium Salutis: Grundriss heilsgeschichtlicher Dogmatik.* Volume 3. Cologne: Benziger.

Lonergan, Bernard J. F. 1977. *The Way to Nicea: The Dialectical Development of Trinitarian Theology*. Philadelphia: Westminster.

Lubac, Henri de. 1953. *Méditation sur l'Église*. 3rd ed. Paris: Aubier.

———. 1965. *Le mystère du surnaturel*. 3rd ed. Paris: Aubier.

———. 1974. *Pic de la Mirandole*. Paris: Aubier.

———. 1979. *Mistica e mistero cristiano*. In *Opera Omnia*, vol. 6. Milan: Jaca Book.

Maisch, Ingrid, and Anton Vögtle. 1969. *Jesus Christ, I. Biblical*. In Rahner 1969, 174-83.

Martin, R. P. 1967. *"Carmen Christi: Philippians II, 5-11 in Recent Interpretations and in the Setting of Early Christian Worship*. Cambridge: Cambridge University Press.

Martin-Velasco, Juan. 1995. *La experiencia cristiana de Dios*. Madrid: Trotta.

Mascarenhas, Hubert Olympius. 1953. "St. Thomas Aquinas and the Medieval Scholastics." In Radhakrhisnan 1953, 2:149-69.

Massa, Willi. 1995. *Der universale Christus*. Mettlach-Tünsdorf: Neumühle.

May, John d'Arcy. 1990. *Christus Initiator: Theologie im Pazifik*. Düsseldorf: Patmos.

McGinn, Bernard. 1992. *The Foundations of Mysticism*. New York: Crossroad.

Menacherry, Cheriyan. 1996. *Christ: The Mystery in History, A Critical Study on the Christology of R. Panikkar*. Frankfurt: Lang.

Mersch, Émile. 1933. *Le Corps Mystique du Christ*. 2 volumes. Louvain: Lessianum.

———. 1949. *La Théologie du Corps Mystique*. 2 volumes. Paris: Desclee.

Milano, Andrea. 1984. *Persona in Teologia*. Naples: Dehoniane.

———. 1987. "La Trinità dei teologi e dei filosofi: L'intelligenza della persona in Dio." In Pavan and Milano 1987, 1-286.

Mitchell, Donald W. 1991. *Spirituality and Emptiness*. Mahwah, N.J.: Paulist Press.

Molinos, Miguel de. 1976. Orig. ed. 1675. *Guía espiritual*. Critical edition by J. I. Tellechea. Madrid: Universidad Pontificia de Salamanca.

Mommaers, Paul, and Jan Van Bragt. 1995. *Mysticism: Buddhist and Christian*. New York: Crossroad.

Monchanin, Jules. 1985. *Théologie et spiritualité missionaires*. Paris: Beauchesne.

Montefiore, Hugh W. 1966. "Towards a Christology for Today." In *Soundings*, edited by A. R. Vidler. Cambridge: Cambridge University Press.

Moore, Sebastian. 1967. *God Is a New Language*. Westminster: Newman.

Moran, Gabriel. 1992. *Uniqueness*. Maryknoll, N.Y.: Orbis Books.

Mounier, Emmanuel. 1936. *Manifeste au service du personnalisme*. Paris.

———. 1950. *Feu la Chrétienité: Carnets de route*. Paris: Seuil.

———. 1952. *Personalism*. London: Routledge & Kegan Paul.

Mount Saviour Monastery. 1972. *On the Experience of God*. 15 papers by monks of the Order of St. Benedict. *Monastic Studies* 9 (Autumn).

Mouroux, Jean. 1952. *L'expérience chrétienne: Introduction a la Théologie*. Paris: Aubier.

Mühlen, Heribert. 1966. *Der Heilige Geist als Person*. 3rd ed. Münster: Aschendorff.

———. 1968. *Una mystica Persona*. 3rd ed. Munich: Schöningh.

Nédoncelle, Maurice. 1942. *La réciprocité des consciences*. Paris: PUF.

———. 1944. *La personne humaine et la nature*. Paris: PUF.

———. 1970. *Explorations personnalistes*. Paris: Aubier.

Newbigin, Lesslie. 1978. "Christ and the Cultures." *Scottish Journal of Theology* 31, no. 1:1-22.

Nieremberg, Juan Eusebio. 1640. *Diferencia entre lo temporal y lo eterno*. Madrid.

Nishitani, Keiji. 1982. *Religion and Nothingness*. Berkeley: University of California Press.

Nolan, Albert. 1978. *Jesus before Christianity: The Gospel of Liberation*. Maryknoll, N.Y.: Orbis Books.

Nurbakhsh, Javad. 1996. *Jesús a los ojos de los sufíes*. Madrid: Darek-Nyumba.

Ohashi, Ryōsuke, ed. 1990. *Die Philosophie der Kyōto-Schule*. Munich: Alber.

Olschak, Blanche Christine. 1987. *Perlen alttibetischer Literatur*. Wald, Switzerland: Im Waldgut.

Orbe, Antonio, ed. 1985. *Il Cristo*. Volume 1, *Testi teologici e spirituali dal I al IV secolo*. Milan: Mondadori-Fondazione Lorenzo Valla.

Ortega, Augusto Andrés. 1970. "Cristo: su conciencia humana y su persona divina." In Zubiri 1970, 1:91-119.

Ozaki, Makoto. 1990. *Introduction to the Philosophy of Tanabe*. Amsterdam: Rodolpi B. V.

Panikkar, Raimon. 1963. *Humanismo y Cruz*. Madrid: Rialp.

———. 1966. *Māyā e Apocalisse: L'incontro dell'induismo e del cristianesimo*. Rome: Abete.

———. 1972a. *El concepto de naturaleza*. Madrid: CSIC.

———. 1972b. *Salvation in Christ: Concreteness and Universality, the Supername*. Inaugural lecture at the Insitute for Advanced Studies of Theology. Jerusalem: Tantur. Pp. 1-81.

———. 1972c. "'Super hanc petram': Due principi ecclesiologici: la roccia e le chiavi," 135-45. *Legge e Vangelo: Discussione su una legge fondamentale per la Chiesa*. Brescia: Paideia.

———. 1975a. *Spiritualità indù*. Brescia: Morcelliana.

———. 1975b. "El presente tempiterno: Una apostilla ala historia de la salvación y a la teologia de la liberación." In Vargas-Machuca 1975, 133-75.

———. 1975c. "Verstehen als Überzeugtsein." In Gadamer and Vogler 1977, 7:132-67.

———. 1977. *The Vedic Experience: Mantramañjarī*. Los Angeles: University of California Press.

———. 1980. "Che accade all'uomo quando muore? Una riflessione interculturale su una metafora." *Bozze* [Rome] 5/6:117-36.

———. 1981a. "Per una lettura transculturale del simbolo." *Quaderni di psicologia infantile* 5:53-91, 113-23.

———. 1981b. *The Unknown Christ of Hinduism: Towards an Ecumenical Christophany*. Maryknoll, N.Y.: Orbis Books.

———. 1983. *Myth, Faith and Hermeneutics*. 2nd ed. Bangalore: ATC.

———. 1986. "The Threefold Linguistic Intrasubjectivity." *Archivio di Filosofia* [Rome] 54, 1/3:593-606.

———. 1989a. *Trinità ed esperienza religiosa dell'uomo*. Assisi: Cittadella.

———. 1989b. "Reader's Response." *International Bulletin of Missionary Research* 13, no. 2:80.

———. 1990. "The pluralism of truth." *World Faith Insight* 25 (October):7-16.

———. 1991. "Indic Christian Theology of Religious Pluralism from the Perspective of Inculturation." In Pathil 1991, 252-99.

———. 1992. "Are the Words of Scripture Universal Religious Categories? The Case of the Christian Language for the Third Millenium." *Archivio di Filosofia* [Rome], 377-87.

———. 1993a. *The Cosmotheandric Experience: Emerging Religious Consciousness*. Maryknoll, N.Y.: Orbis Books.

———. 1993b. *Ecosofia: La nuova saggezza per una spiritualità della terra*. Assisi: Cittadella.

———. 1994a. "Neither Christomonism nor Christodualism." *Jeevadhara* [Kottayam] 24, no. 142 (July):336-38.

———. 1994b. *La nuova innocenza II*. Milan: CENS.

———. 1996. *El silencio del Buddha*. Madrid: Siruela. Eng. trans. of 1st ed., *The Silence of God: The Response of the Buddha* (Maryknoll, N.Y.: Orbis Books, 1989).

———. 1997. *La experiencia filosófica de la India*. Madrid: Trotta.

Parappally, Jacob. 1995. *Emerging Trends in Indian Christology.* Bangalore: Indian Institute of Spirituality.

Parente, Pietro. 1951. *L'io di Cristo.* Brescia: Morcelliana.

———. 1952. *Unità ontologica e psicologica dell'Uomo-Dio.* Rome: Urbaniana.

Pathil, Kuncheria, ed. 1991. *Religious Pluralism: An Indian Christian Perspective.* Delhi: ISPCK.

Pavan, Antonio, and Andrea Milano, eds. 1987. *Persona e Personalismo.* Naples: Dehoniane.

Pelikan, Jaroslav. 1965. *The Finality of Jesus Christ in an Age of Universal History: A Dilemma of the Third Century.* Richmond: John Knox.

———. 1987. *Jesus through the Centuries: His Place in the History of Culture.* New York: Harper & Row.

Peterson, Erik. 1983. *Il monoteismo come problema politico.* Brescia: Queriniana. German original, 1935.

Pienda, Jesús Avelino de la. 1982. *Antropología transcendental de Karl Rahner.* Oviedo: Universityof Oviedo.

Pieris, Aloysius. 1988. *An Asian Theology of Liberation.* Maryknoll, N.Y.: Orbis Books.

Poupard, Paul, et al., eds. 1984. *Dictionnaire des Religions.* Paris: PUF.

———. 1990. *Grande dizionario delle religioni.* Assisi: Cittadella. Casale Monferrato: Piemme.

Quell, Gottfried. 1967. "Pater." In Kittel and Friedrich 1964–, 5:959-74.

Radhakrishnan, Sarvepalli, ed. 1952-53. *History of Philosophy Eastern and Western.* 2 volumes. London: Allen & Unwin.

Rahner, Hugo. 1964. *Symbole der Kirche.* Salzburg: Müller.

Rahner, Karl, et al., eds. 1969. *Sacramentum Mundi: An Encyclopedia of Theology.* New York: Herder & Herder.

Rahner, Karl, and Wilhelm Thüsing. 1972. *Christologie: Systematisch und exegetisch.* Freiburg: Herder.

Ratzinger, Joseph. 1993. "Le Christ, la foi et le défi des cultures." *La documentation catholique,* 2120, 16.VII.1995.

Ravier, A., ed. 1964. *La mystique et les mystiques.* Paris: Desclée.

Ravindra, Ravi. 1990. *The Yoga of the Christ in the Gospel According to St. John.* Longmead: Element Books.

Renwart, Lion. 1993. "Image de Dieu, image de l'homme." *Nouvelle Revue Theologique* 115:85-104.

Ricoeur, Paul. 1990. *Soi-même comme un autre.* Paris: Seuil.

Ringgren, Helmer. 1973. "ᵓab-Galâ." In Botterweck and Ringgren 1973, vol. 1, cols. 1-19.

Robinson, John A. T. 1973. *The Human Face of God.* Philadelphia: Westminster.

———. 1979. *Truth Is Two-Eyed.* London: SCM.

Rombach, Heinrich. 1991. *Der kommende Gott: Hermetik—eine neue Weltsicht.* Freiburg: Rombach.

Rosenberg, Alfons. 1986. *Jesus der Mensch: Ein Fragment.* Munich: Kösel.

Rovira Belloso, Joseph Maria. 1984. *La humanitat de Déu: Aproximació a l'essència del cristianisme.* Barcelona.

Ruh, Kurt. 1990. *Geschichte der abendländischen Mystik.* Volume 1, *Die Grundlegung durch die Kirchenväter und die Mönchtheologie des 12. Jahrhunderts.* Munich: Beck.

———. 1991. Vol. 2.

———. 1996. Vol. 3.

Ruhbach, Gerhard, and Josef Sudbrack, eds. 1984. *Grosse Mystiker.* Munich: Beck.

Rupp, George. 1973. "Religious Pluralism in the Context of an Emerging World Culture." *Harvard Theological Review* 66:207-18.

————. 1974. *Christologies and Cultures: Towards a Typology of Religious World-views.* The Hague: Mouton.

Sala-Balust, Luis, and Baldomero Jimenéz Duque, eds. 1969. *Historia de la espiritualidad.* 4 volumes. Barcelona: Flors.

Santiago-Otero, Horacio. 1970. *El conocimiento de Cristo en cuanto hombre.* Pamplona: University of Navarra.

Scheeben, Matthias Joseph. 1941. *Die Mysterien des Christentums.* Edited by J. Hofer. Freiburg: Herder.

Schestow, Leo [Le Sesto/Chesto]. 1994. *Athen und Jerusalem.* Munich: Matthes & Seitz.

Schillebeeckx, Edward. 1963. *Christ: The Sacrament of the Encounter with God.* New York: Sheed & Ward.

————. 1985. *The Schillebeeckx Reader.* Edited by Robert J. Schreiter. New York: Crossroad.

Schiwy, Günther. 1990. *Der kosmische Christus: Spuren Gottes ins Neue Zeitalter.* Munich: Kösel.

Schmaus, Michael, and Alois Grillmeier, eds. 1965. *Handbuch der Dogmengeschichte.* Volume 3. Freiburg: Herder.

Schnackenburg, Rudolf. 1970. "Christologie des Neuen Testamenten." In Feiner and Loehrer 1970, 3:227-388.

Schoonenberg, Piet. 1971. *The Christ: A Study of the God-Man Relationship in the Whole of Creation and in Jesus Christ.* New York: Seabury.

Schreiter, Robert J., ed. 1991. *Faces of Jesus in Africa.* Maryknoll, N.Y.: Orbis Books.

Schrenk, Gottlob. 1967. "Pater." In Kittel and Friedrich, 1964–, 5:945-59, 974-1022.

Schüssler Fiorenza, Elisabeth. 1994. *Jesus, Miriam's Child, Sophia's Prophet: Critical Issues in Feminist Christology.* New York: Continuum.

Sherrard, Philip. 1992. *Human Image, World Image: The Death and Resurrection of Sacred Cosmology.* Ipswich: Golgonooza.

————. 1995. *The Greek East and the Latin West (A Study in the Christian Tradition).* Limni, Greece: Denise Harvey. Original ed., Oxford University Press, 1959.

Simonson, Conrad. 1972. *The Christology of the Faith and Order Movement.* Leiden: Brill.

Smet, Richard de. 1976a. "The Discovery of the Person." *Indian Philosophical Quarterly* 4, no. 1:1-23.

————. 1976b. "The Rediscovery of the Person." *Indian Philosophical Quarterly* 4, no. 3:413-26.

Smith, Huston. 1992. "Is There a Perennial Philosophy?" In *Revisioning Philosophy*, edited by J. Ogilvy, 247-62. Albany: State University of New York Press.

Soares-Prabhu, George. 1981. "The Historical Critical Method: Reflections on Its Relevance for the Study of the Gospels in India Today." In Amaladoss 1981, 314-67.

Sobrino, Jon. 1976. *Cristología desde América Latina.* Centro de Reflexión Teológica, Mexico. Eng. trans., *Christology at the Crossroads* (Maryknoll, N.Y.: Orbis Books, 1978).

Sophrony (Archimandrite). 1978. *His Life Is Mine.* London: Mowbrays.

Stöckli, Thomas, ed. 1991. *Wege zur Christus-Erfahrung.* Dornach: Goetheanum.

Strack, Hermann L., and Paul Billerbeck. 1922-28. *Kommentar zum Neuen Testament aus Talmud und Midrasch.* 6 volumes. Munich: C. H. Beck.

Sudbrack, Josef, and Gerhard Ruhbach, eds. 1984. *Grosse Mystiker.* Munich: Beck.

Sugirtharajah, R. S., ed. 1993. *Asian Faces of Jesus.* Maryknoll, N.Y.: Orbis Books.

Swidler, Leonard. 1988. *Jeshua: A Model for Moderns.* Kansas City: Sheed & Ward.

Teresa de Jesús. 1967. *Obras Completas.* Edited by Efrén de la Madre de Dios and O. Steggink. Madrid: BAC.

Thibaut, René. 1942. *Le sens de l'Homme-Dieu.* Paris: Desclee.

Thiselton, C. A. 1974. "The Supposed Power of Words in the Biblical Writings." *Journal of Theological Studies* 25:283-99.

Thomas, M. M. 1987. *Risking Christ for Christ's Sake*. Geneva: WCC Publications.

Thompson, William M. 1985. *The Jesus Debate: A Survey and Synthesis*. Mahwah, N.J.: Paulist Press.

Tilliette, Xavier. 1990a. "Cristo e i Filosofi." In Poupard 1990, 424-30.

———. 1990b. *Le Christ de la philosophie*. Paris: Cerf.

———. 1993. *Le Christ des philosophes*. Namur: Culture et Verité.

Tomatis, Francesco. 1994. *Kenōsis del logos*. Rome: Città Nuova.

Trebolle, Julio. 1995. "La otra teodicea bíblica: el mal que procede de Dios." *Iglesia Viva* 175-76, 139-49.

Tresmontant, Claude. 1983. *Le Christ hébreu: la langue et l'âge des Evangiles*. Paris: Oeil.

Turoldo, David Maria. 1996. *La parabola di Giobbe: "L'inevitabile mia storia."* Servitium, Sotto il Monte (Bergamo).

Unno, Taitetsu, ed. 1989. *The Religious Philosophy of Nisihitani Keiji*. Berkeley: Asian Humanities Press.

———. 1990. *The Religious Philosophy of Tanabe Hajime*. Berkeley: Asian Humanities Press.

Vannini, Marco. 1989. "Praedica Verbum: La generazione della parola del silenzio in Meister Eckhart." In Baldini and Zucal 1989, 17-31.

Vannucci, Giovanni. 1978. *Il libro della preghiera universale*. Florence: LEF.

Vargas-Machuca, Antonio, ed. 1975. *Teología y mundo contemporaneo*. Madrid: Cristiandad.

———. 1992. "Jesus ¿fundador del Cristianismo?" *Biblia y Fe* 54:301-12.

Vempeny, Ishanand. 1988. *Kṛṣṇa and Christ*. Pune: Ishvani Kendra and Anand: Gujarat Sahitya Prakash.

Venkatesananda (Swami). 1983. *Christ, Krishna and You*. San Francisco: Chiltern Yoga Foundation.

Vermes, Geza. 1973. *Jesus the Jew*. London: Collins.

Waldenfels, Hans. 1985. *Kontextuelle Fundamentaltheologie*. Paderborn: Schöningh.

Ware, Robert C. 1974. "Christology in Historical Perspective." *The Heythrop Journal* 15, no. 1:53-69.

Weischedel, Wilhelm. 1975. *Der Gott der Philosophen*. 2 volumes. 3rd ed. Darmstadt: Wissenschaftliche Buchgesellschaft.

Witherington, Ben. 1990. *The Christology of Jesus*. Minneapolis: Fortress.

Wilfred, Felix, ed. 1992. *Leave the Temple: Indian Paths to Human Liberation*. Maryknoll, N.Y.: Orbis Books.

Wilke, Annette. 1995. *Ein Sein—Ein Erkennen*. Bern: Lang.

Williams, Anna N. 1997. "Deification in the *Summa Theologiae*: A Structural Interpretation of the Prima Pars." *The Thomist* 61, No. 2 (April): 219-55.

Wong, Joseph H. P. 1984. *Logos-Symbol in the Christology of Karl Barth*. Rome: LAS.

Woods, Richard. 1992. "'I am the Son of God': Eckhart and Aquinas on the Incarnation." *Eckhart Review* [Eckhart Society, London] (June): 27-46.

World Scriptures. 1991. *A Comparative Anthology of Sacred Texts*, edited by International Religious Foundation. New York: Paragon.

Xiberta, Bartholomeus. 1954. *Tractatus de Verbo Incarnato*. 2 volumes. Matriti: CSIC.

———. 1955. *Enchiridion de Verbo Incarnato*. Matriti: CSIC.

Zubiri, Xavier. 1970. *Homenaje a Xavier Zubiri*. 2 volumes. Madrid: EMC.

———. 1975. "El problema teologal del hombre." In Vargas-Machuca 1975, 55-64.

Index

Abba
  meaning of, 90-106
  See also Father; God; Trinity
Abhinavagupta, 44
  on the ultimate, 40
ādhyātmic approach, 67-74
advaita experience, 23. *See also* nonduality
advaitic harmony, xi
angels, 145-46
  and cosmology, 162
  fallen: redeemed by Christ, 163
anthropology
  ādhyātmic (pneumatic), 67-74
  individualistic, 55-60
  personalistic, 60-67
anuttaram (that which cannot be
  transcended), 40
Aristotle
  on consciousness of self, 72
  on human soul, 167
  and Thomas Aquinas, 110-11
Athanasius
  on Christ becoming Man, 16
ātman (self), Son as, 138
Augustine, St.
  on Christian religion, 168
  and christology, 5
  on discovering meaning of past, 45
  on image of vine and branches, 95
  on law of faith written on hearts,
    117n. 63
  on *opinari, credere,* and *intel-
    legere,* 90
  on relationship of God to human
    person, 114n. 59
  on restlessness of human heart,
    107
  on Son's relationship to Father,
    114

  spiritual tradition of, 72
  on Trinity, 97-98, 186
  on unknowability of God, 23
avatāra (descent of the divine), 146
  animal as, 68-69
  Christ as, 107, 146

bhakti (love), 23
  and *jñāna,* 155
biblical criticism, 52n. 28
bodhisattva (one who has achieved
  liberation): Buddha as, 107
Böhme, Jakob, 155
  on relationship of God and Christ,
    114
Bonaventure
  on filiation, 96-97
  on nature of Jesus Christ, 147-48
  on Son's relationship to Father,
    114
  spiritual tradition of, 72
brahman, 72
  God as, 138
Buddha: as *bodhisattva,* 107

Catherine of Siena, on Holy Spirit,
  126n. 77
Chalcedon, Council of
  on two natures of divine person,
    65
  on relation between Jesus and
    Christ, 150
Christ. *See* Jesus/Christ
Christian, recognizing Christ, 149-52
Christianity
  claim of, to be historical and uni-
    versal, 171
  as historical religion, 173-74
  inculturation of, 171
  and monoculturalism, 6

christic experience, following from
    christophany, xvi-xvii
christocentrism, 124, 185
    and Trinity, 147
christology
    from above and from below, 84-
        85, 185
    from center, 185
    and christophany, 9-13
    of first centuries, 3-4
    and identification of Jesus, 154
    limits of, 6-8
    and monotheism, 7
    pneumatic, 185
    as product of Western culture, 4, 7
    of religions, 52n. 27
    and situation of world, 5-6
    traditional images of, 4
    transcended by christophany, 161-
        64
    tribal, 161-62
    and understanding of Christ, 3
    from within, 185
christophany
    as actualization of true identity,
        125
    and christology, 9-13
    cosmovision of, 19-20
    and historicity of Jesus, 162
    and humanization of God, 17
    as manifestation of Christ, 19
    meaning of, xiii, 9-13
    pluralism of, 173-75
    and political problems, 174
    as symbol of conjunction of divine,
        human, and cosmic reality, 180-
        84
    task of, 9-17
    and theology, 13
    transcending historical christology,
        161-64
    and Trinity, 165
Chuang-zu, 125
church, Christian
    christological consciousness of,
        145-46
    as Christ's spouse, 177
    coexisting with universe, 177

cosmic, 176
    and Jesus Christ, 126
    as mystery of universe, 176
    and salvation, 177
    as site of incarnation, 176-79
    Spirit active in, 176
circumcision, abolished by First
        Council of Jerusalem, 149
circumincessio. See perichōrēsis
Clement of Alexandria
    on church, 177
    on God's Word becoming Man, 16
    on humans as images of reality, 31
colonialism
    calendar and, 173
    essence of, 170-71
communion: persons and, 65
consciousness, human
    of intentional nature of humans,
        167
    of self, 70-74
    of spatial dimension of world, 167
    as temporal, 166-67
Copernican cosmography, 162
cosmology
    heliocentric, 170
    modern: evolutionistic mentality
        of, 171
    scientific, 146
cosmovision, 18-20
    christological assertions of, 163
    heliocentric, 170
    of patristic period, 145-46
    of poor: and liberation theology,
        166
    Ptolemaic, 162
    of Vatican II, 162-63
councils of the church
    Chalcedon, 65, 150
    First Council of Jerusalem, 149
    Lateran, 182
    Toledo, 101, 182
    Vatican II, 4-5
creation
    continuous, 128, 169, 179
    and *perichōrēsis*, 110
culture, as preamble to faith, 7-8
Cyprian, St.: on church, 177

dalits (oppressed), 45
death, meditation on, 120-21
deification, doctrine of, 95n. 17
Descartes, 71
   and individualism, 66
Dionysius the Areopagite, 39
discerning
   between temporal and eternal, 136
   versus thinking and understanding,
     89
divine manifestation, 15-17
divine nature, participation in, 94-95
Dōgen, Eihei, 7-8
dualism, 34
   and knowledge, 70
   versus monism, 63
   See also nonduality
Durgā, 78

Ebionites, 146
Eckhart, Meister
   on Christ becoming Man, 16, 55n.
     33
   on continuous creation, 179
   on detachment, 139
   on incarnation and dignity of man,
     147
   and mystical language, 25
   on Son generated from Father, 113
   on Spirit, 73
   veil of being of, 31
ecosophy, 6, 168
Erasmus, on man, 59
eucharist
   as *incarnatio continua*, 128, 169
   meaning of, 124
   as real presence of Christ, 151,
     172
experience
   of Christ-event, 44n. 8
   christophanic, 18-35; and
     eucharistic life, 24-25
   and christophany, 11
   cosmotheandric, 181, 183
   and existential inquiry, 74-88
   and faith, 21
   of incarnation, 128
   and interiority, 21

   meaning of, 40-41
   mystical, 41, 67-68, 104; of Jesus
     Christ, 135-40; silence and, 140
   and mystical knowledge, 90
   personal, 78-82
   spiritual, 120
   theanthropocosmic, 183
   of ultimate reality, 104
   universal, 137
eye
   first (senses), 23
   second (mind), 24
   third (spirit), 24, 31; and christo-
     phany, 174; and modern philoso-
     phy, 153

faith
   and experience of union, 21
   preambles to (*preambulae fidei*), 7
Father
   God as, 93
   meaning of word, 104
   relationship of, to Son, 93, 180
   See also Abba; God; Trinity
Ficino, Marsilio: on beauty, 5
fides quaerens intellectum (faith seeking understanding), 11
First Council of Jerusalem, 149

gnōsis, 152. *See also* knowledge
gnosticism, as spirit/matter dualism,
   70
God
   as *brahman,* 138
   as Father, 93-106; one with Jesus,
     106-14; relationship with human
     person, 114-20
   humanization of, 17, 145
   life of, as trinitarian, 129
   natural desire to see, 46n. 16
   omnipotence of, 105n. 32
   participation in nature of, 94-95
   relationship to God, 23
   unknowability of, 23
Gospel of John, 107-9, 121-24
Gospel of Thomas, 30, 135
Gregory of Nazienzen
   on Christ becoming Man, 16

Gregory of Nazienzen (*cont.*)
  on *praxis* and contemplation,
    112n. 48
  on Trinity, 112n. 47
Gregory of Nyssa, on Christianity,
    95n. 18
Gregory the Theologian, St., on God
    becoming Man, 16

heart, human
  law inscribed in, 117
  purity of, 58
  Spirit in, 117
Heisenberg, Werner, 153
hellenistic world, as context of early
    Christianity, 52
Hinduism, 45-46
historiolatry, 170
history
  incarnation and, 170-75
  as myth, 162
Holy Spirit. *See* Spirit
humans
  activity of: three classical moments
    of, 14n. 7
  intentional nature of, 167
  See also man; person
Husserl, Edmund, 57, 154-55

identification, versus identity, 57-58,
    153-55
identity
  versus identification, 57-58
  of Jesus Christ, 75, 153-55
  sharing of, 57
Ignatius of Antioch
  on church, 177
  on silence, 41
immanence
  and relationship of God and man,
    23
  and transcendence, 30
incarnation
  of Christ, 147 (*see also*
    Jesus/Christ)
  Christian: and dignity of man,
    147; as trinitarian vision of cre-
    ation, 128
  church as site of, 176-79

continuous, 128, 169
  as cultural event, 170
  as historical event, 164, 170-75
  as inculturation, 170-75
  and *Logos,* 170
  and pantheism, 163-64
  as trinitarian vision of creation,
    128
inculturation
  and incarnation, 170-75
  and liberation theology, 175
India, social structures and historical
    situation of, 45-46
individual: versus person, 77
individualism
  as anthropological approach, 55-
    60
  and question of Christ's human
    consciousness, 66
  versus personalism, 61-62
interiority, world of, 20-25
Irenaeus
  on church, 177
  on Word of God becoming Man,
    16, 101
iṣṭadevatā (divine icon), 81, 102, 140

Jaspers, Karl, 14
Jerome, and Ebionites, 146
Jerusalem, First Council of, 149
Jesus/Christ
  and *Abba,* 92-99 (*see also Abba*)
  activity of, 48
  as *ātman,* 138
  as center of universe, 170
  and church, 126
  context of, 49-50
  cosmic, 147, 170
  cosmotheandric, 147
  as creator, 165-66
  departing from world, 120-34
  docetic view of, 10
  doctrines of, 48-49
  eschatological, 168-69; and
    eucharist, 169
  experience of God of, 99-101, 104
  filiation of, 94, 96-97 (*see also*
    Trinity)
  as glorifier, 165-66

historicity of, 162
human consciousness of, 65-66, 86
humanity of, 126-27, 140
identity of, 75, 119, 153-55
impact of, on human life, 75
incarnation of, 94
as Jesus and Christ, 150-51, 161
kerygma of, 126-28
knowledge of, 156-60
life of, 47-48
as Lord, 150
manifestation of, 19; in other religions, 157-60
as Messiah, 149-50
mystery of, 3, 12, 22, 140 (*see also perichōrēsis*)
mystical body of, 163-64
mysticism of, 46-49, 135-40
one with Father, 106-20, 180 (*see also Abba; Father*)
as *pantokratōr*, 3
person of, 84-88
personal encounter with, 77, 151-52
as redeemer, 165-66
and resurrection, 127
and salvation, 161
as servant, 127
as symbol for whole of reality, 144-48
and trinitarian mystery, 15
and Trinity, 94
unity of, 165
as Word, 94
jñāna (knowledge), 23
and *bhakti*, 155
Jñāneśvar, 155
John Damascene, St., 65n. 55, 183
John of the Cross, on man as microcosm, 115n. 60
Judaism, and Christianity, 171
justice, and truth, 123
Justin, and christology, 5

Kant, Immanuel, and individualism, 66
kenōsis (emptying), 29
and Asian religions, 118

of Christ, 117-18, 137, 138
as divine annihilation, 120
of ego, 139
knowledge
of Christ, 85; available to all, 156-60
Christ's, 3
dualism and, 70
experiential, 152
kinds of, 3, 88
mystical, 90
of other persons, 59, 69-74
and purity of heart, 58
symbolic, 144
koinōnia (communion), 95
Kṛṣṇa (Krishna), 24
as manifestation of God, 107, 146-47

language
meaning of, 27
mystical, 25-35
Lao Tze, 125
as wise man, 107
Lateran Council, on Trinity, 182
Leo, St. (pope), on Christ's equality with Father, 180
liberation theology, 45
and christology from below, 185
and cosmovision of poor, 166
and inculturation, 175
life
authentic, 58
Greek words for, 130n. 87
meaning of, and person of Jesus, 75-76
uniqueness of, 137-38
logomonism, 173
Logos
and incarnation, 170
and Trinity, 10
love
as nondualistic, 57-58
origin of, 103
Luther, Martin, and scholasticism, 19

māhāvākyāni (great sayings), 88n. 96, 107, 131, 133-34, 139

man
    anthropologies of, 54-74
    dignity of: and incarnation, 147
    divinization of, 15-17, 120, 145;
      and salvation, 147
    as pilgrim, 30
    relationship to God, 23; and *Abba*,
      90-106
    role of, in universe, 178
    as self-conscious being, 72-74
    See also humans; person
Marius Victorinus, on relationship of
    Father to Son, 139
Mary, mother of God, 4
Maximus the Confessor
    on continuous creation, 179
    on five great conjunctions in
      Christ, 183
    on incarnation, 16
Messiah
    Christ as, 149
    meaning of, 149
Mirandola, Pico della, on creation of
    man, 15
Molinos, Miguel de, on mystical
    knowledge, 90
monism, versus dualism, 63
monoculturalism, and Christianity, 6
monotheism
    and christology, 7
    and Thomism, 110-11
    and Trinity, 139
multiculturalism, and Christianity, 6
mystery, church as, 176
mystical body of Christ, 163-64
mysticism
    and experience of ultimate reality,
      104
    and idealizing man, 32-33
    of Jesus Christ, 46-49
    and language, 27
    meaning of, 40
    rooted in Jesus's experience, 44
myth
    history as, 162
    meaning of, xiii

Nieremberg, Juan Eusebio, 136
noēma (understanding)

love and, 57
    versus *pisteuma*, 78, 87
nonduality, 113, 129, 182
    love and, 57
    and mystery of Christ, 172
    and reality, 33
    and Trinity, 182-83

ontonomy, 119
Origen
    on church, 177
    on creation, 146

panchristism, 124-25
pantheism
    Christian fear of, 62
    and incarnation, 163-64
pantokratōr, Christ as, 3
patēr. See Abba
perichōrēsis
    and creation, 110
    and love, 103
    and mystery of Christ, 22
    and relationship of Jesus to Father,
      110
    trinitarian, 73, 95, 134; Jesus as
      symbol of, 128; and universe,
      147
person
    and communication and commu-
      nion, 77
    encountering Christ, 151-52
    meaning of, 64-67
    mystery of, 75
    relationship with God as Father,
      114-20
    versus individual, 77
    See also humans; man
personalism
    as anthropological approach, 60-
      67
    versus individualism, 61-62
phania (manifestation to human con-
    sciousness), 11
    christophany as, 25
phenomenology, religious, 154-55
philosophy, 7, 11
pisteuma, 154-55
    versus *noēma*, 78, 87

Pius XII (pope), on church, 177
Plato
    meditation on death of, 120
    on monism versus dualism, 63
    on self-consciousness, 70
    on ultimate, 40
Plautus, on man, 59
Plotinus, 34
    on self-consciousness, 70
pluralism, and christophany, 173-75
praxis
    informed by *theōria*, 5
    as matrix of history, 5
pretext, 50-54
    Christian tradition as, 52-53

Rahner, Karl, on Trinity, 182
reality
    centers of, 125
    Christ as symbol of, 144-48
    consciousness of, 166-67
    meaning of, 40
    mystery of, 140
    as nondualist, 33-34
    as spatial and material, 167
    as trinitarian, 144-45
    ultimate, 41; experience of, 104
relativism, 7
relativity, 7
religions, world
    manifestation of Christ in, 156-60
resurrection, as historical event, 164
Richard of St. Victor
    on love and consciousness, 69

sahṛdaya (man with heart), 58
śakti (energy, power), 44
salvation
    and church, 177
    and divinization, 147
    and Jesus, 161
    not a historical fact, 170
    as sharing divine nature, 178
sat-puruṣa (universal Man), 68
    meaning of, 138-40
    person as, 62
    See also man
scandal, Christian, 151
science, as culturally neutral, 171

Second Vatican Council. *See* Vatican
    II
seeking, 28-35
shivaism, 44
sign
    as epistemic in nature, 144
    versus symbol, 144
silence, and mystical experience, 140
Soares-Prabhu, George M., on bibli-
    cal criticism, 52n. 28
spirit
    and *ādhyātmic* approach, 68-69
    and matter, 63 (*see also* dualism)
Spirit
    active in church, 176
    and christophany, 10-11
    in heart, 117
    and incarnation, 164
    as Paraclete, 132-34
    of Truth, 122-24
subjects, versus objects, 70-71
sūtra, meaning of, 143
symbols
    knowledge and, 144
    as ontological in character, 144
    versus sign, 144

taboric light, 17, 151
Tagore, Rabindranath, on life, 130
Teresa of Avila, St.
    on hearing and believing, 90
    and mystical language, 27-35
Tertullian
    on believing, 88
    on church, 177
    problematic of, 18
    on Trinity, 182
theanthropocosmic intuition, 183
theōria, informing *praxis,* 5
theōsis
    as participation in divine nature,
        147
    as realization of incarnation, 120
    See also incarnation; man:
        divinization of
thinking, versus discerning and under-
    standing, 89
Thomas Aquinas
    and Aristotle, 110-11

Thomas Aquinas (*cont.*)
  on being and non-being, 121n. 68
  on church, 177
  on consciousness of self, 86n. 92
  on creature as nothing, 97-98
  on discerning, thinking, and
    understanding, 89-90
  on divine absoluteness, 110
  on filiation, 96n. 20
  as greatest Muslim theologian,
    96n. 19
  on image of vine and branches, 95
  on incarnation, 69, 96n. 19, 163
  on law inscribed in heart, 117
  on nonduality, 129
  on philosophy, 7
  on relationship of God to creation,
    110
  on teaching of Jesus, 117
  on Trinity, 98n. 26, 129, 133-34n.
    90
  on truth and scripture, 47
time, human consciousness of, 166-67
Toledo, Council of, 101
  on Trinity, 182
tradition, as hermeneutic key, 52-54
transcendence, and immanence, 30
tribe
  and christology, 161-62
  meaning of, 162
Trinity
  and *Abba*, 95-96, 133-34
  Christ and, 16569
  and christophany, 10
  economic, 182

  as fulcrum of Christian experience,
    120
  immanent, 182
  manifestation of, 165
  as measure of all things, 34-35
  and monotheism, 139
  as pure relationality, 173
  unity of, 111
truth
  and justice, 123
  meaning of, 123-24

understanding, versus discerning and
    thinking, 89
universe
  called to share trinitarian
    perichōrēsis, 147
  Christ as center of, 170
  divinization of, 147
  spatial dimension of, 167

Valla, Lorenzo, 176
Vatican II
  on church, 176
  and Enlightenment rationality,
    162-63
  Gaudium et spes, 5, 99
  Lumen gentium, 176
  on persons as children of God, 99
Vedas, as primordial word, 54

word, significance of, 54
world
  contemporary crisis in, 5-6
  as interval of time, 167

Other Titles in the Faith Meets Faith Series

Toward a Universal Theology of Religion, Leonard Swidler, editor
The Myth of Christian Uniqueness, John Hick and Paul F. Knitter, editors
An Asian Theology of Liberation, Aloysius Pieris, S.J.
The Dialogical Imperative, David Lochhead
Love Meets Wisdom, Aloysius Pieris, S.J.
Many Paths, Eugene Hillman, C.S.Sp.
The Silence of God, Raimundo Panikkar
The Challenge of the Scriptures, Groupe de Recherches Islamo-Chrétien
The Meaning of Christ, John P. Keenan
Hindu-Christian Dialogue, Harold Coward, editor
The Emptying God, John B. Cobb Jr. and Christopher Ives, editors
Christianity Through Non-Christian Eyes, Paul J. Griffiths, editor
Christian Uniqueness Reconsidered, Gavin D'Costa, editor
Women Speaking, Women Listening, Maura O'Neill
Bursting the Bonds?, Leonard Swidler, Lewis John Eron, Gerard Sloyan, and Lester
    Dean, editors
One Christ—Many Religions, Stanley J. Samartha
The New Universalism, David J. Kreiger
Jesus Christ at the Encounter of World Religions, Jacques Dupuis, S.J.
After Patriarchy, Paula M. Cooey, William R. Eakin, and Jay B. McDaniel, editors
An Apology for Apologetics, Paul J. Griffiths
World Religions and Human Liberation, Dan Cohn-Sherbok, editor
Uniqueness, Gabriel Moran
Leave the Temple, Felix Wilfred, editor
The Buddha and the Christ, Leo D. Lefebure
The Divine Matrix, Joseph A. Bracken, S.J.
The Gospel of Mark: A Mahayana Reading, John P. Keenan
Revelation, History and the Dialogue of Religions, David A. Carpenter
Salvations, S. Mark Heim
The Intercultural Challenge of Raimon Panikkar, Joseph Prabhu, editor
Fire and Water: Women, Society, and Spirituality in Buddhism and Christianity, Aloy-
    sius Pieris, S.J.
Piety and Power: Muslims and Christians in West Africa, Lamin Sanneh
Life after Death in World Religions, Harold Coward, editor
The Uniqueness of Jesus, Paul Mojzes and Leonard Swidler, editors
A Pilgrim in Chinese Culture, Judith A. Berling
West African Religious Traditions, Robert B. Fisher, S.V.D.
Hindu Wisdom for All God's Children, Francis X. Clooney, S.J.
Imagining the Sacred, Vernon Ruland, S.J.
Christian-Muslim Relations, Ovey N. Mohammed, S.J.
John Paul II and Interreligious Dialogue, Byron L. Sherwin and Harold Kasimow, edi-
    tors
Transforming Christianity and the World, John B. Cobb, Jr.
The Divine Deli, John H. Berthrong
Experiencing Scripture in World Religions, Harold Coward, editor
The Meeting of Religions and the Trinity, Gavin D'Costa
Subverting Hatred: The Challenge of Nonviolence in Religious Traditions, Daniel L.
    Smith-Christopher, editor
Christianity and Buddhism: A Multi-Cultural History of their Dialogue, Whalen Lai
    and Michael von Brück
Islam, Christianity, and the West: A Troubled History, Rollin Armour, Sr.

Many Mansions? Multiple Religious Belonging, Catherine Cornille, editor

No God But God: A Path to Muslim-Christian Dialogue on the Nature of God, A. Christian van Gorder

Understanding Other Religious Worlds: A Guide for Interreligious Education, Judith Berling

Buddhists and Christians: Through Comparative Theology to Solidarity, James L. Fredericks